Sharing Jesus
in the
Buddhist World

D1113423

Sharing Jesus
in the
Buddhist World

David Lim and Steve Spaulding, Editors

Copyright 2003 by David Lim and Steve Spaulding

All Rights Reserved

No part of this publication may be reproduced, stored in a retrieval system, or transmitted in any form or by any means—electronic, mechanical, photocopy, recording, or any other—except for brief quotations embodied in critical articles or printed reviews, without prior permission of the publisher.

Cover design by Rachel Snodderly

Copyediting: Marybeth Tewksbury

Published by
William Carey Library
1605 Elizabeth St.
Pasadena, California 91104

ISBN 0-87808-506-8

Printed in the United States of America

Contents

Introduction

David Lim and Steve Spaulding

A group of evangelical mission theologians and practitioners who are concerned with developing more biblical and effective ways to evangelize in the Buddhist world are instrumental in having this book produced. Our objective is to bring together a set of well-researched works that will help the global church reach the peoples in the Buddhist megasphere for Christ.

We hope we can publish one similar book per year through the annual holding of a missiological forum that specifically focuses on this theme. We thank God that we were able to hold the first Forum at the start of the fourth assembly of SEANET last March 18-19, 2002, in Bangkok, Thailand.

For the past three years, SEANET had been holding annual assemblies that brought together various key leaders (church leaders, mission leaders, missiologists, missionaries, and pastors) to reflect, discuss, and plan programs and projects that will help in the evangelization of Buddhist peoples and nations. Even in the first assembly, the group already discerned that there needs to be three strategic foci for our consideration:

(1) prayer mobilization,

(2) research and training, and

(3) strategy development.

It was during the 2000 assembly that the idea surfaced of holding a regular missiological forum (with its papers published widely) to provide the global church with knowledge and understanding of the Buddhist world and how to reach it for Christ. No one was ready to put it into action then, but in the 2001 assembly, David Lim accepted the challenge to get it organized, while the Steering Group (led by Steve Spaulding) committed itself to finding the resources to help make it happen. We praise God that we found a foundation (which humbly asked not to be recognized) that was more than willing to provide all the funds needed for the event and the publication of its papers!

For the forum, fifteen evangelical researchers, theologians, and missiologists were asked to contribute a paper each. Ten accepted to try, and nine made it. And what an impressive combination of excellent and creative works they were! These were received very well by the more than forty people who registered (we were expecting only fifteen to twenty participants to start with!). We hope that the publication of these papers in a book will be warmly welcomed and appreciated by the global church.

The nine papers in this compendium have three major themes:

(1) One is a "situationer" on the global context of the Buddhist world. *David Burnett*, who heads the Center for Buddhist Studies at All Nations, U.K., presents this paper on "The Challenge of Globalization of Buddhism," which shows the historical contextualizations that Buddhism has undergone since its beginnings to the present.

(2) Four papers are on the second theme: "Issues in Theological Contextualization," that is, how do we engage the Buddhist worldview in the twenty-first century.

  (a) *Kang San Tan*, a Chinese missiologist based in Malaysia, outlines the "Elements of a Biblical and Genuine Missionary Encounter with Diaspora Chinese Buddhists."

  (b) *Alex Smith*, an OMF missionary in Thailand for almost thirty years, shows the "Missiological Implications of the

Key Contrasts Between Buddhism and Christianity," while

(c) *Johannes Aagaard*, head of the Dialog Center in Denmark, which reaches out to Buddhists worldwide, presents his "Reflections on Suffering and Salvation in Buddhism and Christianity." And

(d) *David Lim*, a biblical theologian cum mission mobilizer who has ministered among the Chinese Diaspora in the Philippines, gives the challenge to work "Towards a Radical Contextualization Paradigm in Evangelizing Buddhists."

(3) The other four papers are missiological reflections on "case studies" of actual missions to Buddhists. Two are on our host culture in Thailand:

(a) *Dr. Ubolwan Mejudhon*, who heads the Cross-Cultural Communication Training Center and the Muangthai Church in Bangkok with her husband, presents "An Integrated Model of Evangelism to Buddhists Using Theology, Anthropology, and Religious Studies," the result of a nine-year research for her D. Miss. with Asbury Seminary. And

(b) *Paul DeNeui*, a missionary in Thailand, now finishing his D. Miss. at Fuller Seminary, narrates with his colleague, the head of the Isaan Covenant Church, how they did "Contextualizing with Thai Folk Buddhists."

Then on another folk Theravadan context,

(c) *Steve Bailey* shares his model of "Communication Strategies for Christian Witness among the Lao." Finally,

(d) *Mark Dominey*, an OMF missionary who has a D. Miss. from Dallas Seminary, shows the challenge of the "Problem of Japanese Self-Identity."

During the forum, some more issues were raised for future fora. These may be classified into two main sets:

(1) On theological challenges are: limits to contextualization, value and limits to dialogue, Tantric Buddhism, "transfer of merit" in folk Buddhism, "theology of suffering" compared, and new Buddhist religious movements. Three papers in this area have also been volunteered: "The Use of Ecclesiastes in Evangelizing Buddhists," "Christian Creation Worldview for University Students in Buddhist Contexts," and "The Attraction of Buddhism in the West and How to Respond."

(2) The second set consists of (practical) missiological models. Among them are: "Spiritual Perspectives in Evangelizing Buddhists in South Asia," "How to Facilitate Group Decisions for (Birthing) People Movements," "Implications for Theological Education," "Identity and Role of Expatriate Missionaries," and some general topics like: indigenous arts and communication, conversion of monks, models of partnership, and models of church-planting movements (CPMs).

Also requested are papers to give "situationers" on Buddhism in Asia, in the West, and especially on Buddhist persecution of Christians. All these look very promising for a second book, to come next year. Readers who are interested in participating in the Forum and/or this publication series may contact the publishers.

Please pray and work with us as we look forward to an annual forum on Christian missions to the Buddhist world, as well as an annual publication of the papers presented in each forum. May God find our circle of partners and colleagues faithful in facilitating the sharing of the "best theologies" and the "best practices" of Christians, particularly evangelicals worldwide, in reaching Buddhist peoples for Christ in their various contexts—until all shall hear and have a chance to be saved.

DAVID LIM and STEVE SPAULDING, editors

Quezon City, Philippines

June 4, 2002

The Challenge

of the Globalization of Buddhism

David Burnett

Most religions experience a tension between the desire to hold to the original patterns of their founders, and the need to innovate to accommodate changing situations. This is because religions emerge from one historical and social context and generally address the needs of that particular situation. However, religious aspirations are never exclusive to one community, so the teaching and practice has the potential to spread into similar societies. As they spread beyond their original community there is a continual process of reinterpretation and adaptation. Thus, missionary religions are continually faced with the dilemma of holding to traditions or contextualizing to the new. In order for a new religion to expand, it must allow freedom for local expressions.

This paper first examines the reasons for the early expansion of *dharma* in India. Second, it considers the process of contextualization of Indian Buddhism to China. Third, the analysis will look at the way Buddhism has entered Western society, and explore the contemporary process of adaptation that is currently taking place.

Expansion of Buddhism in India

This paper argues that Buddhism has been more open to adaptation than most religions. This is probably because Buddhism is

1

not merely a philosophy, but a religious discipline that leads to an awakening to the true nature of reality. The Buddha taught that by direct experience he had come to understand the human condition, and had discovered a means of transcending it. The human condition is one of continual rebirth into *samsara,* a state characterized by suffering impermanence. Within the cycle, the various states of being (god, human, animal, ghost or hell-being) are directly conditioned by one's previous actions and thoughts. What keeps us in this state is our own craving and ignorance of the nature of things. If one can eliminate these things one achieves a state of perfection, liberation, and peace known as *nirvana,* and one is never reborn in samsara again. Craving and ignorance are eliminated by responsible moral behavior, discipline of mind through meditation techniques, and insight into the truths the Buddha discovered. It is not so much a philosophy about life as practical advice on how to live life based on the Buddha's own personal experience.

There were several significant topics on which the Buddha refused to speak. These were issues on which one would expect most religious philosophies to comment, and were discussed by the ascetics of his time.1 First, the Buddha refused to speculate whether the world had a beginning or an end. He would not be drawn into the discussion as to whether the universe was eternal or not. Secondly, he refused to speculate as to whether the universe was finite or infinite. Is there an edge to the world? Thirdly, is the existence of a living being strictly identified with the physical body, or is it something separate? Fourthly, when an enlightened being dies, can he be said to exist or not exist? The failure to address these questions provided much room for speculation in later years.

The Buddha always claimed that he taught his followers everything they needed to know, summarized in the Four Noble Truths. One of the Buddha's famous parables illustrates this teaching. A man was shot with a poisoned arrow and refused to let the surgeon remove the arrow until he had the answers to everything about it—the nature of the wood and metal from which the arrow was made, the color and length, the family background of the man who shot the arrow, and the type of bow that was used. While asking these irrelevant questions the man died. Similarly one could spend one's whole life asking philosophical questions, but would die in the same predicament.

When the Buddha died he was confident his followers had been told and had assimilated everything they needed to know. The *dharma* had been preached for forty-five years and there was a well-established oral tradition and hundreds of *Arhats* who could teach. The Buddha did not appoint a successor, and a written canon was not produced for some hundreds of years. However, soon after his death there is evidence that his disciples began to dispute the content of his teaching. For example, at the first Council at Rajagaha (c. 483 B.C.) soon after the Buddha's *paranirvana.* Ananda mentions that the Buddha had said that not all the precepts were necessary. When the council asked him which ones were not so important, Ananda had to admit he had not asked the Buddha. The assembly were annoyed with him for this failure and finally decided to keep all the precepts. As the council was coming to a close, the great Arhat Purana is said to have arrived with 500 disciples. Purana said that he remembered the teaching of the Buddha perfectly and did not need the consensus of the council.

In the second council (c. 383 B.C.) the tension between the conservative and liberal wings of the movement became evident. The monks at the *Sangha* in Vaisali had modified some of the existing practices. Although these modifications were condemned by the council, this is often seen as the beginnings of the split between the *Sthavira* ("elders" or "conservatives") and *Mahasamghika* ("great Sangha") schools. However, by the time of the third council (c. 270 B.C.) the sectarian movement was well advanced. From out of the Sthavira, several schools emerged but only the Theravada remains today. From out of the reformed school, a whole range of new religious texts was to emerge and form what was to become known as the Mahayana tradition. Although scholars talk of different "sects," monks from different groups could be found living side by side in the same monastery, and the differences may have been irrelevant to many lay Buddhists. Tradition has it that there were eighteen different schools in the first few centuries of Buddhism, but many scholars suggest that there might have been more. Professor Williams has argued, "For Buddhists 'schism' is nothing to do with doctrinal disagreements as such, but is the result of divergence in monastic rule."[2]

In spite of its internal divisions, Buddhism spread rapidly in India and beyond. By the third century B.C. it was a major religion in India and had already spread to Sri Lanka. There are a variety of reasons that have been proposed for this expansion:

> The teaching was not related to local deities or sacred places, but offered a skillful way of living and a hope for salvation. It was not a tribal religion, but one that was potentially universal in its appeal.

> At that time the people were dissatisfied with the dominant role of the priests and their rituals. The dharma allowed the individual to question religious authorities and choose their own spiritual path.

> The Buddha did not explicitly condemn other religious traditions, so people were free to continue to worship their traditional gods if they so wished.

> The Sangha was a visible demonstration of those who were successfully following this new spiritual path with its peaceful lifestyle.

> The dharma impressed many intellectuals with its coherent analysis of the human predicament, and its offer of a distinct moral rule of life that resulted in social stability.

> These advantages appealed to several monarchs (i.e. King Ashoka) who supported Buddhism and encouraged its spread.

However, the factors that make Buddhism attractive can also make it vulnerable. The decline of Buddhism in India is usually attributed to two things: conquest and assimilation. Its peaceful nature makes Buddhists open to military conquest, which happened in India and central Asia with the Muslim invasions. More recently, Communism has been able to dominate many Buddhist nations. The second factor is that the flexibility and tolerance allowed the folk tradition to become indistinguishable from the existing religious traditions. The decline of support for the Sangha results in a decline in the teaching of the dharma.

Contextualization of Buddhism to Chinese Society

The introduction of Buddhism into China was one of the great events in Chinese history, and provides a remarkable example of cultural borrowing by one civilization from another. This was all the more remarkable since the Indian civilization was so different from China, and China was so dismissive of all that was foreign.

The first known Buddhist missionary was Shih-kao, a Parathian prince who, after his arrival in about 148 A.D., spent more than twenty years in China. Growth was slow under the Han dynasty. This in part was due to the way in which the emperor was viewed as the "Son of Heaven" and was the focus of the empire in Confucian ideology. Supernatural sanctions held power, position, and prestige in correct balance for all members of society.

In addition, there were several major difficulties in communicating Buddhist ideas, and the only way a translation could be attempted was through Taoist terminology. A word like *Tao*, for example, was used to translate *marga*, or "path." This automatically carried with it many Taoist overtones unintended in the original Sanskrit scriptures of India. It seems that Buddhism was initially regarded in China as a sect of Taoism, and as such, there was probably a mixing of Buddhism and Taoism in this early period.

Points of similarity between Buddhism and Taoism included:

a) Many of the assistants of early translations were Taoist scholars.

b) There were similarities in the rituals such as the absence of any animal sacrifices.

c) Emphasis upon meditation.

d) Abstinence from certain foods.

e) Concern about immortality.

Even so, Buddhism was criticized by Taoists, and in the T'ai P'ing Ching text that is attributed to Yu Chi (fl. A.D. 126–144), four criticisms are made:

a) It was unfilial, in that young people are encouraged to become monks and leave their parents.

b) It encouraged celibacy and therefore the neglect of wives and children.

c) It permitted the eating of impurities (use of cow's urine for medicine).

d) It promoted begging.

Buddhist teaching clashed with indigenous Chinese culture in several fundamental ways. First, the Chinese held the view that life is good and to be enjoyed, and this was counter to the Buddhist teaching that all is suffering and illusion. Second, the Buddhist practice of celibacy conflicted with the Chinese emphasis upon family life and the need for many children. Third, the mendicant monk was an object of scorn to those who believed that all able-bodied people should be engaged in productive labor. Four, the idea of a monastic community possessing its own government and passing its own laws was contrary to Confucian teaching that held to the unity of the empire under one supreme ruler.

During the period of the Han dynasty, there was little opportunity for mass response to Buddhist teaching, but it did allow the introduction of the new teaching into society. Many of the Buddhist texts were translated into Chinese, especially after the fall of the Han dynasty. Most attention seems to have been given to the shorter texts dealing with meditation or trance (*dyana*), probably because of its similarity to the Taoist techniques.

In 581, the great ruler Yang-chien unified both north and south to form the Sui dynasty. He relied on Buddhism to help in the unification and consolidation of the empire. He initiated a series of measures including establishing monasteries at the foot of each of the five sacred mountains, and on the sites of famous battles. Under various emperors, Buddhism was patronized on a lavish scale, though not always for religious reasons. The result was a period of creative activity in all of Buddhist thought and practice. Central Asia regained its role as a transit area between China and India until the late seventh century. The result was an upsurge of pilgrimage, the most famous being that of Hsuan-tsang (c. 559–664). Throughout this period, Chinese Buddhism was continually being renewed by contact with India.

The great T'ang Empire (618–907) was, on the whole, favourable to Buddhism, although some of the early emperors claimed descent from Lao-tzu and so followed Taoism. The expansion of the empire into central Asia, and the opening of trade routes, brought many foreigners into China. Among these were Nestorian Christians from the Middle East, and later Muslims.

Eventually, the T'ang rulers saw the need to bring the growing Sangha under the control of the state. Throughout the eighth century, several measures were introduced to regulate the Buddhist monks, but the religion was by then too well established to be seriously affected. The dazzling images, colorful ritual, and beautiful temples impressed the people. Monasteries served as charitable institutions, caring for the old and sick. The monks ran dispensaries and hospitals, arranged for the feeding of the poor, and engaged in community projects such as building roads and digging wells. These were all ways in which merit might be accumulated to ensure entrance into Amitabha's heaven.

As long as the T'ang state prospered, it was able to tolerate the immense Buddhist community, but when, later in the dynasty, it faced political turmoil and economic crises, anticlericalism became evident. In 845, a census was taken of all Buddhists monastic communities, which revealed that there were some quarter of a million monks and nuns, 4,600 temples, and over 40,000 lesser shrines. The order was given to destroy all Buddhist buildings apart from one temple in each major prefecture and four temples in each capital city. The majority of monks and nuns were forced to leave the monastic life and take secular occupations. Although the persecution did not last long, it had a disastrous effect, from which Buddhism in China never fully recovered.

Another significant aspect of Buddhism in China was that of martial arts. It is likely that martial arts were practised in China long before the arrival of Buddhism, but it is interesting how it was associated with Buddhism. The myth of the origin of Buddhist martial arts attributes it to an Indian scholar Bodhidharma who is said to have travelled to China in the latter fifth century. He taught a new style of meditation known as *Ch'an*, and according to tradition he instructed his followers about breathing and yogic-based martial moves known as the "Eighteen Hands of the Lohan." The story associates him with the Shaolin temple in Henan near Loyang. There are many associations of Buddhism with the martial arts, and sword and warrior imagery abound in Buddhist texts. The ethical teaching invoked the concept of "skillful means" to justify violent actions in order to protect the innocent or the dharma and its representatives. Popular ballads, stories, and novels have portrayed the exponent as a "Chinese knight errant."

Lawrence summarizes the introduction of Buddhism into China as follows:

> The transplantation of Buddhist thought to China is one of the great intercultural movements of history. Among the many lessons we may draw from that movement is that accommodation of a foreign culture is only accomplished as a result of many modifications and reinterpretations that make it comprehensible and even naturalize it. In the case of Buddhism, one must recognize that first there was Indian Buddhism; then there was Indian Buddhism in China; and finally, after many centuries of adjustment there was Chinese Buddhism. [3]

It is now possible to return to the question of why the Chinese people accepted Indian Buddhism. Covell summarizes the reasons under eight factors. [4]

1. The relative ease of access by land into China by zealous missionaries able to relate well to Chinese life within the general Asian milieu.

2. A Han China open to new ideas and needing revitalization.

3. An available role as a "sect of Taoism," asserting no exclusive claims.

4. A popular movement among a great number of people, such that there was little social dislocation.

5. A philosophy seen by the Chinese as adequate to deal with the incredible human misery and suffering experienced during the period.

6. No external power base that could pose a threat to the Chinese state.

7. A flexible methodology adequate to exploit differing opportunities in northern and southern China.

8. Chinese society was penetrated by Buddhism at all levels of society—linguistically, economically, socially, politically, and artistically. Submitting to the state politically was of crucial importance.

As Covell comments, "none of these several advantages were available to the same degree to the emissaries of the Christian faith. Apart from the Nestorians in the seventh century, they came by the sea route—distances were great, communication with the home base was poor, they were not Asians, it was the 'ocean of faith' (*yang jiao*) or 'foreign faith' ... Christianity was an exclusive faith." [5]

To summarize, Buddhism appears to have entered Chinese society for two primary reasons. First, Chinese society was facing social dislocation and Buddhism offered a non-threatening option. As Smart writes, "Its very foreignness was an advantage, for it brought something new and difficult into Chinese civilization, and the resultant dialectic with native forces could be very fruitful." [6] Second, Buddhism was contextualized to Chinese society in such a way that socially unacceptable elements were removed or transformed.

Buddhism Goes West

Today it seems surprising that only 150 years ago there was little knowledge of Buddhism in Europe. European travelers and especially Jesuit missionaries to Tibet, China, and Japan made record of an obscure cult of the "false god" called "Bod." The coming of Buddhism to western Europe can be described as four movements. The process is slightly different for North America with the large Chinese community that settled along the West Coast at the beginning of the twentieth century.[7]

1. Theravada Tradition (1900 onward)

With British colonization of India, Burma, and Ceylon, missionaries began to evangelize Buddhists. This required not only knowledge of the local language, but also an understanding of *Pali*, the religious language. For this reason, in 1824 the Wesleyan missionary Benjamin Clough published the first grammar book of the Pali language in Colombo. This stimulated a lot of interest in academic circles, and in 1881 the Pali Text Society was established to collect, translate, and publish more of these texts.

It was also in Colombo, in 1899, that Gordon Douglas was ordained as the first known Westerner to become a Buddhist monk. He was given the Buddhist name Asoka, but he died a few years later in 1905. The second European to become a monk was Alan Bennet McGregor (1872–1923), a former member of the Golden Dawn occultist association, who entered a Burmese monastery in 1901 and took the name Ananda Metteyya. He returned to Britain in 1907 leading a small mission from Burma. The Buddhist Society was formed at this time to support this mission, and it was later joined by the influential Christmas Humphreys. A German who was ordained in Sri Lanka in 1903 under the name Nyanaponika became a prolific writer on Buddhism. The first Western Buddhist "nun" was a German ordained in 1926. The Buddhist Society of America was formed in 1930.

The Theravada regained popularity in Britain through the Thai master Ajahn Chah (1918–1992). He founded the Chithurst Forest Monastery in West Sussex in 1978, which was the first successful Theravada monastery with Western members. Under its British abbot, Ajahn Sumedho (formerly Robert Jackman), other centres were established in Britain, Germany, Italy, and Switzerland.

2. Zen Buddhism (1945 onward)

The Second World War marked a halt to Buddhist activities within Europe, but rapid new developments occurred in the USA. The Japanese Buddhist scholar, D. T. Suzuki (1870–1966), published a number of books in English on Zen, and these became popular in the West. Zen caught the imagination of many young people in the USA during the "beatnik" generation of the 1960s, and books such as *Zen and the Art of Motorcycle Maintenance* gained cult status. Zen spread into many areas of popular Western culture. However, more serious practitioners of Buddhism criticized the superficial presentation of the religious tradition to the wider public. Meditation stimulated this popularity. Initially only the better educated were attracted to Buddhism, but the practice of meditation opened it to a wider class of the university students who were, at this time, increasing in number.

Other events that occurred in the 1950s included the mass conversion to Buddhism in 1956 of many *Dalits* in India who were followers of Dr. Ambedkar. A second wave of conversions occurred in 2001, and more are likely to occur in the near future.

3. Tibetan Tradition (1960 onward)

A third wave of interest came to the West with the flight of the Dalai Lama from Tibet in 1959. With the Dalai Lama came many leading teachers, who settled in Nepal and northern India. The Dalai Lama made his home in Dharamsala, which quickly became the centre of Tibetan religion and culture. The cooler climate of the mountainous region attracted many Western "hippies" of the period, and they came into contact with the colorful art and rituals of Tibetan Buddhism. A desire for peace and love was common, as evidenced in the anti-Vietnam-War demonstrations in the USA, and "Ban the Bomb" campaigns in UK. The Westerners felt a real empathy with the displaced Tibetan people, and a respect for their fundamental belief in the use of non-violent methods to solve their problems.

The Indian government was not oblivious to the presence of these Westerners, and in the early 1980s decided to tighten its tourist policy. Along with requiring British visitors to have visas for the first time, the government staged local clean-up operations in all areas where Westerners were known to live. Dharamsala was no exception, and by 1985 the majority of those Westerners who had lived there for over ten years were sent back home. They returned home with a natural desire to share what they had learned from Tibetan Buddhism. They therefore invited various lamas to live and teach in Europe and America.

There are four main schools in Tibetan Buddhism. The *Gelug* School, headed by the fourteenth Dalai Lama, has established study and practice centres in Switzerland and Germany, and by 1990 had more than fifty centers. Following his first visit to the West in 1973, the Dalai Lama has made many visits and has inspired his Western followers. The *Kagyu* School also has been very successful. The sixteenth head of the Kagyu school was Gyalwa Karapa (1923-1981), and he made his first visit to Europe and North America in 1975, and more than fifty centres are claimed to have been founded by him throughout Europe. The seventeenth head of Kagyu, although still a young man, has been accepted by the Chinese and was officially appointed in 1992.

4. New Movements (1970 onward)

In 1967, Venerable Sangharakshita, an Englishman, founded the Friends of the Western Buddhist Order (FWBO) in Britain. This is the first Buddhist tradition to be founded in Britain and stresses the basic unity of all forms of Buddhism rather than the collection of oriental customs that have grown up around it. The FWBO itself is a new way of taking Buddhist practice seriously, providing ordination that does not involve adopting the traditional life-style of a monk or nun. It sees itself as a practical form of Buddhism suited to the Western urban world. It has also shown not only a tolerance but an acceptance of homosexuals. Many gay men have found it be a spiritual home.[8]

The 1970s and 1980s have seen the introduction and growth in popularity of *Nichiren* Buddhism. The emphasis on practical results in material as well as spiritual success has been of particular appeal. In Japan, there are two popular lay organizations based on Nichiren Buddhism. The largest is Soka Gakkai, which has some ten million followers throughout the world, and the other is Rissho Kosei-kai.

Contextualization of Buddhism to the West

Two different types of Buddhists may therefore be identified in the West today. First, there are those groups patterned on Asian Buddhist traditions, and propagating Buddhism in a particular Eastern cultural context. Second, there are those who are seeking to express Buddhism in new forms that are relevant to the contemporary urban world. I want to show that both types have to contextualize to a greater or lesser extent.

Ancient Asian Traditions

For Westerners, it has often been the exotic quality of ancient Buddhist traditions that have woven their particular fascination. There is something exciting about chanting in an ancient foreign language, or performing colorful rituals from distant parts of the world. Even so, Asian traditions have to address practical issues in order to manifest themselves in the West. Sometimes the accommodation has been begrudging, but in other cases it is seen as the way of making Buddhism relevant for industrial urban society.

The Theravada tradition has generally been one of the most conservative. However, the Forest Tradition, taught by Ajahn Chah, has had to make changes in order to adjust to the colder climate of northern Europe. The British monks have adopted the use of a jacket that has been designed for them to wear under their robes. Celibacy is still carefully adhered to, and marked social boundaries are maintained. A radical change however is the institution of an order of nuns, which is generally unknown in Sri Lanka and Thailand. The nuns, who are called "sister," wear white robes and take a submissive role behind the monks. Even so, some have shown themselves to be significant exponents of the dharma and dedicated meditators. Kornfield, in his study of American Buddhism, comments that feminization is the most important change going on within the Sangha. [9] The increasing number of nuns in this order raises significant questions as to the future developments of the Forest tradition in the West.

Serene Reflection Meditation has similarly sought to retain its Asian heritage, following much of the Japanese tradition, such as their distinctive methods of meditation. Even so, various modifications have been made, such as the shifting of the festival celebrating the Buddha's enlightenment from the 8th to the 25th December. Buddhist texts are chanted in English to the accompaniment of an organ in medieval plainsong. These changes have not always been simply to accommodate the tradition for Western followers. For example, in Japan monks are able to marry, whilst those with Serene Reflection Meditation remain celibate. This raises questions as to how much of these changes are cultural adaptation, and how many result from the particular views of the Western founder.

Geshe Kelsang Gyatso has sought to express the ancient *Gelukpa* School of Tibetan Buddhism in English, so that Western people may be able to understand the teaching without the obstacle of having to learn Tibetan. [10] In his prodigious writings he has tried to express Buddhist terms in English, so that his followers can appreciate the ancient teaching. It is not surprising that these movements that have deliberately sought to contextualize themselves to the West have been subject to criticism by more conservative schools of Buddhism. [11] The New *Kadampa* Tradition (NKT) has been vigorous in its own defence. It has also been bold enough to criticize the Dalai Lama, but strangely, for a school that is trying to contextualize itself, it has condemned the Dalai Lama for rejecting ancient rituals. The argument has been especially vocal over the oracle Dorje Shugden. [12] The fourteenth Dalai Lama has tried to ban Shugden worship on the grounds that it is dangerous to practitioners of Buddhism and to Tibet as a country. The on-going conflict has led to accusations of physical persecution among the Tibetan communities in North India.

New Western Tradition

One of the most notable examples of deliberate adaptation of Buddhism to Western society is the Friends of the Western Buddhist Order (FWBO), founded by Sangharakshita. He made it his aim to deliberately translate Buddhism into the Western urban scene. To do this, the FWBO has abandoned ancient Asian traditions, and formulated a new tradition that draws upon elements of several Buddhist traditions. The FWBO was the first Buddhist tradition to be founded in Britain and although basically Mahayana in outlook, the movement stresses the basic unity of all forms of Buddhism rather than the collection of oriental customs that have grown up around it.

The FWBO sees itself as a new way of taking Buddhist practice seriously, providing ordination that does not necessarily involve adopting the traditional life-style of a monk or nun. It sees itself as a practical form of Buddhism suited to the Western world.

Sangharakshita argues that Western culture, as a whole, is quite incompatible with Buddhism and there can be no question of Buddhism being expressed in terms of Western culture. It is a question, therefore, of Western Buddhism finding expression in a *new* Western culture, a culture which would in its own way help people to develop, if not spiritually, then at least psychologically. In creating that culture, Buddhists would keep the best elements of the traditional Western culture, but a lot would have to go. [13]

The special emphasis that is placed on the "going for refuge" and the observance of the ethical precepts represent in Sangharakshita's words "a return to and renewed emphasis upon the basics of Buddhism." [14] The FWBO calls its interpretation of Buddhism "interdenominational Buddhism." The growth of the FWBO has been hindered by questions over the historical accuracy of the account of the life story as told by the founder and some of his moral practices. More individualistic practitioners of Buddhism tend to regard the FWBO as a "cult."

Buddhism in Western Culture

Buddhist ideas have also been absorbed into popular Western culture without people actually becoming Buddhists. There are many who retain their allegiance to another religion, including Christianity, but find Buddhist meditation techniques helpful. Buddhist references can be found in novels, songs, and films. Recent opinion polls reveal that twenty-five percent of the population of Britain now believe in reincarnation, and this would be typical of many Western nations. Films such as *Seven Years in Tibet* and *Kundun* have resulted in a positive attitude in Western people toward Tibetan refugees and their ancient heritage. [15] *The Matrix* has achieved a cult following with its haunting question of what is the really real?

In the 1960s, Buddhism was closely related to the emerging New Age movement in the West, but in recent years, Western Buddhists have been firm in making a clear distinction. New Agers have been blamed for portraying Buddhism as one path among many, all of which are open to personal choice in the post-modern world. A vague, relativist attitude finds some aspects of Buddhism attractive. This can be seen from the first encounters of the West with Buddhism in the nineteenth century when Madam Blavatsky brought some Buddhist teaching into Theosophy. Later in the 1950s, the beatniks and hippies appropriated aspects of the dharma. Today, Buddhism in the West has come to be seen as a trendy religion that is followed by stars of screen and television.

Conclusion

It has been shown that cultural accommodation is not new in the history of Buddhism. This was one of the main reasons why Indian Buddhism eventually became accepted into China, and became one of the "Three Religions" (Confucianism, Taoism, and Buddhism) of the Empire. Similarly when Buddhism moved into Japan, it eventually adopted its own character and distinctive teaching there. Now Buddhism is adapting to Western society. There is one major difference with the current situation, and that is that Western culture now has a global quality. Tibetan lamas use modern jets to travel the world. Most Buddhist leaders have their own website, as do many leading monasteries. E-mail provides a way that a teacher can give guidance to his students scattered around the world. New Buddhist publishing houses have been established to meet the increasing demand for teaching on meditation and ancient wisdom.

In the West, Buddhism has become the "trendy" religion. Unlike the terrorist attacks of Muslim fundamentalists and the military response of the Christian West, the Dalai Lama has advocated peace, saying, "I believe violence will only increase the cycle of violence." [16] Buddhism has the potential to greatly affect the global world that is emerging.

Notes

1 For example, *Majjhima Nikaya*1:63.

2 Paul Williams, *Buddhist Thought* (London: Routledge, 2000)

3 L. G. Thompson, *Chinese Religion* (Wadsworth: Belmont, 1989), 113.

4 R. R. Covell, *Confucius, The Buddha, and Christ* (Orbis: Maryknoll, 1986), 147.

5 Ibid.

6 N. Smart, *Buddhism and Christianity: Rivals and Allies* (Hawaii: University of Hawaii Press, 1993), p. 34.

7 Emma McCloy Layman, *Buddhism in America* (Chicago: Nelson-Hall, 1978).

8 "Karma Chameleons," *The Times Magazine*(9 Feb 2002): 22–26.

9 J. Kornfield, "Is Buddhism Changing North America" in *Buddhist America: Centres, Retreats, Practices*, ed. Don Moreale (Santa Fe: John Muir Publications, 1988), xi-xxviii.

10 D. Kay, "The New Kadampa Tradition and the Continuity of Tibetan Buddhism in Transition," *Journal of Contemporary Religion* 12 (1997): 277-293.

11 Geshe Kelsang Gyatso, *Universal Compassion* (London: Tharpa Publications, 1997).

12 R. N. Ostling, "Monks vs. Monks," *Times.com* 11 May 1998

13 Sangharakshita, *New Currents in Western Buddhism* (Glasgow: Windhorse, 1990), 66.

14 Sangharakshita, *The History of my Going for Refuge* (Glasgow: Windhorse, 1988), 115.

15 D. S. Lopez, *Prisoners of Shangri-La* (Chicago: University of Chicago Press, 1999).

16 Dalai Lama, *Dharma Life* Winter 2001:6.

Elements of a Biblical and Genuine Missionary Encounter with Diaspora Chinese Buddhists in Southeast Asia

Tan Kang-San

What Is a Diaspora Chinese Buddhist?

Chinese people can be divided demographically into three main categories: Chinese in mainland China, Chinese who live in Hong Kong and Taiwan, and "overseas Chinese" who live outside these three nations. The last category, "overseas Chinese," may also be termed "Diaspora Chinese," a concept deriving from the Greek word, "diaspora" meaning dispersal or dispersion. It is estimated that there are 1.2 billion Chinese in mainland China and another 200 million overseas Chinese.

Most Chinese consider themselves Buddhists, although they practise a heterogeneous mixture of Chinese religious beliefs derived from Buddhism, Taoism, and Confucianism (Wee and Davies 1998, 80). In reality, one cannot strictly separate a Chinese Buddhist from the teachings of these Chinese religious beliefs. Instead of strict categories, it is more helpful to draw a continuum of a Chinese Buddhist religiosity according to the degree of its mixture with Chinese traditional beliefs.

It would be drawn as follows:

Chinese Folklore » Taoism/Confucianism » Inclusive Buddhist » Exclusive Buddhist.

The focus of this paper is on the last two categories, Buddhist-influenced Chinese, whose dominant belief systems tend toward Buddhist teaching in its varied forms. Although there is no initiation ceremony to become a Buddhist, a "born again" or practicing Buddhist may undertake a commitment to the Three Refuges. In essence, it can be said that a Buddhist is one who takes the Buddha, Dhamma, and Sangha as guides to life and thought.

Although loosely defined, the term "Chinese Buddhist," or "Chinese Buddhism," is an established term in academic circles. [1] In his study on the development of Buddhism in Singapore, "Buddhist Development in a Secular State," Trevor Ling noted that there is an increasing trend for teachers of Buddhism to distinguish pure Buddhist teachings from those of other Chinese religions (1993, 71). Similarly, the writers below argue that Buddhism is growing at the expense of Chinese religions:

> The early Chinese migrants drew nourishment from oral rather than canonical traditions … The high rate of literacy among Chinese overseas of the 1990s has contributed significantly to the decline of Chinese religion and to the concomitant rise of canonical religions, in particular Christianity and Buddhism (Wee and Davies 1998, 82).

Counting Diaspora Chinese Buddhists?

Although I am aware of the difficulties in estimating the number of Buddhists and the lack of statistics on number of Diaspora Chinese, I think it is helpful for us to provide a rough "guesstimate" of the number of "Chinese Buddhists" in East Asia (see table below). I put an estimate of about fifty-six million Diaspora Chinese in these East Asian countries of which thirty-seven million may be Buddhist influenced or practitioners (excluding pure Chinese religionists). The table below is provided to give an idea of the tremendous challenge and opportunity facing Christian mission among Buddhists. If one includes mainland China, the Chinese Buddhists may conservatively represent over 660 million people!

Country	Chinese Population	Estimated % Buddhist	Estimated No. Buddhist	Dominant School
Cambodia	550,000	80%	440,000	Theravada
Hong Kong	6,700,000	70%	4,690,000	Mahayana
Japan	252,000	80%	201,000	Pureland, Zen
S. Korea	234,000	60%	140,500	?
Malaysia	5,561,000	70%	3,893,000	Mahayana
Myanmar	1,368,000	70%	1,000,000	Theravada?
Indonesia	8,520,000	40%	3,408,000	Mahayana
Philippines	1,500,000	50%	750,000	Mahayana
Singapore	3,143,000	50%	1,571,600	Mahayana
Taiwan	21868,000	70%	15,307,600	Mahayana
Thailand	6,000,000	95%	5,700,000	Theravada
Vietnam	800,000	50%	400,000	Mahayana
Total Diaspora Chinese	56,496,000	66%	37,501,000	

China	1,253,567,000	50%	626,783,500	Mahayana, Lamaistic

Table 1: The Diaspora Chinese Buddhists of East Asia [2]

Malaysian Chinese as a Contextual Example of Chinese Diaspora [3]

Within the limits of this paper, I now seek to illustrate the socio-historical context of a Chinese Diaspora community by focusing on the Malaysian Chinese Buddhists. [4]

Before 1970, religious data were seriously defective because the Malaysian government census committee wrongly assumed that all Europeans were Christians, all Malays were Muslims, and all Chinese were Buddhists (see discussion in Sidhu and Jones 1981, 234-236).

Most Chinese in Malaysia practice a mixture of Taoism, Confucianism, and Buddhism. They borrow from, and freely integrate their folk religious practices with, the three Chinese religions to fulfill the practical needs of family, finances, and business. It is common for Chinese homes to have a kitchen god, family ancestor altar, as well as Buddhist or Confucius deity. Although the Malaysian population census did not distinguish between Mahayana and Theravada Buddhists, Ackerman and Lee rightly assume that most Chinese in Malaysia are adherents of the Mahayana tradition (1988, 47). Many Mahayana religious groups are affiliated with the Malaysian Buddhist Association. Apart from many small temples scattered throughout the country, a few Mahayana temples such as Kek Lok Si (a Pure Land Sect temple), bring symbolic unity to Buddhists. Many of the temples are run by families or by a committee of lay leaders. Increasingly, as more Mahayana monks are being trained (mostly in Taiwan), these temples may appoint a resident monk.

Theravada Buddhism received its influence and funding mostly from Thailand and Sri Lanka. Through the Buddhist Missionary Society, there was a resurgence of missionary interest among university students during the early 1970s. There were other groups such as the Japan-based Nichiren Daishonin Buddhist movements and the nonsectarian Dhamafarers' Movement that emerged during this period of Buddhist revivalism.

Elements of a Genuine Missionary Encounter with Diaspora Chinese Buddhists

Christian missions have been active in Buddhist heartlands for centuries. Despite the relative freedom (compared to missions among Muslims) given to Christian missionary work, we have not seen major breakthroughs of Chinese Buddhists coming to Christ. Various approaches and strategies have been developed, mostly on how to penetrate the Buddhist world as people groups. To these approaches, I hope to contribute a more fundamental orientation, phrased by way of the following questions: is there a genuine encounter with Buddhist worldviews? [5] And, what constitutes a genuine and biblical missionary encounter? These questions assume it is possible to be engaged in religious chatter where the underlying belief systems of

Buddhists are not being addressed. In the remaining section, I will outline key elements of a genuine missionary encounter between Christian and Buddhist in a Diaspora Chinese context.

Dialogical

If there is to be a genuine encounter between the Christian and Buddhist, the religious exchange need to be dialogical, in contrast to being a one-sided presentation of the gospel. The Christian and the encounter partners interact as equals. Instead of the traditional image of the evangelist/missionary as the "teacher" who has all the answers and the Buddhist as the "student" who has nothing to contribute, encounter takes "the subject and person seriously" (Stott 1975, 61). It recognizes that both the Christian and the Buddhist have something to contribute to the interreligious encounter. Dominance and control are abandoned, and the Christian, in particular, does not determine the agenda of encounter.

If Christians take the dialogical element seriously, then studying Buddhist belief systems becomes an essential prerequisite. Books such as *The Teaching of Buddha*, Rupert Gethin's *Foundations of Buddhism*, and Smart and Hecht's *Sacred Texts of the World: A Universal Anthology* must become standard reading, not only for potential missionaries but also for the average thinking Christian. In addition, views on Jesus Christ and about Christianity from a Buddhist perspective are invaluable. In academic studies, the *Buddhist-Christian Studies Journal* is another example of essential reading. [6]

Person Centered

A dialogical approach is audience sensitive in the sense that the unique qualities of individuals, not abstract theory, guide the process. In addition, it is flexible and acknowledges that there is no one right method or strategy for encountering people of other faiths. Whenever the Christian-Buddhist encounter is person centered, the interreligious exchange becomes dynamic rather than "steps" in a lock step procedure. In the Asian context, how one encounters overseas Chinese must be highly differentiated from the way that same individual interacts with Buddhists. Similarly, different evangelistic approaches are needed for reaching Theravada Buddhists than for reaching Zen Buddhists and for reaching English-educated Chinese than for reaching Chinese-educated Chinese. Instead of applying a reductionistic approach, the Christian takes the individual person and his Buddhist worldviews seriously. Recognizing the close identification of being Chinese with being a Buddhist, a person-centered element will increase the sensitivities of the Christian partner.

Incarnational

Another element of a genuine encounter is that it is incarnational. Incarnation takes seriously both Christianity and the Buddhist culture in the interreligious encounter. Increasingly, mission theoreticians are realizing the intimate relationship between "culture" and "the Christian faith." The Christian faith needs to be expressed in people's lives through symbols and modes native to the Buddhist culture. Only then will the gospel be a source of transformation for the Diaspora Chinese cultural context. The vision is for each Chinese cultural expression of the Christian faith to be capable of renewing and enriching the universal Christian community.

Verdict Oriented

Genuine missionary encounter is verdict oriented. The pluralist model that shuns the evaluation of competing truth claims is not a genuine encounter because there is nothing at stake. Partners in dialogue do not engage in genuine dialogue but mere religious chatter. Paul J. Griffiths, Professor of Philosophy of Religions at the University of Chicago Divinity School proposes the principle of the necessity of interreligious apologetics, defined as:

> If representative intellectuals belonging to some specific religious community come to judge at a particular time that some or all of their own doctrine-expressing sentences are incompatible with some alien religious claim(s), then they should feel obliged to engage in both positive and negative apologetics vis-à-vis these alien religious claim(s) and their promulgators (1991, 3).

For example, there is a seeming contradiction between the Buddhist claims that 1) there are no spiritual substances (soul), and 2) each person is reborn many times. Genuine encounter mean the Christian must be willing to point out the contradictions of some Buddhist beliefs. Too many pseudo-dialogues are involved in mutual admiration exchanges rather than genuinely encouraging honest expressions of what we find troubling in the other traditions.

Religious encounter between the Christian and Buddhist will at some point require truth validation. Genuine and biblical encounter must include both elements of 1) *negative* (or defensive) *apologetics* whereby the Christian is concern with the attacks upon the truth of Christianity and responding to show that such truths are defensible, and 2) *positive* (or offensive) *apologetics* whereby the Christian is concerned to show that non-Christians also ought to accept the truth claims of Christianity (Netland 1994).

Ten Ground Rules for a Genuine Missionary Encounter with Buddhists

How will the above elements of a genuine missionary encounter with Buddhist be applied in practice? What will a genuine biblical encounter look like?

The first four of the following ground rules for encounter are adapted from Swidler (1983, 1-4), while the second six rules are developed specifically from an Evangelical perspective.

Rule one: The first purpose of encounter is to listen so that we can grow in our understanding about others and about what God is doing in their lives. "We enter into dialogue so that we can learn, change, and grow, not so we can force change on the other" (Swidler 1983, 2).

Rule two: Interreligious encounter must be a two-sided discourse within each religious community and between the religious communities. Both sides determine the direction and agenda of the missionary encounter.

Rule three: Encounter can take place only on the basis of mutual trust. Each participant must come to the encounter with complete honesty and sincerity and must assume a similar honesty and sincerity in the other individual—in brief: no trust, no encounter. Encounter, ideally, must be formed in a context of authentic reciprocal friendship.

Rule four: People entering into interreligious encounter must be at least minimally self-critical of both themselves and their own religions. Swidler explains:

> A lack of such self-criticism implies that one's own tradition already has all the correct answers. Such an attitude makes encounter not only unnecessary, but even impossible, since we enter into dialogue primarily so we can learn—which obviously is impossible if our tradition has never made a misstep, if it has all the right answers (1983, 3).

Rule five: Where possible, parameters for encounter should be considered and identified as clearly as possible. This rule is particularly crucial in formal encounters. Such clarification serves a three-fold purposes: (1) it delineates the different expectations that participants have over the dialogical encounter, (2) it demarcates certain encounters (such as a common search for spiritual and mystical truth) as outside the boundaries for evangelicals, and (3) it helps to avoid the predictable propensity many have to shift from encounter into sermonic monologue.

Rule six: Participants should speak from the perspective of their faith and personal religious conviction ("encounter of life"). Encounter must not be content with mere propositional statements but should move into a deep sharing of faith commitments. Evangelical encounter must eventually include witness about the lordship of Jesus Christ and persuasion that all humankind needs to put their faith in him. Here, proclamation is not incompatible with encounter.

Rule seven: True and genuine encounter will not only include mutual witness but also critical evaluation of all truth claims. In the first rule above, the immediate purpose of encounter is to understand and change. From an evangelical perspective, however, encounter must go beyond understanding and include witness (rule six) and critical appraisal of truth claims (rule seven). Where possible, common criteria for evaluating truth claims should be developed together.

Rule eight: "New" insights from encounter must be subjected to various cumulative tests. In particular, the Bible serves as the standard against which all dialogical practices and truth claims are measured, and the church acts as a hermeneutical community where new insights from dialogical encounters are critically appraised. Similarly, other religious communities will subject their dialogical insights to their respective sources of authority.

Rule nine: Encounter, in the final analysis, will include an invitation for personal response. Whatever the form or level of response invited, the practical intent of the encounter is to enable participants, by God's grace, to make historical choices about the praxis of religious faith in the world.

Rule ten: Encounter must be engaged as a spiritual battle, with prayer and conscious dependence on the Holy Spirit. The real enemy is not the encounter partner, but Satan, who has blinded the eyes of unbelievers. Evangelical encounter is really a trialogue, with God as the third partner (Verkuyl 1993, 78).

Limitations of an Evangelical Missionary Encounter

For evangelicals, there are certain types of encounter that border on syncretism and thus are incompatible with Scripture. Such syncretistic encounters seek to combine truths from conflicting religious systems and to manufacture a "third" or new truth. That "truth," however, invariably contradicts God's truth as presented in Scripture.

The various dangers surrounding certain types of encounters should not be used as excuses by evangelicals to avoid interreligious encounter with people of other faiths. Rather, in order to overcome such dangers, evangelicals should root their missionary encounters in firm theological truth. In his discussion on contextualization, Hiebert suggests the following checks against syncretism: the Bible, the Holy Spirit, and the Church as a hermeneutical community (1994, 91-92). Similarly, the same filters can be applied to the outcomes of encounter.

Throughout the process of encounter, evangelicals should be aware of at least four limitations surrounding encounter:

First, encounter should not follow a Hegelian model of searching for "new" truth. Instead, encounter should be viewed as a way of understanding others and what God has done and is doing in their lives. Doing so allows us to change our misconceptions and to grow in our understanding of God and others. All truths, furthermore, should be received and assessed critically within the biblical revelation. The Bible, as God's special revelation, is the final authority for the Christian in encounter.

Second, encounter must not turn into a reductionism of all religious truths. "The intention is not to arrive at some lowest common denominator in the hope of reaching an irenic common ground of religious affirmations" (Sheard 1987, 282). There must be no preconditions that require participants to discard their fundamental beliefs. Evangelicals must be allowed to enter into encounter with firm convictions shaped by the gospel, just as Muslims and other religionists must also be free to enter into encounter with their own religious convictions.

Third, Evangelicals do not enter into encounter to experience other religions "from within." We seek to understand our dialogical partners' worldviews, not to mystically experience their religions. We need to acknowledge that, as outsiders, we will never fully understand other religions as insiders do, but that does not mean we cannot understand the basics of their religions. We can learn by listening and asking questions. But we will not engage in the worship practices of other faiths.

Fourth, encounter, by itself, does not fulfill God's Great Commission in Matthew 28:19-20. In an open environment, proclamation is primary. In restrictive and problematic situations, evangelicals should, at an appropriate stage and context of encounter, witness about the truth of the gospel and call people to put their faith in Jesus Christ. Some Chinese Buddhists are ready and receptive to the gospel. Others might have assimilated deep Buddhist values and beliefs. In any event, encounter cannot replace the preaching of the gospel as God's appointed means of bringing salvation to the lost.

Closing Comment

The Buddhist world has not been well represented in missions mobilization and education among evangelical missions. The average Chinese Christian, though living in a Buddhist world, knows very little about the basic beliefs of his or her Buddhist neighbor. The occasional ventures into evangelism have tended towards one-sided invitations to come to church. The culture, symbols, and thought patterns of Chinese worldviews, as integrated and shaped by Buddhist philosophies and teachings, remain largely unchallenged. In mission preparation, for missionaries working among Buddhists, there are many gaps to be filled, particularly in understanding Buddhist beliefs and practices.

Genuine missionary encounter will not be a one sided proclamation of the gospel. Neither will genuine missionary encounter be mere religious chatter over a cup of tea. The central thesis of my paper is that the effectiveness of Christian mission among Buddhists in the coming decades will be directly related to the church's willingness to enter into genuine and biblical missionary encounter, shaped by these basic elements: that it is dialogical, person centered, incarnational and verdict oriented. All these elements must ultimately be God-centered, undergirded by a spirit of dependence upon the Lord expressed through humble and agonizing prayers. May His kingdom come, His will be done on earth as it is in heaven!

Notes

1 See Knight 1959 for an early usage of the term "Chinese Buddhism" and a good historical background of how Buddhism became integral to Chinese religious practice. Another excellent study is Jones 1999.

2 Database on Johnstone and Mandryk 2001.

3 A cursory survey of Buddhism in these Asian countries will confirm the great diversities of local features of Buddhism due to political and socio-historical factors in each country. There is an urgent need for a country-specific survey of the development of Buddhism in Asia.

4 A good reference for other Diaspora Chinese Communities is edited by Lynn Pan (1998).

5 For further study on worldviews, see Burnett 1990.

6 Paul J. Griffiths' *Christianity Through Non-Christian Eyes* gives a selection of non-Christian perceptions of Christianity. The editors of the *Buddhist-Christian Studies Journal*, Rita M. Gross and Terry C. Muck, brought together contributions by six Buddhist and six Christian scholars in an excellent study, *Buddhists Talk about Jesus and Christians Talk about the Buddha* (2000).

References

Ackerman Susan and Lee Raymond. 1988. *Heaven in Transition: Non-Muslim Religious Innovation and Ethnic Identity in Malaysia*. Honolulu: University of Hawaii Press.

Burnett, David. 1990. *Clash of Worlds*. Crowborough: MARC.

Gethin, Rupert. 1998. *Foundations of Buddhism*. Oxford: Oxford University Press.

Griffiths, Paul J. 1991. *An Apology for Apologetics*. Maryknoll: Orbis Books.

——. 1994. *Christianity through Non-Christian Eyes*. Maryknoll: Orbis Books.

Gross, Rita M. and Terry Muck. 2000. *Buddhists Talk about Jesus and Christians Talk about the Buddha*. New York: Continuum.

Hiebert, Paul. 1994. *Anthropological Reflections for Missiological Issues*. Grand Rapids: Baker Book House.

Jones, Charles Brewer. 1999. *Buddhism in Taiwan: Religion and History, 1660–1990*. Hawaii: University of Hawaii Press.

Johnstone, Patrick and Jason Mandryk. 2001. *Operation World*. Cumbria: Paternoster.

Knight, Arthur F. 1959. *Buddhism in Chinese History*. Stanford: Stanford University Press.

Ling, Trevor. 1993. *Buddhist Development in a Secular State. Buddhist Trends in South East Asia*, ed. Trevor Ling. Singapore: Institute of South East Asian Studies.

Netland, Harold A. 1994. Truth, Authority and Modernity: Shopping for Truth in a Supermarket of Worldviews. *Faith and Modernity* eds. Philip Sampson, Vinay Samuel and Chris Sudgen. Oxford: Regnum Books International.

Pan, Lynn, ed. 1998. *The Encyclopedia of the Chinese Overseas*. Singapore: Archipelago Press.

Sheard, Robert B. 1987. *Interreligious Dialogue in the Catholic Church Since Vatican II: An Historical and Theological Study*. Lewiston: Edwin Mellen Press.

Sidhu, M.S. and Gavin W. Jones. 1981. *Population Dynamics in a Plural Society: Peninsular Malaysia*. Kuala Lumpur: University of Malaya Press.

Smart, Ninian and Richard D. Hecht. 1997. *Sacred Texts of the World: a Universal Anthology*. New York: Crossroad.

Stott, John. 1975. *Christian Mission in the Modern World*. Downers Grove: Inter-Varsity Press.

Swidler, Leonard, ed. 1987. *Toward a Universal Theology of Religion*. Maryknoll: Orbis Books.

Verkyull, Johannes. 1993. The Kingdom of God: Test of Validity for Theology of Religions. *The Good News of The Kingdom: Mission Theology for the Third Millennium*, eds. Charles Van Engen, Dean S. Gilliland, and Paul Pierson. 71-81. Maryknoll: Orbis Books.

Wee, Vivienne and Gloria Davies. 1998. Religion. *The Encyclopedia of the Chinese Overseas*, ed. Lynn Pan. Singapore: Archipelago Press.

Missiological Implications
of the Key Contrasts
between Buddhism and Christianity

Alex Smith

Introduction

Karma, nirvana, reincarnation, the Dalai Lama, sand mandalas and the Buddha are well known and commonly used terms, even among Christians in this twenty-first century. Burgeoning Buddhism increasingly influences the cultures of our global village. In some countries, it permeates all from education to environment. In the West, "Buddhism in the boardroom" is common. The January 2000 issue of *Civilization* magazine claims a "Buddha boom" is saturating Western culture. Society and modern business integrate Buddhist practices, if not its tenets. Its popularity is enhanced by its celebrity status in Hollywood. Peoples' identities are tied to it. Buddhist temples sprout like mushrooms in the West and East alike. The variegated mosaic of many varieties of Buddhism opens the door for popular "People's Buddhism." The eclectic nature and doctrine of assimilation within Buddhism tolerate selective expression of individuals seeking their own Buddhahood. This mixture of Buddhist precepts with other beliefs produces Folk Buddhism. Followers of Folk Buddhism now number about one billion worldwide.

Contemporary Growth

This considerable growth of Buddhism in the last half century is quite evident, especially in the West. First, some of this expansion rides on the wave of the popularity of Folk Buddhism. Buddhist exhibitions, such as the one in Sydney, Australia in November 2001, focus on introducing people to "this multiple world of Buddha, this sense that Buddhahood is not a being, but it's a state that exists within us all" (*The Courier Mail*, Saturday, November 3, 2001). Buddhism is said to be the fastest growing religion in Australia today.

Second, some growth also comes from renewed efforts of missionary outreach by Buddhists. In 2001 a new Theravada Buddhist Missionary Training University was opened in Yangon, Myanmar. It is already drawing international students from many lands. In Thailand, the *Bangkok Post* in July issues of 2000 and also 2001 featured front-cover pictures of mass ordinations of two hundred hill tribesmen entering the monkhood at Wat Benjamabopit in the Dusit district of Bangkok. These events were organized by the Public Welfare Department to promote Buddhism. Last year, a Thai woman was ordained in Sri Lanka into the Buddhist Order. This may become a new growing trend.

Third, expansive growth has also been fostered through building huge, ornate, and expensive temples. Malaysia, an Islamic State, now has the largest sitting Buddha in Southeast Asia. It was opened recently at Wat Machimmaram in Tumpat in the eastern state of Kelantan (*Bangkok Post*, September 11, 2001). Around this same time, Muslim Taliban in Afghanistan were destroying two towering ancient Buddhist statutes, while nearby Tajikistan, also an Islamic land, restored a huge terra cotta figure of a reclining "Buddha in Nirvana" (*The Oregonian*, Tuesday, March 27, 2001; Wednesday, April 4, 2001). Last year while traveling in China about two hours south of Kunming, Yunnan, I observed the massive construction of a large Buddhist complex of three tiers up a mountainside. In the Buddhist state of Myanmar, two thousand of the five thousand pagodas around ancient Pagan have been refurbished in recent years. On August 18, 2001, "the largest Buddhist temple outside Asia—the Great Stupa of Dharmakaya which Liberates Upon Seeing" was consecrated at the Rocky Mountain Shambhala Center in Red Feather Lakes, just two hours from Denver Colorado, USA. This stupa commemorates the resting place of Chogyam Trungpa Rinpoche, the Tibetan meditation master and the father of Shambhala Buddhism. He was a powerful figure in spreading that religion in the Western world, first in Britain and later in North America. He also developed a network of 150 meditation centers around the world (*The Economist*, August 18, 2001).

Another significant movement into Buddhism in the last forty-five years occurred primarily in the four Indian states of Maharastra, Orissa, Uttar Pradesh, and Bihar. In it, ten million Dalit, low-caste Hindus have turned en mass to Buddhism. This turning to New Buddhism is among the largest People Movements of modern times and is still growing. It was started by their leader, Dr. Bhimrao Ramji Ambedkar, a lawyer, statesman, activist, and one of the drafters of India's Constitution, following India's independence from Britain. He was of the Dalit, or scheduled untouchable caste, and sparked this emancipation movement around 1956 when he became a Buddhist just a few months before his death. (For more details check www.lclark.edu~canwell/thali.)

Fifth, Buddhist revival is spreading in China, where many youth and young professionals can be seen making offerings of candles and incense sticks as they visit the Buddhist shrines throughout the Peoples Republic of China. Possibly some of this overall growth of Buddhism is riding on the wave of the new spirituality being ushered in during postmodern times.

Concerns for the Church

Not only does this modern expansion of Buddhism raise difficulties for control by the traditional Buddhist hierarchy, but it also causes concerns for the church. It even affects governments like China's, where the popular Falungong Buddhist explosion has been outlawed.

First, church leaders seek illusive answers to the question of why many churches have failed to reach out effectively to droves of people experimenting with a new spirituality and flocking to Eastern religions in this postmodern era.

Furthermore, some from the Christian camp are now calling themselves "Jesus Buddhists." As Terry Muck pointed out, People's Buddhism, particularly in the West, with its "emphasis on individual practice has led to a kind of eclectic spirituality that comingles Buddhist practice with Christian, Jewish and even Sufi forms of spirituality" (*Missiology: An International Review,* Vol. XXVII No.1, January 2000, 42). Muck points out that some of these "Buddhist Christians" use forms of Buddhist meditation as they worship in Christian churches. "Christian Buddhists" may attend Christian churches to embrace certain aspects of Christianity without abandoning Buddhism. Nowadays some denominations and churches in the USA are holding Christian-Buddhist seminars in their facilities during Sunday School. Some churches have been bought and converted into Buddhist temples. This "interpenetration of Buddhism and Christianity" is what Arnold Toynbee predicted would mark the late twentieth century. This new fact of pluralism raises tensions among traditional churches and theologians as the growing trend of folk religion, including eclectic folk Christianity, increases.

Third, many Christians are confused with such a mixture, lacking clarity of understanding for either true Buddhism or real Christianity. Many terms used in both seem similar whereas, in fact, when these terms are carefully defined, there is considerable discrepancy in meaning. Of grave concern is the question, "What attitudes should Christians have towards Buddhists and those of other faiths?" In the Spirit of Christ, Christians should exhibit a merciful attitude, offer a loving apologetic, and yet humbly, without shame, maintain their biblical beliefs. In *Christianity among the Religions of the World,* Arnold Toynbee makes a crucial point suggesting "that we can have conviction without fanaticism, we can have belief and action without arrogance or self-centeredness or pride" (1957, 110).

Lastly, the vital issue is one of communication. Can the church effectively communicate with Buddhists—whether in Asia, or in their own back yards? This is a real challenge, particularly for the Asian church, which is usually a tiny Christian pool in a huge majority, Buddhist pond. More attention should be given to developing indigenous drama and native music appropriate to those cultures, both for evangelism and for worship. Significant symbols and cultural festivals need also to be analyzed and addressed and, where appropriate, adequate functional substitutes should be developed. Above all, in Buddhist Asia, the mode of teaching, preaching, and communicating should focus much more on the use of storytelling, parables, and riddles. Local drama and music are also valuable tools. A potent illustration of the power of this occurred two years ago when the Muang Thai Church did an indigenous musical presentation adapted from Thai culture for a group of overseas people, myself included. Afterwards one of the Thai Buddhist waiters who served our tables expressed his feelings: "As I listened the hairs on my arms stood up. I felt that music very deep down inside of me."

Context of History

A review of some selected broad strokes from history may help to understand the development of Buddhism, stemming from its Hindu roots. Around 1525 B.C., Aryans from Central Asia invaded and migrated throughout the Indus Valley during the beginning of the Vedic age in India. (Around the same time the Hittites sacked Babylon and the Shang Dynasty ruled in China.) By 1400 B.C. Hinduism had taken root in India. The Rig-Veda was written in 1300 B.C., just before the Exodus of Israel from Egypt occurred (Carling 1985).

Some of the key concepts that were developed in Hinduism became foundational to Buddhism later. In 900 B.C. the principle of *karma* was developed and *The Upanishads* were written. By 800 B.C. the concept of "a single world spirit of Brahman" was prevalent. This monistic concept became integral to many Eastern religions.

While Daniel, the Israelite prince, was in early exile in a palace in Babylon under King Nebuchadnezzar, Siddhartha Gautama was a prince in a palace of the Kingdom of Kosala in today's Nepal. About thirty-five years later, Gautama found Enlightenment in 528 B.C. His new religion of Buddhism was heavily influenced by the parent beliefs of Hinduism. He borrowed *karma*, adapted transmigration of soul to become reincarnation, and espoused monistic ideas. He also rejected all gods, spiritual entities, and the caste system.

Other Eastern religions besides Buddhism and Jainism arose around this same time. Later, they received interaction with and considerable influence from Buddhism. The Confucian tradition of morality and duty had already begun in 595 B.C., with Taoism following about 100 years later.

Carling's History Chart indicates that by 295 B.C., Buddhism had entered China. Shortly afterwards, Emperor Asoka of India consolidated his vast conquests and simultaneously sent Buddhist missionary priests throughout the kingdom, bringing that religion to Ceylon (Sri Lanka), and spreading it eastwards into Southeast Asia.

Around 195 B.C. the Epics of *Ramayana* and *Mahabharata* arose. The Hindu poem, *Bhagavad Gita*, was written soon after. By about 95 B.C., India had developed a legal code and the earlier class system, instituted in 700 B.C., had become an entrenched caste system. Buddhism was still a significant influence throughout the Indian sub-continent.

Within a decade or so of Christ's birth, Buddha had become deified in the East. By then, ornate Buddhist temples and artistic sculptures were prevalent. Around 95 A.D. a new thrust of Buddhism into Central Asia and China occurred.

One hundred years later, while Buddhism was flourishing throughout much of Asia, it was in decline in India. Towards the end of the fourth century A.D., the golden age of Hinduism arose. Hinduism continued to reclaim India over the next millennium.

Significantly, after the first few centuries of the early entrance of Christianity into India, in 495 A.D. several key new Hindu gods arose, notably: *Brahma* (creator), *Vishnu* (preserver), *Shiva* (destroyer), and *Parati* (Shiva's wife). Then in 605 A.D., *Khrisna*, the incarnation of Vishnu, arrived on the scene, followed by multitudes of other gods and heroes.

Observe that key concepts were developed and added to the Hindu-Buddhist milieu over time, including later adaptations through contact with and reactions to Christianity as it expanded.

By 700 A.D., the Buddhist kingdoms of Srivihaya in Indonesia and the Khmer of Cambodia were in full power. About that time, Buddhism also spread into Nepal and Tibet. In the seventh century A.D., the Islamic religion arose, and by the early eighth century invaded northern India from Arabia, introducing Islam to India. The first Muslim rule in India was established soon after. By 1200, Islam had started to replace Buddhism in Sumatra and Java, Indonesia.

Throughout the colonial period, Asian religions continued to encounter Christianity but remained largely entrenched and relatively unaffected by it. The advance of Catholic missions in the sixteenth and seventeenth centuries saw only moderate response. The modern Protestant missionary movement of the nineteenth century also encountered small increases for the church in Asia. In the twentieth century, increased growth of Christianity occurred, but was still quite minimal among most Buddhist peoples, with the notable exception of those in Korea, and later, China.

At the end of the nineteenth century, through the efforts of Colonel H.S. Olcott, along with Madam Blavatsky, a Buddhist renewal was sparked in Ceylon. This also influenced the strengthening of Buddhism throughout Southeast Asia.

In 1891 Olcott formulated fourteen "Fundamental Buddhistic Beliefs." Later in 1945, Christmas Humphreys developed "Twelve Principles of Buddhism." These provided a codified foundational platform for agreement among all of the Buddhist sects: Theravada, Mahayana, and Vajrayana or Tibetan forms.

Concepts in Contrast

Significant differences in foundational beliefs and teachings exist between Buddhism and Christianity. In other ways, there are many similarities which have been observed and explored by writers elsewhere. In today's climate of eclectic choices and unfortunate ignorance of the fundamental teachings of these great religions, a chance to revisit them is warranted. Twelve key contrasting elements are summarized below, but only the first nine will be discussed in this paper:

1. Source of Creation: Impersonal Karma or Personal God

2. Nature of Things: The Universe—Transitory Illusion or Concrete Reality.

3. Nature of Christ: Human Only or God-Man

4. Nature of Humans: Soullessness or Eternal Soul-Spirit

5. Nature of Sin: Karmic Consequences or Rebellion against the Holy God

6. Source of Salvation: Self or God

7. Provision of Redemption: Earned Merit or Christ's Substitution

8. Basis for Spiritual Life: Reincarnation or Regeneration

9. Destiny and Finality: Nirvana or Eternal Life

10. Authority of Scriptures: Open Canon or Closed Revelation

11. View of Suffering: Basic Nature of Existence or Primary Effect of Evil

12. Principle of Expansion: Assimilation or Exclusiveness

1. Source of Creation: Impersonal Karma or Personal God.

Buddhism has little specific teaching on creation. It primarily accepts an evolutionary viewpoint, if any. The universe resulted from karma, a kind of cycle of cause and effect. In his helpful *What Buddhists Believe*, Dr. K. Sri Dhammananda, one of the leading Buddhist scholars of today, writes: "According to Buddha, it is inconceivable to find a first cause for life or anything else. For in common experience, the cause becomes the effect and the effect becomes the cause. In the circle of cause and effect, a first cause is incomprehensible." He points out therefore that "Buddhism does not pay much attention to theories and beliefs about the origin of the world" (1998, 113-114).

So the Christian God, the self-existent One, as personal Creator existing outside of the universes and all things He created, is inconceivable to Buddhists. Another leading Buddhist authority, Bhikkhu Buddhadasa Indapanno, in his *Christianity and Buddhism* lectures, equated God with impersonal *karma*, thus rejecting God's eternal personality and His purposeful relation to His created world. Indapanno argues that if God is the cause of all things then He must be equated with *karma* (1967, 66-67). Instead of the Creator God being separate from and outside of His creation, Buddhists take a monistic view that espouses *karma* and all things as parts of creation itself.

Indapanno also proposed a second view of God by equating Him with *avijja* meaning lack of knowledge, or ignorance. He argues that if God caused all things to exist, then He is the cause of suffering. In Buddhist views, suffering is caused by ignorance of the Four Noble Truths of the enlightened Buddha.

The Christian viewpoint, of a supreme personal Creator God of holy character, infinite grace, and eternal being, is found in Scripture from Genesis through Revelation. Genesis 1:1 declares, "In the beginning God created the heavens and the earth..." (NIV, See also Revelation 10:6). Then, towards the end of the Bible, an angel is sent to proclaim an eternal gospel to all nations and peoples on the earth saying, "Fear God and give Him glory...and worship Him who made the heaven and the earth and sea and springs of water" (Rev. 14:7 NASB).

The key issue at stake is the very existence of God. My interaction with students in Asia has often started by their challenge, "You show us God and then we will believe." I immediately ask for clarification, "By that, do you mean that if you cannot see things, they do not exist?" Following the students' affirmation, I then ask them to explain to me what the scent of a rose looks like. Then I encourage them to stop breathing, because the air they depend on cannot be seen, so does not exist! I ask, "Please explain to me what electricity actually looks like." They usually describe the power poles and the electric lines, not the electricity, which is invisible. Finally, I ask them if they've ever seen a ghost or spirit. Their answer frequently is, "Well, no. But I have a friend who did." Then I affirm that I believe in the spirits, including evil demons and the Holy Spirit of God, who is the Creator of all. Usually by this time, they realize there are things that do exist though they cannot be seen.

A couple of missiological implications arise here. First, in approaching Buddhists, we need to be aware that the concept of God is very difficult for them to grasp. Often our evangelism starts with John 3:16 or the Four Laws, both of which start with the word, "God." We encourage people to accept Jesus without the context of the Creator God who sent Him.

Second, new believers need to be taught, in terms that they can comprehend, the greatness and importance of the theology of God: His holy character, His powerful nature and His high attributes.

One of the most exciting indigenous contextualizations of the Person and power of God, especially showing Jesus as God, was produced in a circle of paintings created by a Sherpa in Nepal. The Buddhist cycle of life is portrayed, but the resurrected Christ is seen breaking out of that cycle of life. Inside that cycle are panels or sections of painted scenes portraying the miracles and key events in the life of Christ. Right in the center of the whole is a smaller circle, showing His power over nature. Christ is walking on the water in the midst of the storm. That is a powerful expression of contextualizing the all-powerful God of Creation. Unfortunately, when this painting was printed as a poster, well-meaning missionaries replaced that small central circle with a drawing of the cross, even though the crucifixion scene was already in one of the picture panels. Thus, the powerful Creator was sadly and inadvertently dismissed from the indigenous portrait of the God-Man.

2. Nature of Things: The Universe—Transitory Illusion, or Concrete Reality.

The notable scholar Dr. Dhammananda summarizes Buddhist thinking on the state of the universe (1998, 86-87):

- As creation is an empty void of nothingness, so the nature of the universe and all within it is illusionary, and constantly changing.

- "The Buddha described the world as unending flux of

becoming. All is changeable, continuous transformation, ceaseless mutation, and a moving stream. Everything exists from moment to moment. Everything is a recurring rotation of coming into being and then passing out of existence." Life is a continuous movement of change towards death.

- "Nothing on earth partakes of the character of absolute reality." By his law of impermanency "the Buddha denies the existence of eternal substances."

- Both matter and spirit are regarded as "false abstractions" in Buddhism. "What exists is changeable, and what is not changeable does not exist."

- All material forms, including human beings, animals and all gods—everything—"is subject to the law of impermanency." All vanishes away. Even perception is a mirage.

Within Christian cult circles there are some mind-science groups, such as Christian Scientists, who believe disease, sin, and death have no real existence, and are purely caused by mental error.

Traditional Christians would hold to a view of a created material world and real universes, comprised of provable material elements and forces that make them up. They also believe in absolutes, eternal laws, and truth, as well as things of substance and forces that are measurable scientifically.

I have often handed my wristwatch to my Buddhist friends during the discussion of the transitory illusion and changeable nature of all things. First, I suggest that this watch had no creator. It just came into being by itself. "That is impossible," they reply. Second, I ask them to handle it and see if it really works. They feel it, look at it, and check it out. Is it real? Does it exist? Third, I ask them if they understand the value of the watch, in terms of its usefulness. Finally, I remind them how important it is to care for the watch and use it wisely. Each of these points helps in discussing the nature of all things. Natural revelation can also be helpful in discussing the beauty of the created world, as well as its usefulness and value.

The conclusion by King Solomon in *Ecclesiastes* is helpful.

Referring to death, Solomon says, "The dust will return to the earth as it was, and the spirit will return to God who gave it. 'Vanity of vanities,' says the preacher. 'All is vanity'" (Eccl. 12:7-8 NASB). His vital summary of this matter is potent: "The conclusion, when all has been heard, is: fear God and keep His commandments, because this applies to every person. Because God will bring every act to judgment, everything which is hidden, whether it is good or evil" (12:13-14 NASB).

There are two issues for application concerning nature. First, since many things in life are intangible and transient, humans should be careful not to be attached to the material world. On that point we can agree with the Buddhists.

A second missiological application relates to the possible connection for both Christians and Buddhists in the area of ecology. Buddhists are careful about protecting all forms of life, though in practice they have done little better than Christians in exploiting God's resources. Therefore working together in ecological projects, such as reforestation, cleaning up pollution, and caring for the water is most admirable. In China, the government encourages Christians, as good members of society, to be involved in such activities. However, it is important to remember that the viewpoint of the world, which Buddhists hold, contains concepts of monism, which is very different from the Christian creationist view. Buddhists see only one ultimate substance, in which all things are a dependent part. Christians see the independent units of God's creation, set apart from Himself. The Lord said in Genesis 1 and 2 that He created each species to reproduce "after their kind." These differing viewpoints should not work against Christians sharing in harmonious ecological projects with Buddhists.

3. Nature of Christ: Human Only or God-Man

As I frequently discussed Christ with Thai-Buddhists, I often asked them the question, "Who do you think Jesus really is?" Common responses were "a good man," "the founder of the Christian religion," "a wonderful prophet," "a great leader like Buddha," or surprisingly, "the younger brother of Buddha." Thus Buddhists view Jesus only from the human side, not the divine. None of these responses ascribe any deity to Christ. In Jesus' day, the disciple Peter responded to the same question, "Thou art the Christ, the Son of the living God" (Matthew 16:16 NASB).

Among the Buryiat people of Mongolia and Siberia is an old oral legend. Its source probably pre-dates the entrance of Buddhism among them, but has been influenced by it also. The Buryiat legend says that their god of light, called Tenger, looked down on the world and saw a great war going on between the East and the West. So, he sent Gesar, his beloved son, down to set the people free and to rescue humanity. King Gesar was born as a man, not a god, in a simple teepee. King Gesar did not use any of the weapons of heaven on the enemies of his people because he did not believe in killing. He achieved his goals by other means (Becker 1992). This old Buryiat epic has many varieties of endings, some Buddhistic, some Shamanistic, others political. Of course, from the Buddhist viewpoint, this king could only be human, never divine.

But the Apostle Paul describes the Lord Jesus Christ as the image of the invisible God, the first-born of all creation, the "creator of all things," seen or unseen, and the One who pre-existed all things, which are held together through Him (Col. 1:13-20).

The missiological implications of Buddhists viewing Christ as being human only calls Christians to have great care and diligence in portraying Him more accurately during evangelism and discipling. True, we should emphasize the fact that He was very human, partaking of common suffering, such as temptation and eventually the ultimate pain of death on the cross, but we must also teach and recognize Him as the God-man, the pre-existing One, Creator of all, incarnated through the virgin birth, and without sin or *karma*, qualifying Him to be the true Redeemer of mankind. This careful teaching of the nature and character of Christ, not only from the human side, but also His divine side, is essential especially for seekers and new believers.

4. Nature of Humans: Soullessness or Eternal Soul/Spirit

One of the oldest and most fundamental teachings of the Buddha concerns the *anatta* doctrine. *Anatta* could be translated " No-Soul, No-Ego, No-Self or soullessness". There is nothing eternal or unchangeable in humans. Buddhists believe there is no eternal ego-entity that exists in humans past death. Dr. Dhammananda writes, "The Buddha taught that what we conceive as something eternal within us, is merely a combination of physical and mental aggregates or forces." These comprise five *khandhas* body or matter, sensation, perception, mental formations, and consciousness. These forces are constantly in a state of "flux of momentary change". Together they are the component forces "making up the psycho-physical life." When the Buddha analyzed this, "He found only these five aggregates or forces. He did not find any eternal soul." In the Mahayanan School of Buddhism the *anatta* doctrine is known as *sunyata* or voidness. Buddha rejected the two concepts of soul or self, and the Creator God or eternal Spirit (1998, 117-119).

In his *Buddhism and the Claims of Christ*, Dr. D. T. Niles gives excellent descriptions for understanding the Buddhist concepts. He clarifies the basic Buddhist doctrines of *annicca* (impermanance or transitoriness), *anatta* (soullessness or absence of self) and *dukkha* (sorrow, suffering). He writes:

> "If we do not start with God we shall not end with Him, and when we start with Him, we do not end with the doctrines of *annicca, anatta* and *dukkha*
> The existence of God means the existence of an order of life, which is eternal—*nicca* (permanence). It means that there is postulated for the soul—*natta*—an identity which is guarded by God's sovereignty, and that sorrow—*dukkha*—is seen to consist, not so much in the transitoriness of things, as in the perverseness of our wills, which seeks these things instead of the things that are eternal. The circle of the Christian faith can thus be described as that which starting with God leads man to the realization that God alone affords the most adequate base for a most meaningful explanation of life's most significant facts" (1967, 27).

The classical Buddhist view of no-soul/spirit has produced some disagreement within the Buddhist priesthood. There are those who espouse some form of soul entity. In the last couple of years one of these groups at Wat Dhammakaya in Bangkok was severely censured for "corrupting the doctrine and discipline of Theravada Buddhism." Their teaching that "*Nirvana* is a permanent heaven, thus possessing *atta*, or self" was judged to be negating the teachings of Buddha. Other charges proscribed their "commercialization of Buddhism, monk's misconduct, and opaque business investments" (*Bangkok Post* February 19, 1999).

Buddhists seem to have a spiritual hunger, recognized in their dedicated seeking after release from suffering, and by their great efforts in doing good works and making merit. Yet their *khandhas* disintegrate at death, and no entity of self-soul, self-ego, or self-spirit carries on into the next reincarnation. It seems, therefore, that since no personality of soul is reincarnated, the only thing that really is recycled is the accumulated *karma* from past and present lives.

From the biblical perspective, the creation of humans with soul or spirit indicates the high value and the great dignity the Creator put on human beings, made in the *Imagio Deo*.

Here is another significant difference that Christians should observe. They need to treat their Buddhist neighbors and associates with the same human dignity and value as those created in that image of God. This will especially affect their attitudes and approaches to Buddhist peoples when relating to them or while presenting Christ to them humbly, meekly, and respectably.

5. Nature of Sin: Karmic Consequences or Rebellion against the Holy God

The basic five laws or *Sila* that Buddhists commonly follow are often practiced only occasionally by many lay persons. I have often heard my Buddhist friends say, "Well, I followed the five laws today, being perfect in thought, word and deed." But what about overcoming their failures during the other 364 days of the year? There is no way to remit them.

I remember meeting one fine Buddhist woman in North Thailand who said, "I have never sinned." Primarily, when Buddhists say this they mean they have not killed life. From the Buddhist viewpoint, man is neither sinful by nature nor seen to be in rebellion against God. "In each human is a vast store of good as well as evil." Dr. Dhammananda writes, "According to Buddhism, there is no such thing as sin as explained by other religions. To the Buddhists sin is unskillful or unwholesome action—*Akusala, Kamma,* which creates *Papa*—the downfall of man. The wicked man is an ignorant man. He needs instruction more than he needs punishment and condemnation. He is not regarded as violating God's will or as a person who must beg for divine mercy and forgiveness. He needs only guidance for his enlightenment" (1998, 183). The biblical teaching of the Fall of humankind, whereby humans are sinful by nature and therefore produce sinful actions, words, and deeds, is thereby rejected by Buddhists. To Buddhists there is no accountability to any higher power, or to a Creator God. One is only accountable to oneself and one's own *karma*, which will affect future existences through any infractions of *Sila* or other laws.

In April 1977 I had the privilege to interview an elderly Thai Pastor in Chiang Mai, not long before he died. Reverend Boomee Rungruangwongs shared with me that he frequently cited the Buddhist *Sila* law in talking with his friends, to convict them of their sin and failure. Many admitted they had not kept even the five *Sila*, so to accept that they felt like sinners was no problem. Of course, biblical sin is much deeper than that. Significantly, there is a close parallel of the five *Sila* in the last five commandments of the Decalogue. Equally significant in Buddhism, there are no laws equivalent to the first five commandments, which primarily focus on man's relationship to God.

Among folk Buddhists, the feeling of sinfulness or failure is not hard to discover. Primarily this is produced by the high level of the fear of death and of being consigned to one of the seven Buddhist hells. These are indeed most graphically and frighteningly portrayed, particularly in Mahayana Buddhism.

In a survey of many Christian Thai who came from Buddhist backgrounds, my research indicated that the fear of going to hell was a high factor in their accepting the redemption that was offered in Christ Jesus—equal to 22.6 percent of them (1977, 172-173). The influence of their Buddhist concepts of hell prepared them to seek salvation in the gospel, even though missionaries had done little preaching of "fire and brimstone" to them.

6. Source of Salvation: Self or God

The first of the *Twelve Principles of Buddhism*, summarized by

Christmas Humphreys, sets the stage for all Buddhist practice: "Self-salvation is for any man the immediate task." Professor Dhammananda quotes "Each and every person must make the effort to train and purify himself toward attaining his own salvation by following the guidance given by the Buddha" (1998, 19). Reaching *nirvana* relies on his own efforts alone, causing the Buddhist to feel that both his present life and future lives depend completely on himself alone. "One's self, indeed, is one's saviour, what other saviour should there be?" (Dhammapada 166) In it Buddhists must rely entirely on themselves, not on any external god, savior, or even the Buddha. One must overcome one's own accumulated *karma* himself alone.

In contrast, the Christian source of salvation is God alone. Works, merit, or personal goodness cannot abrogate sin, unrighteousness, or wickedness. The Christian source of salvation is in God, and through His grace and unmerited favor it is freely given. "For by grace are you saved through faith; and that not of yourselves, it is the gift of God; not as a result of works, that no one should boast" (Eph. 2:8-9 NASB). Succinctly stated, "The Father sent the Son to be the Savior of the world" (I John 4:14 KJV).

The Buddha taught that one must depend only on oneself. I often discuss this with my Buddhist friends. A brand new baby just born should therefore be taught to depend only on itself, with no help from mother, father, relatives, medical personnel, or anyone. "But that would be disastrous," my friends say, "The baby will die." I ask the Thai farmer, "Do you only depend on yourself?" "Of course," he replies. "Then you have no need of the family to help in the planting? Or your friends to assist in the harvesting? Or the rice-millers to mill your grain? Or the merchant middleman to market your rice?" To those in financial need and crisis, I ask, "Why do you go to the bank, or to your friends and relatives to borrow money? Is that not depending on others, instead of only on yourself?" Of course, in reality, these are normal circumstances that show us it is impossible in life just to depend only on oneself.

Interestingly there is a hope among Buddhists about a future savior to come. Just before he passed away, the Buddha spoke to Ananda about a future Buddha known as *Maitreya*, saying, "I am not the first Buddha to come on earth, nor shall I be the last. In due time, another Buddha will arise in this world, a Holy One, a Supremely Enlightened One, endowed with wisdom, in conduct auspicious, knowing the universe, an incomparable leader of men, a master of devas and men. He will reveal to you the same Eternal Truths, which I have taught you. He will proclaim a religious life, wholly perfect and pure; such as I now proclaim" (Dhammananda 1998, 45-46). Other words for this future savior include *Sian* or *Phra See An* and *Phra Pho Thi Sat*, as well as *Phra Sri Areya Maitreya*. In Inta Chanthavongsouk's booklet *Buddha's Prophesy of the Messiah,* he discusses this context and applies it to Christ the Messiah. Referring to the Tripidok Buddhist Scriptures, Inta describes the interview between Brahman and the Buddha, who said, "In the Saviour who will come to save the world, you will see puncture wounds like a wheel in the palms of his hands, and the bottom of his feet. In his side there is the mark of a stab wound, and his forehead is full of scars" (1999, 25).

The Buddhist monk's response, in a chant to the devoted ones offering food early in the morning, includes: "May all the charities you have done lift you up to heaven. May you be filled with merit until you see the face of *Sian* (Messiah)" (Chanthavongsouk 1999, 36). Professor Dhammananda summarizes a further interesting belief of Buddhists who follow the meritorious deeds of the committed religious life. They "will have a chance to be reborn as human beings in the time of *Maitreya* Buddha, and will obtain *Nibbana* identical with that of Gautama Buddha." (1998, 46) In *Buddhism through Christian Eyes*, I note this *hope of the Maitreya Buddha, which seemed to be particularly alive a* century ago among the Lao people of Northern Thailand and Laos (Smith 2001, 15-18).

While some Christians see significant points of contact in this concept, and some Buddhists have studied it in relation to Christ, more discussion is needed. Many Buddhists would see Christ as a Buddha. Others would not accept Him as Maitreya Buddha, because they claim this is still the age of Gautama Buddha, and that Maitreya Buddha is still to come. In recent years some Buddhists have been teaching that the next Buddha will be a woman, and this has enhanced the popularity of the Kwan Yin cult, although originally

Kwan Yin was a male figure adopted from India.

7. Provision of Redemption: Earned Merit or Christ's Substitution

In Buddhist terms, it is already noted that you are on your own. Your salvation depends entirely on yourself through thousands of reincarnations, hopefully working yourself up out of your *karma* into achieving the perfection of nirvana. No one can substitute for you. That is inconceivable. Technically no one can provide merit for you.

In Mahayana Buddhism, however, the *Bodhisattvas* are believed to have a way of helping humans by delaying their own entry into *nirvana* thus postponing their release from *samsara*.

One other exception is a diversion from traditional Buddhism in the Japanese cult of Amida Buddhism (Amitabha). This group, founded as Jodo by a twelfth century monk named Genku, believes that only through Amida Buddha can a person be saved and enter the "Pure Land." Salvation cannot be gained by one's own efforts alone, but only through calling on Amida in prayer.

God's provision of redemption is in Christ our substitute, the one Mediator between God and man, the man Christ Jesus. He is the Redeemer who shed His blood for the salvation of mankind.

As already stated, substitution is impossible and inconceivable to the Buddhist mind. However, I have discovered a few key illustrations within Thai history and legend that help lay a foundation for understanding the possibility of substitution. First, in Chiang Mai, North Thailand, there is a Chedi dedicated to Pi Ang near the bank of the Mae Ping River. Legend says that the king from the south once attacked the king of Chiang Mai. Not wanting to see the city destroyed, the two kings met and agreed that a contest would be held. One man each from north and south would participate in a diving contest to see who could remain under the water the longest. If the north won, Chaing Mai would be left alone. But if the south's representative won, the city would capitulate to the forces of the south. Uncle Pi Ang volunteered for the north. The contest was held. After several long minutes the south's representative emerged, gasping for breath. The city was saved. But Uncle Pi Ang was nowhere to be found. The king sent divers in to discover what had happened. They found that Pi Ang had tied his leg to a submerged branch of a tree and had literally given his life to save his beloved city.

The second key historical incident from the Ayuthaya Period of Thailand is found in most schoolbooks. The Burmese had attacked the old Thai capital, and the Thai monarch came to fight the enemy. Unbeknown to the Thai king, his favorite queen, Phra Nang Siriyothai, disguised herself as a warrior and rode out to the battle. At one stage, the Burmese king was gaining the advantage over the Thai king and was about to cut him down. The queen saw the danger and deliberately drove her elephant between the Burmese king and her Thai husband. She consequently was slain by the Burmese, but the Thai king escaped. In honor of her bravery and sacrifice the king built a special pagoda for her. It is still a busy tourist attraction to this day. In early 2002, a Thai film that had just been made about this heroine of Thai history was released. The queen gave her life as a substitute for her royal husband.

A third illustration of substitution and grace usually occurs on the birthday of His Majesty, the King of Thailand. On that day the King often remits the sentences of certain criminals who are then allowed to go free. They are saved by his mercy and grace extended to them without paying the full penalty for their crimes, though condemned by the law.

These illustrations are good stepping-stones toward making the possibility of Christ's substitution conceivable to the Buddhist mind.

Christian salvation is like a gift freely offered. The step of faith and acceptance appropriates that gift. Buddhists reject such a concept. In *What Buddhists Believe,* Dr. Dhammananda writes, "Faith in the theistic sense is not found in Buddhism because of its emphasis on understanding. Theistic faith is a drug for the emotional mind and demands belief in things which cannot be known. Knowledge destroys faith and faith destroys itself when a mysterious belief is examined under the daylight of reason" (1998, 197).

In the film *Indiana Jones,* Harrison Ford portrays taking "a step of faith" while seeking the Holy Grail. Confronted with a seemingly impossible chasm that impedes his advance, he remembers "the word of faith" from Scripture, and in obedience, by stepping forward into the air, finds an invisible way appear by which he crosses the frightening chasm.

One of my South American friends once told me of a huge Condor that was captured in one of the villages. It had been hurt. The villagers decided to tie it to a stake in the middle of the square, so that everyone could observe it. After some time, the huge bird seemed to be healed. Convicted about holding one of God's beautiful creatures in captivity, the villagers decided to release the Condor. They untied the cord binding its leg to the stake. For weeks the Condor had walked in a circle at the extreme extension of that cord tied to that stake. Even though it had been freed, it continued to walk around the stake as usual for quite some time. Eventually the Condor took some steps of faith beyond its formerly bounded circle. Seeing one of its fellows flying high above the mountain, it began to flap its wings. It was soon soaring high above the mountain.

8. Basis for Spiritual Life: Reincarnation or Regeneration

In Buddhism, *karma* is the iron law from which there is no escape. Bad *karma* might be equated with sin. A common Buddhist's expression is, "Do good, get good. Do evil, get evil." During the discussion between Brahman and the Buddha on how men might save themselves from sin, the Buddha repeatedly responded, "Even though you give alms, observe the five commandments governing everyone, the eight commandments governing a fervent Buddhist, and the 227 commandments governing the conduct of a bonze (a high Buddhist official), join your hands in prayer a billion times, and meditate five times a day, you will not be saved. Even if you do these things every day, you will only receive merit equal to one eighth of a split hair" (Chantavongsouk 1999, 24-25). This shows the difficulty of overcoming *karma* and therefore the necessity of endless reincarnation. The self-reliance and self-deliverance of Buddhists seems to be a very long road indeed before salvation is found.

In contrast, there is the instant regeneration available through Christ, and the total forgiveness for accumulated sins of the past. Accepting His vicarious atonement for humanity gives the one who trusts present peace and hope for the future. For spiritual growth, the Buddhist must depend only on himself. For Christians, that dependence is only on Christ. Here is another seemingly irreconcilable contrast, which would make it truly impossible to be either a Buddhist Christian, or a Christian Buddhist.

9. Destiny and Finality: Nirvana or Eternal Life

Buddhists obviously believe in life after death through the process of reincarnation caused by *karma*. They also strive for *nirvana*, which is a most complex and difficult concept to grasp. Earlier definitions of *nirvana* tended toward an extinction. Many scholars indicated that this is not entirely accurate. In his discussion of *nirvana/nibbana*, Christmas Humphreys in *Buddhism* writes that it "means to the Theravardin the dying out of the three fires of Greed, Anger and Illusion. It is negatively expressed, being the extinction of undesirable qualities." (1958, 157) *Nirvana* "is the end of woe. It is logically inexpressible." *Nirvana* "is the extinction of the not-Self in the completion of the Self" (1958, 127-128). In the Mahayana viewpoint, emphasis is laid on the "Self to be obtained, rather than the Not-Self to be stamped out." So *nirvana* "is not the goal of escapism, a refuge from the turning Wheel; it is the Wheel" (1958, 157). Professor Dhammananda says this final goal of Buddhism "is quite unexplainable, and quite indefinable." It is not nothingness or extinction, nor is it paradise. It is not a place, but is more like a state or experience. "*Nibbana* is a supra-mundane state of unalloyed happiness." It is "an end of the craving which caused all the sufferings." It is "the extinction of those relative physical and mental sources" (1998, 103-105). This is the final goal of Buddhism—a kind of extinction-cum-nothingness "consciousness."

Nor is there any resurrection from this state. "Buddhists do not believe that one day someone will come and awaken the departed persons spirits from their graveyards or the ashes from their urns, and decide who should go to heaven and who should go to hell" (1998, 176).

While Buddhists' finality and destiny are epitomized in *nirvana*, a kind of cessation of existence, the Christian's destiny is everlasting life with the added anticipation of the resurrection. In Buddhism, no one is responsible or accountable to an external higher being. In Christianity we are accountable to God, before whom we shall all stand.

By way of contrast, "In Buddhism there is no personal judge either to condemn or to reward, but only the working of an impersonal moral causation and natural law" (1998, 266). Again, here are a number of irreconcilable differences between Christianity and Buddhism. The Buddha "rejected both extremes of eternalism and nihilism" (1998, 111).

While Buddhists do not accept the Christian concepts of heaven and hell as eternal, they do believe there are heavens and hells—not only beyond this world, but also in this very world itself. But these are only temporary states or places where, on one hand, "those who have done good deeds experience more sensual pleasures for a longer period," and on the other hand, "those evildoers experience more physical and mental suffering" (1998, 303-304). These temporary states are therefore only part of the long process of *samsara* on the endless way to final *nirvana*.

Conclusion

These two systems of salvation are poles apart. While Christianity is theistic, the basis of Buddhism is monistic, atheistic (nontheistic), and humanistic. Since their beliefs are diametrically opposed, they seem irreconcilable without destroying the foundational premises of each. These differences are significant and pose difficult missiological challenges.

Three suggestions for serious concentration and contemplation are proposed. First, a strong focus on the ultimates or end goals of each should be considered. In 1981 Dr Ninian Smart's *Beyond Ideology: Religion and the Future of Western Civilization* already suggested that if they are to talk at all, Christians and Buddhists "must talk about ultimates" (Neill 1984, 157). The goal of peaceful bliss and finality rests in God for Christians and *nirvana* for Buddhists. But is there any possibility of real reconciliation between the two?

Second, more study and discussion should be undertaken on enlightenment. This concept certainly speaks of the quest of seeking after truth, understanding it, and especially acting upon it in both religions, though from differing sources. The "eyes of understanding being enlightened" is an intriguing focus as seen for instance in Psalms 19:8 and Ephesians 1:8. Buddhists are working towards ending *karma*, erasing desire and passion, evading suffering, escaping endless rebirth, and exiting to *nirvana*—all by enlightenment. Christians trust God's provision for all of these by being enlightened through His Scriptures, enduring suffering by His grace, and accepting forgiveness through His Son.

Third, Christians must be serious about expressing a life of love to Buddhists, not just being zealous about witnessing to their faith. They must practice being exemplary models of genuine concern, proclaim Christ by meekness and humility through their lives, and provide an understanding of God's love. This they can do by showing true gentle kindness in loving "their neighbors as themselves" and by sensitively expressing the power of the Spirit of Christ who indwells them to those who differ in belief orientation.

References and Bibliography

Becker, Jasper. 1992. *The Lost Country, Mongolia Revealed* London: Hodder & Stoughton.

Carling, R.H. 1985. *The World History Chart* Vienna, VA: International Timeline Inc.

Chanthavongsouk, Inta. 1999. *Buddha's Prophecy of the Messiah*. La Mirada, CA: The Lao Conference of Churches.

Dhammananda, K. Sri. 1998. *What Buddhists Believe* Kuala Lumpur, Malaysia: Buddhist Missionary Society.

Humphreys, Christmas. 1958. *Buddhism*. London: Penguin Books.

Indapanno, Bhikkhu Buddhadasa. 1967. *Christianity and Buddhism*. Bangkok: Sinclaire Thompson Memorial Lectures, Fifth Series.

Muck, Terry C. 1967. Missiological Issues in the Encounter with Emerging Buddhism. *Missiology: An International Review*, Vol. XXVIII, No. 1.

Neill, Stephen. 1984. *Christian Faith and Other Faiths*. Downers Grove, IL: IVF Press.

Niles, D. T. 1967. *Buddhism and the Claims of Christ*. Richmond, VA: John Knox Press.

Smart, Ninian. 1981. *Beyond Ideology: Religion and the Future of Western Civilisation.* London: Harper & Row

Smith, Alex. 1977. *Strategy to Multiply Rural Churches: A Central Thailand Case Study.* Bangkok: OMF Publishers.

———. 2001. *Buddhism through Christian Eyes.* Littleton, CO: OMF International.

Toynbee, Arnold. 1957. *Christianity among the Religions of the World.* New York: Charles Scribner's Sons.

Suffering and Salvation in Buddhism and Christianity: Negations and Positions

Johannes Aagaard

Religious projects are an attempt to draw up *positions* that can correspond to *negations*. We must scrutinize the negations that negatively determine such positions if we are to understand these positions in their innermost nature.

When the oriental religions—in particular Buddhism—define the negation of life so unequivocally as *suffering*, it is imperative to understand the content of this word, otherwise the *positions* of Buddhism are themselves not meaningful. Since Christian churches, for their part, define the crucial problem of life as *sin*, it is equally important to penetrate into this negation in order to understand the Christian *position*.

Only in a superficial sense can suffering be defined as merely "feeling bad." Buddha himself enjoyed life to the full. According to one legend, he was the son of a king, newly married, and the father of a baby son. According to other legends, he had several wives and lived the sweet life of an oriental prince. So it was neither pain nor misery that troubled him personally.

It was, as we know, *the suffering of others* that set him going. Through his confrontation with disease, poverty, and death, he was

57

awakened to a realization of suffering in life. The formulations of his thought as they are handed down to us do not reflect the indignation of a social reformer.

Buddha's reflections are not a stimulus for him to use his power and influence to reduce poverty in his father's kingdom, or to secure help for the sick, or to dignify death as the fitting end to a good life. That is not the tone that characterizes Buddha's teachings.

It seems as though the confrontation with other people's actual sufferings elicited in his mind the *sense* of suffering. We might even interpret it by simply saying he had been traumatized by what he saw. His mind had been damaged by these not-especially-terrible experiences, so that his emotions had seized up. Yet this too is not confirmed by his teachings.

His insight, achieved through these confrontations, seems rather to have triggered the insight in him that all of life, even the very fact of existence, is incomprehensible and, in reality, quite absurd. It is *suffering through the lack of meaning* that speaks out of the teachings of Buddha. There is no rational sense in existing at all, he says, let alone existing forever!

A contributing factor to Buddha's "fear of life" was his belief in *samsara*, that is, the conviction that the life-death cycle is endless, and that not even death brings freedom from the wheel of destiny. It is reasonable to assume that his belief in samsara was of a theoretical nature until these confrontations with the realities of life and death filled out the empty theory and turned it into a stark insight into the meaningless absurdity of life and death. Taken this way, his negation adds perspective to his teachings and makes them meaningful precisely in the light of this negation. Buddha's teachings are not fully meaningful in themselves, but require a series of presuppositions of the type outlined here, for them to acquire full meaning.

The Victory over Sin and Death

The Christian negation that corresponds to suffering in Buddhism is sin. The experience of life that finds expression in an acknowledgement of sin does not differ as much as we might imagine from Buddhism's experience of suffering. Yet its nature is quite different. The Christian experience of sin lies in the acknowledgement that there is an everlasting distance between reality in God's sense and reality in man's sense. And indeed Jesus himself experienced sin when he cried from the cross, "My God, my God, why have you abandoned/betrayed/failed me?"

The prerequisite for this experience was his faith in God as the cause and nature of all reality. To judge from our sources, Jesus always lived *within* this experience, and his experience of death was just like his experience of life. It was the conclusion of his life, for his life was characterized—if we look to his teachings—by an intense and warm experience of unity with God. All the parables, for instance, speak of this unity with God as love's innermost nature. Jesus was never outside this love. Indeed, he lived completely within it and mediated it to others, so that 1 Corinthians 13 has rightly been called a biography of Jesus.

Jesus' experience of sin, however, when he took it upon himself and nailed it to the cross as the death he must die for the world's sake, was precisely an experience of *sin as a foreign power*. To understand Jesus' negation we must realize that he never attributed sin to life itself. It is not the fault of life, nor even of man, that sin has arisen and has entered the world; it is the result of the work of the Evil One. For Jesus, the true reality of evil is of a personal character; it arises from trans-personal and trans-cosmic forces gathered in the Enemy's (Satan's) name. The world and man are possessed by this evil power with whom they collaborate. The salvation to which Jesus saw himself as the Way was therefore synonymous with liberation from this evil power. That is why the prayer for liberation from the Evil One is the heart of the matter in the words of the Lord's Prayer. Salvation's victory over the Evil One therefore had to take concrete form in Jesus' vicarious suffering, death, and resurrection.

We find no parallel to this in Buddha's teachings. Jesus' *negation* is a negation of the occupational force of the Evil One, so to speak. And his *position* is the liberating force of the Good One, that is, God's power. Using an expression from Zen Buddhism, all these occupying forces are "foreign powers." In this connection, our own powers are powerless. As Martin Luther says in *A Safe*

Stronghold Our God Is Still, "With force of arms we nothing can,/ Full soon were we down-ridden,/But for us fights the proper Man,/Whom God himself hath bidden."

In contrast, Buddha's suffering does not lead to salvation. It is, rather, a reaction to the negation of having to suffer life and death for all eternity. Buddha's suffering cannot therefore be seen as a *parallel* to Jesus' suffering and death, for Buddha experienced suffering and death as the condition of man, including his own condition. He then found the way out of samsaric suffering, as a cosmic phenomenon of everlasting rebirth, to be facing up to its illusory nature. No human soul can suffer and be reborn. Buddha's teaching on *athman* (man's innermost core) is that it does not exist: *anathman,* no soul. No one therefore can suffer. Suffering is the circumstance of living, but it is not bound up with reality itself, which is pure emptiness without origin or creation. This is the "gospel" of Buddhism: one can take one's own self out of the game.

When this teaching is converted to the dimensions of Mahayana (i.e. the northern traditions of Buddhism in China, Tibet, and Japan in particular) and the mediated teachings of Amida Buddha and the many Boddhisattvas, it no longer centres on man's own powers. Northern "higher" Buddhism recognizes that our own powers cannot lead us to liberation from the constraint of endless suffering. So "foreign powers" are brought into play. Liberators must come into being before liberation from the illusion that *anyone* can suffer can take place.

We are speaking here of a *loyalty in suffering* which, in its nature, is quite different from the vicarious nature of Jesus' suffering. Loyalty in suffering is full of sympathy and mercy, but it is not true compassion. This is because, at the deepest level, all the forms of Buddhism maintain the teaching, not only of no-soul, but also of no-God, for everything is and will remain emptiness—in the innermost as in the outermost.

God Is Closer to Us than We Are to Ourselves

Thus with Buddhism and Christianity, we find ourselves in two different worlds, aligned towards two different forms of positions, determined by two quite different negations. The negations and positions of Buddhism rest entirely on the tenet of the trans-migration of souls and its cosmic absurdity. Buddhism cannot be transplanted into religious contexts where samsara is not the foundation. Conversely, the Jesus-communion of Christianity cannot be transplanted to a religious context where samsara is determinative. The samsaric circling in on itself (*incurvatus in se*) finds its parallel in the circle of sin that can only be burst open by the reality of the resurrection.

Buddhism is absolutely meaningful and understandable. In no way can its religious project be equated with that of the many New Age inventions in current vogue. There is face and profile, character and genuine life-experience in Buddhism. But that does not bring it closer to God's revelation in Jesus Christ than it does to others of man's religious projects. For we are all—Buddhist, New Age, and Christian alike—always alienated from God, and on our various flight routes away from him. The gospel is not that some have gotten closer than others, but that God always comes right in close to us. And "us" means all of us—Buddhists, New Agers, and Christians. God is closer to us than we are to ourselves. This is not merely a fact that one can take on board or leave alone. It is a reality of faith that arises, that comes into being, that is created when we trust that our distance to God has become God's nearness to us, solely because Jesus himself took our distance upon himself when he screamed it out to the empty sky. God's name is Jesus. God's nearness becomes reality "in Jesus' name."

Addendum: An-athman as the Consequence of Athman's Deficit

Buddhism's an-athman is a necessary consequence of the acknowledgement of athman's deficit, for athman is not the soul as acting subject, the soul that constitutes the person and the conscience. Athman is not therefore the person through whom God acts, nor is it the conscience as the reality that acknowledges good and evil. Neither of these is represented by athman, since athman is not an acting subject but is over and above all difference.

An-athman simply means that there is nobody at home. As in Homer's *Odyssey*, it is a question of "Nobody!" Of course, this is a language question, as is all religion, down to its details. But here, the language is plain and clear. In an-athman the end is a cul-de-sac—that is, emptiness, nothingness, *sunyatha*—since athman, by definition, does not function and is not active.

Thus we can see that just as athman contains *brahman*, so must an-athman contain no-brahman. If there is no soul, there can be no divine reality. And if there is no innermost subject, then there is no outermost, ultimate subject. Conversely, it is also true that if there is sunyatha instead of God, then, of necessity, there is an-athman. For nothing rhymes with nothing.

Similarly, God rhymes with soul. It is possible to reach unity between the soul and God. God and the soul belong together, and if they are apart, it is a sin for the soul. This is the point: only what is sin for the soul separates it from God. It is not God who separates himself from the soul, and even sin cannot separate God from the soul, only the soul from God. God alone can overcome this schism by forgiving the sin. This can only happen through a reconciliation, which comes solely through an atonement. But that has happened.

So the soul and God are in fact united. It is only a fiction and an illusion that separates the soul from God—the idea that the sin is not forgiven, redeemed, atoned. Faith is acknowledgement and confession of this ultimate truth.

On the Transmigration of Souls and Identity

How can we now speak of the transmigration of the soul when there is no soul? We are speaking of Buddhism, now, not of Hinduism. The answer is plain and simple: the only thing that binds life and existence to previous and future lives and existences is karma, alias *samskaras*. It is causality at work. There is no identity between the twice nothing.

But this is not the real truth. For Truth is therapeutic if it is Buddhist. It is perfectly logical: To recognize that neither athman nor brahman exist means that souls cannot transmigrate. To recognize that the Hindu brahman-athman identification is a fiction means that the goal is achieved. The Nirvana involved is precisely the stopping of the fiction by perceiving that it is an illusion.

It is not so much suffering that is an illusion as it is the lack of awareness of the cessation of suffering, which is a fiction, that is already realized by perceiving its illusionary character. It does not need to be brought to cessation, for it has ceased when one realizes that it was and is fictive.

Again we ask, how can we speak of the transmigration of the soul when there is no soul? Buddhists do not use the word "transmigration" when they are in the state of enlightenment where they realize that transmigration of the soul is the uttermost suffering and thus the uttermost illusion. Endless suffering in the circle of existence is just as fictive, indeed more so, than the many earthly sufferings that every Buddhist knows to be an illusion. But only those who realize that the uttermost illusion is the uttermost suffering, and vice versa, have *already* passed over from something to nothing and are free, that is, freed not by a savior and a liberator but by an awareness of the illusion that one is not free, that is, samsara.

Buddhism is thus salvation from the transmigration found in Hinduism. Also, today true Buddhism is salvation from the illusion of transmigration. In this regard, Buddhism and Christianity actually stand together against Hinduism. Both agree that the transmigration of souls is a nightmare, a fiction, an illusion that one must see through and be released from.

On the Transmigration of Souls, and Identity, the Tantric Way

The tantric insight (in Hinduism and Buddhism) is both simple and unnerving: Samsara *is* nirvana, and nirvana is samsara, until you wake up to the realization that nirvana is, of course, just as much an illusion as samsara. Liberation from samsara is therefore also liberation from nirvana, and vice versa. This is clear and consistent.

Nirvana means precisely that one awakes from the nightmare in which one is tortured by samsara, longing with suffering and pain for nirvana. One awakes, one is awakened. But one is not enlightened! That is a misunderstanding. Nirvana does not mean enlightenment; it means (verbatim) to "blow out the light," to "extinguish" it, so that all emptiness and nothingness are acknowledged.

If it is only samsara that is illusion, one is only half liberated, only half out of the dark. But when everything, including salvation, is seen as an illusion, then darkness is finally overcome and liberation realized.

It is clear that this cannot happen in popular Buddhism and Hinduism. It is part of the nature of Hinduism and Buddhism that popular Buddhism is a continuation of Hinduism, though with significant differences. But in Tantrism, both are fulfilled and overcome analogously.

Popular Forms of Buddhism and Hinduism

Nirvana, in popular Buddhism, and *samadhi*, in popular Hinduism, are transformed into paradises—in the plural, for there are a number of them. They represent the expectation of salvation for the ordinary Buddhist and Hindu, salvation from the many hells.

Paradise is the goal of the longing for salvation among the Buddhist laity. It is reached with the aid of merit, achievement and good deeds. The same is more or less true of the expectation of paradise in Hinduism.

Nirvana from a Buddhist point of view means the ultimate death, corresponding closely to *nirvikalpa samadhi* in Hinduism, which means death "without any form," the full extinction. Nirvana means the full "awakening," but, strangely enough, is often translated as the full "enlightenment," a peculiar word when one realizes that "nirvana" means to "extinguish the light," extinction. The translation, "enlightenment," is best avoided because it is misleading.

The Two Truths

The explanation for the relationship between Hinduism and Buddhism is found, in particular, in the two truths. In both religions, there is a difference between the meritorious, mythological beliefs of the laity and the gnostic, yogic beliefs of the monks and yogis.

In both religions, there are two quite different attitudes towards those with knowledge and those without it.

Ultimately there is one single truth; relatively there is quite another truth. This is balanced from situation to situation. It often serves as a means to explain away something. One shifts the weight on one's legs, so to speak, according to circumstances.

One speaks of God, for instance. The Dalai Lama often does this, even though God is naturally understood as being relative. For ultimately there is no God, only gods, who are merely superhumans. This is true in both Hinduism and Buddhism.

Buddhism even speaks of the soul, but again this is only understood relatively. It speaks of the transmigration of souls, knowing full well that ultimately there are no souls that transmigrate.

In both religions it is the link between the ultimate and the relative that makes understanding difficult, more so in Buddhism where the concept of nirvana is in the foreground, whereas for the most part nirvikalpa samadhi concerns only a small circle of Hindu yogis.

Occultization Destroys the Balance

A comprehensive occultization has long taken place in Hinduism. This has meant that the ultimate world of the gurus has been invaded, and largely conquered, by popular Hinduism's relative world with its emphasis on power and success. There are still gurus who are not wrapped up in sex and money but they are few and far between. In numerous Hindu ashrams, there is a growth in occultism that clearly does the trick, and more than manages to pay its way. Such gurus are frowned upon by critical Hindus.

The same is now happening in Buddhism. There are still Buddhist masters who have not sold their souls—the souls that ultimately they do not possess—but a great number of them are no better than the worst gurus, as regards sex and money, fraud, repression, and exploitation.

This occultization is, in principle, of the same kind as the occultization of Hinduism and is the result of a direct influence. It led the patriarch of Thailand to refuse visas to Indian participants travelling to a recent Hindu conference. This, of course, happened through his influence, rather than his intervention, but it must be seen as an attempt to avoid the identification of Buddhism with

Hinduism, despite an awareness of the link between them.

In Buddhism, there is a possibility of control from above barely available in India in relation to the dominant popular religion. In Thai Buddhism, for instance, there is a joint leadership that can function as a corrective, and can exercise discipline in relation, say, to certain Buddhist monks known for their activities with the opposite sex.

On the other hand, the patriarch will not even speak to the reformers who directly oppose popular Buddhism's occult businesses, peddling amulets and other forms of magic. This is protected by official state Buddhism, since it constitutes the popular and financial basis for real Buddhism.

The situation is quite different in Taiwan. Here there is no patriarch, and, as far as is known, no common structure for Buddhists. Here therefore occultisation is well advanced and out of control.

Many Taiwanese masters—women, and especially men—are outside the Buddhist tradition and simply follow the laws of power, sexuality, and money. This may lead to the total destruction of Buddhism in Taiwan, but for the time being, the population is not apparently troubled to any great degree.

The situation in Japan is harder to depict. We know that *Aum Shinri Kyo* prospered, and still functions, as a totally occultised religion that is Buddhist in name only, but otherwise builds on a cocktail of all manner of religious flotsam. By all accounts, it is rarely criticized publicly by the other Buddhist communities. Its master, Ashahara, also received royal treatment at the hands of no less than the Dalai Lama, until the whole world was made to realize that he was rotten to the core.

Buddhists in Japan have no system to protect them from corruption. Their religion exists in almost total isolation between its various constituent parts.

However, there are signs of change. In the latest issue of their periodical, *Kadjyapa*, Danish Buddhists take issue with the secrecy surrounding the numerous examples of sex abuse by Buddhist masters. This is only a modest beginning in relation to what is happening in reality.

Bibliography on Buddhism and Buddhist-Christian Dialog

Buddhism and Christianity:

Baptist, Egerton C. *Nibbana or the Kingdom*. Colombo: M.D. Gusanena & Co., Ltd., 1953.

Buddhadasa. *Appearance and Reality—Being a Review of Christianity and Buddhism*. Bangkok: The Sublime Life Mission, 1971.

Chai-Shin Yu. *Early Buddhism and Christianity*. Delhi: Motilal Banarsidass, 1981.

Dumolin, Heinrich. *Begegnung mit dem Buddhismus*. Freiburg: Herder Taschenbuch Verlag, 1991.

Indapanno, Bhikkhu Buddhadasa. "Sinclaire Thompson Memorial Lecture, Fifth Series: Christianity and Buddhism." Bangkok: Thailand Theological Seminary, 1967.

Küng, Hans and Heinz Bechert. *Christentum und Weltreligionen III: Buddhismus*. München: Gütersloher Verlagshaus Gerd Mohn, 1988.

Masutani, Fumio. *A Comparative Study of Buddhism and Christianity*. Tokyo: Bukkyo Dendo Kyokai, 1967.

Peiris, William. *The Western Contribution to Buddhism*. Delhi: Motilal Banarsidass, 1973.

Phra Sobhon—ganabhorn. *A Plot to Undermine Buddhism*. Bangkok: Defendants of Security of Buddhism, 1984.

Vajirananavongse, Krom Luang. *The Purpose of Religion*. Bangkok: Mahamakut Rajavidyalaya Foundation Press, 1972.

Williams Jay G.. *Yeshua Buddha: An Interpretation of New Testament Theology as a Meaningful Myth*. Wheaton: The Theosophical Publishing House, 1978.

Buddhism:

Amaro, Ajahn Yantra. *The Bliss of Peace*. Bangkok: n.p., 1993.

Bhikku, Bhuddadasa. *Handbook for Mankind*. Bangkok: The Dhamma Study & Practice Group, 1980.

———. *The 24 Dimensions of Dhamma*. Bankok: Vuddhidhamma Fund, 1991.

———. *Heart-Wood from the Bo Tree*. Bangkok: Suan Usum Foundation, 1985.

———. *Messages of Truth from Suan Mokkh*. Bangkok: Vuddhidhamma Fund, 1990.

———. *Key to Natural Truth*. Bangkok: The Dhamma Study & Practice Group, 1988.

————. *Buddha-Dhamma for Students*. Bangkok: The Dhamma Study & Practice Group, 1988.

————. *The A, B, C of Buddhism*. Bangkok: The Sublime Life Mission, 1982.

————. *Paticcasamuppada Dependent Origination*. Bangkok: Vuddhidhamma Fund, 1986.

————. *No Religion*. Bangkok: n.p., [1967?]

Bhikku, Mettanando. *Meditator's Handbook*. Bangkok: Dhammakaya Foundation, 1991.

Bhikku, Yantra Amaro. *The Heart of Void*. Bangkok: Pim-Pun Printing Limited Partnership, 1992.

Chandrkaew, Dr. Chinda. *Nibbana—the Ultimate Truth of Buddhism*. Bangkok: Kurusapha Ladprao Press/Mahachula Buddhist University, 1979.

Conzse, Edward, trans. *Buddhist Scriptures*. Harmondsworth: Penguin Books, 1984.

Dhammananda, Sri. *What Is This Religion*. Hong Kong: From Saha to Nirvana´ Dharmaduta Activities, 1987.

Holt, John Clifford. *Buddha in the Crown—Avalokitesvara in the Buddhist Traditions of Sri Lanka*. New York: Oxford University Press, 1991.

Jayatilleke, K.N. *The Buddhist Attitude to Other Religions*. Chiangmai: The Buddhist Publication Foundation, 1987.

Keawkungwal, Dr. Sriruen. *Therapeutic Approaches in Theravada Buddhism and Existentialism: A Comparison*. Chiengmai: Department of Psychology, 1987.

Manich Jumsai, M.L.. *Understanding Thai Buddhism*. Bangkok: Chalermnit Press, 1980.

Moti Lal, Pandit. *The Fundamentals of Buddhism*. New Delhi: I.S.P.C.K., 1979.

————. *The Essentials of Buddhism*. New Delhi: TRACI Publications, 1994.

————. *Being as Becoming—Studies in Early Buddhism*. New Delhi: Intercultural Publications, 1993.

————. *Beyond the Word—Buddhist Approach to Knowledge and Reality*. New Delhi: Intercultural Publications, 1997.

————. *Transcendence and Negation—a Study of Buddhist Compassion and Christian Love*. New Delhi: Munshiram Manoharlal Publishers Pvt., Ltd., 1999.

————. *Buddhism in Perspective*. New Delhi: Munshiram Manoharlal Publishers Pvt., Ltd., 2001.

Nyanasamvara, Somdet Phra. *Faith in Buddhism*. Bangkok: The Office of the Supreme Patriarch's Secretary, 1993.

Nyanatiloka. *Buddhist Dictionary—Manual of Buddhist Terms and Doctrines.* Colombo: Frewin & Co., Ltd., 1972.

Price, Leonard. *To the Cemetery and Back—Dark Ages, Golden Ages.* Sri Lanka: Buddhist Publication Society, 1983.

Rajavaranumi, Phra. *Thai Buddhism in the Buddhist World.* Bangkok: Mahachulalongkorn Buddhist University, 1990.

Sangharakshita, Maha Sthavira. *The Spiral Path.* Pune: Triratna Grantha Mala/Dr. Ambedkar Society, 1983.

Santacitto (Stephen Saslav), Ven.. "Love and Attachment." *Seeing the Way—Buddhist Reflections on the Spiritual Life.* England: Amaravati Publications, 1989.

Sobhonganabhorn, Phra. *What Buddhism Gives Us.* Bangkok: The World Fellowship of Buddhist Youths, 1986.

Streng, Frederick J. *Emptiness—a Study in Religious Meaning.* New York: Abingdon Press, 1967.

Sumedho, Ajahn. *Mindfulness: The Path to the Deathless.* England: Amaravati Publications, 1987.

Towards a Radical Contextualization Paradigm in Evangelizing Buddhists

David S. Lim, Ph.D.

As we enter the twenty-first century and the third millennium, evangelical missiology faces a critical challenge to craft a "mission paradigm" that is truly biblical and relevant to the issues raised by the spread of information technology, post-modern thinking, and pluralistic contexts, especially in regard to the resurgence of traditional religions. Some even see "the need to drastically reconceptualize a major part of evangelical missiology, if not its entirety,"[1] hence the boldness of the title and aim of this paper: to delineate what it sees to be a *radical* (i.e., deep into the basic roots) mission paradigm which consists of the best missiological *theory* (biblical-theological) and the best missionary *strategy* (practical), especially in relation to doing missions in Buddhist contexts.

The biggest challenge was presented by Samuel Escobar at the Iguassu Missiological Consultation, held last October 1999 in Brazil by the World Evangelical Fellowship Mission Commission, when he criticized the "managerial missiology" that served as the main evangelical mission paradigm during the last two decades of the twentieth century. He called for a "critical missiology from the periphery." "The question for this missiology is not how much missionary action is

71

required today but what kind of missionary action is necessary."[2] He concludes: "The missiologist in the Third World cannot avoid the evaluative questions not only for the defense of missionary work as it stands today, but also for the formulation of a missionary strategy for the coming decades" (Escobar 2000, 114). Having grappled with the missiological issues from my Asian (Chinese Filipino) context, I venture to show a mission paradigm (called "radical contextualization") that I believe fully reflects the best of evangelical missiology.

This mission paradigm is then applied to the challenge of resurgent Buddhism, especially as it is showing much socio-cultural relevance to Asian societies today. In the past two years, the Beijing government has had to determine to persecute the quasi-Buddhist, Falungong cult, which claims to have about eighty million followers in China. Since November last year in India, a mass conversion movement among the Dalits show that they see in Buddhism their best hope to find socio-political liberation. In Taiwan, Buddhists have set up hospitals, universities and welfare programs, which they have exported to many other lands, including China, Vietnam, and the Philippines (cf. Ruiz 1998). It looks like there will be more contextualized forms of Buddhism, with more generous and compassionate faces, promoting tolerance and non-violence in our rapidly changing world (cf. Seamands 2000, 24-25, 29, 38; M. Tan 2001).

The "radical contextualization" paradigm will be shown to cover three important dimensions of missions: missiological strategy, Christological message, and ecclesiological structure. This paper also suggests that this is a "whole package," for a biblical missiology that is truly Trinitarian:[3] As the Father sent the Son into the world (as the model of incarnational missions), as the Son became the Savior of the world (as the message of the gospel), and as the Holy Spirit empowers the church to be his witness in the world (as the servant of his Kingdom), so all these three (missiology, Christology, and ecclesiology) make up a consistent whole. Any missing component becomes a deficiency in a radically contextualized "Trinitarian missiology." Further, in showing how these apply in Buddhist contexts, we will also refer to examples, similar to this paradigm, in mission work among other religions, like animism,[4] Islam (Love 2000; Parshall 2000; Woodberry 1989), Hinduism (H. Richard 1999; Hedlund

2001; cf. Sunder Raj 2001), and folk Catholicism (Bjork 1997; Boff 1986; Bonino 1995; Padilla 1999; P. Richard 1987).

This paper shows that "radical contextualization" (RC) consists of incarnational missiology, dialogic (or dialectic) Christology, and diaconal (or servant) ecclesiology, reflecting Jesus Christ as the *way* (that saves the world, John 1:29), the *truth* (that enlightens the world, John 1:9), and the *life* (that his body/church shares in the world, Eph. 3:7-13). This threefold paradigm calls for quite a shift indeed from the dominant evangelical "managerial missiology" to a truly "contextualizing (or incarnational) missiology."

1. Incarnational Missiology

The first dimension of RC is in the area of mission strategy: "As the Father has sent me, so I send you" (John 20:21 NRSV). What are the ways or means of mission that best fit the incarnational model of our Lord Jesus? We suggest there are three basic ways: friendship evangelism, church multiplication, and a simple lifestyle, all of which reveal a low-profile approach to missions.

1.1. Friendship Evangelism

The clearest verse on evangelism is 1 Peter 3:15, which teaches that we should treat our contacts "with *gentleness* and *respect*," meaning "as persons or human beings." Since people are multifaceted, and each person is unique, this means the evangelist should take time out to get to know the person and as much of her/his background and situation as possible, and not intrude prematurely or aggressively into her/his (inner and social) world; otherwise an honest "heart to heart talk" becomes almost impossible. Establishing a personal friendship with the other person is prerequisite in evangelism, since the messenger becomes a very important part of the message, at least for the unbeliever. People become more receptive to the gospel when they see and experience the love of God before (or as) they hear about the love of God. [5]

Though the religious background of our contacts is very important in our evangelism, we should be concerned with their total life, not with the religious systems they represent. People are first of all human beings, then Buddhists (or Muslims or Hindus).

Although Asians live in a very religious continent, filled with religious peoples (including all kinds of Buddhists), "there is no such thing as a purely religious encounter in Asia" (K. Tan 2000, 296-299). On the personal level, there are concerns of health, family relations, financial survival or upward mobility, and so forth. On the social level, there are issues of ethnic identity, political affiliation, legal restrictions, modernity (versus traditionalism), social class, historical prejudices, and so forth. As societies modernize and urbanize, for more and more people religion becomes less and less a primary concern. Thus, to these people, turning to religious discussions would immediately turn them off.

Yet we also know it is possible and "relatively easy" to share our faith, since there is a universal "common ground" based on our human nature and existence. Fundamentally, all people are alike. We have the same religious consciousness, needs, longings and aspirations. All have the same physiological needs, the need for security, a need to love and be loved, to belong and be accepted, and the need for self-actualization. Spiritually we need meaning in life, strength to overcome temptations, faith to face death, forgiveness of sins, and communion with God. So the gospel can have universal application to these different needs and interests.

But often the gospel has not been shared effectively merely because it was not done "with gentleness and respect" by not establishing rapport and friendship first. The witness fails to come alongside (or is perceived not to have done so) as someone having the same needs and desires, and receiving the same promises and gifts from God. "It is not the I–You relationship, but the God–Us relationship; not 'I have something for you,' but 'God has something for all of us'" (Seamands 2000, 79).

Practically speaking, in human relations the first rule is to listen first and always (cf. Seamands 2000, 96-97). Being a good listener includes such acts as accepting his/her views *non-judgmentally* (even if they are dead wrong!) at least at the start, spending time doing various activities together, and remaining friends even if she/he rejects our message later.

This "listening" attitude also means "becoming all things to all men," so that we can have a chance to share the gospel with them (cf. 1 Cor. 9:19-23). This means not only trying to learn their language and culture, but also learn about their faith (in our case, Buddhism) as much as possible. And when evangelizing, one cannot assume to know it all. There are myriad types of Buddhists, and each Buddhist people group has its unique kind of Buddhism!

When the issue of faith is raised, in order to gain and maintain the person's friendship, we do not tell that person that his/her religion (or any aspect of it) is false or wrong *at first* (even if it indeed is). We can *correct* them *later*, if necessary, after a loving or friendly relationship has been established. (The *content* of the evangelistic message is discussed in section two below.) Thus, in witnessing to Buddhists (or any religionists),[6] it is best to approach them as plain human beings, and as friends. This increases the chances of our Buddhist contacts becoming receptive to the gospel that is shared as being relevant to their individual need(s).

1.2. Church/Cell Multiplication

Once there is a receptivity to our evangelistic message, the next step is to nurture our converts in such a way that they become God's "first fruits," able to start a church-planting movement among their people. For this to happen, the new converts have to be formed into small disciple-making groups, whereby they can grow in faith in a contextual way. This will ensure not only quality discipleship, but also the multiplication potential for church-planting movements (CPM).

The recent "best practice" in mission circles has shown that the best way to do saturation evangelism, in the fastest way possible, is through the multiplication of small (house) churches (cf. Patterson 1988; Garrison 2000). This also fits the disciple-making patterns used in various student movements, especially in the intervarsity fellowships of the International Fellowship of Evangelical Students (IFES) and the Navigators, as well as by underground churches in restricted countries like China, Vietnam, Cambodia, Cuba, Indonesia, and so forth.

This seems to have been the original mission of Jesus and the early church. Jesus had "twelve disciples" whom he trained through living with them (Mark 3:14-15) and sending them out "two by two" to make twelve disciples each; hence, there were "seventy-two others" in Luke 10:1. If these seventy-two, in pairs, also made twelve new disciples each, there would have been more than 500 disciples before Christ's ascension (hence, 1 Cor. 15:6). And in pairs they could disciple all the 3,000 (who were baptized immediately) converted on the day of Pentecost, in groups of twelve each (cf. Acts 2:41-47, who "broke bread from house to house")! The focus of this pattern is simply to multiply "disciple-making cells" or "house churches" until the whole area is saturated with such groups, with only occasional public gatherings, and even when a majority have already become believers or the threat of persecution has been eliminated. The key is to remember that disciples are made in *small* (not *big*) groups, where they learn from one another how a committed follower of Jesus lives and thinks! After being discipled for a while, each believer can then find a few "faithful men" whom they can disciple also (cf. 2 Tim. 2:2).

Historically, however, Christians have made evangelization so complicated. We think we have to use *multiple* and *diverse* strategies (and *vast* resources) to be able to reach the world. What happens in fact is the "export" or "transplant" of our church structures and mission strategies into different cultures. Such uncontextualized witness has inevitably put up unnecessary barriers, not just for evangelism and discipleship, but also for saturation evangelization.

Thus for CPMs to occur more widely, it seems best to avoid bringing new converts into present church structures (or even into international Christian fellowships in restricted areas). Otherwise, they are likely to be initiated into a traditional Christian sub-culture, which Buddhists consider to be *anti-Buddhist* (most probably *correctly*), thus delineating and de-contextualizing them from their people. In our RC strategy, instead of bringing people to church, we seek to bring the church to the people, and also to disciple them where they are!

Hence it seems best to send among the Buddhists those believers who know how to form functioning and reproducing cells from the converts they will be leading to Christ. Rather than just planting a church, they will be founding CPMs. They should be allowed to establish *Buddhist-convert* churches (or better, CPMs) for the sake of the gospel and the salvation of their Buddhist compatriots. This may be the only way to remove the foreignness and strangeness of Christianity, so as to bring CPMs about among Buddhists.

1.3. Simple Lifestyle

Yet RC's "incarnational missiology" has a third dimension: identification with the poor, hence "simple lifestyle." The redemptive plan of God required that the Son be sent as a poor man (2 Cor. 8:9; Phil. 2:5-8) who identified with the poor (Matt. 25:31-46) and had a clear mission to "proclaim good news to the poor" (Luke 4:18-19; 7:22; cf. Isa. 61:1-2). The apostles followed this simplicity in their incarnational mission (Acts 20:33-35; 2 Cor. 4:7-12; 6:3-10; 1 Pet. 5:1-3).

More and more missiologists are finding out that it is only through being faithful in doing "missions of the poor" that Christian care for the marginalized can be effectively done. In contrast to the dominant "imperialistic mission" that depended on vast resources, the cutting edge of Christian missions has almost always been the "radical" renewal movements that formed flexible and mobile (read: simple) groups, which freely moved out of the centers of mainstream Christianity into the peripheries.[7]

Simplicity is important also for pragmatic reasons. It is almost impossible to be "incarnational" from a position of power and wealth. One not only tends to be aloof and distant with a "superiority complex," but even with the best intentions and methods, one's actions are easily seen to be paternalistic, if not patronizing. Only the "church of the poor" can truly reach out contextually to those who are poor. This is most significant because many (folk) Buddhists are relatively poor. Moreover, "simple lifestyle" can speak also to the richer Buddhists, since their worldview respects those who "forsake the world" to live as monks and nuns.

Further, a "simple lifestyle" may be the only way to achieve the maximum of resources for continuously expanding missions, both locally and globally. By staying simple, the "church of the poor" will be able to send more missionaries and release more resources for ministry—and not just among the poor. Hence, simplicity of lifestyle and modesty in means are important values in this mission paradigm. In our concern for material well being, we often forget the essential issue that should concern us: the building of God's church, committed to the development of others, in the spirit of *self-giving* and *cross-bearing*, including among Buddhists.

These three "incarnational" ways reveal a stark contrast to the "high profile" mission paradigm that evangelicals have been using: evangelistic crusades, healing rallies, mass media (print, radio, television, cable) and recently, the internet. Honestly, how effective (especially in terms of "cost-effectiveness") have these methods been in comparison to this *simple* mission strategy: "incarnational missions" through friendship evangelism, church/cell multiplication, and a simple lifestyle? Perhaps we can try a more *low profile* approach that mobilizes the *whole church* to take the gospel to the whole world, rather than relying on a minority of "experts" in promoting expensive mass rallies and high technology.

2. Dialogic Christology

RC's second dimension has to do with the message: what contextualized forms should the Christian gospel take in order to make sense to Buddhists and elicit the right faith response in them? There seem to be three important ways: radical Christocentrism, dynamic theologizing, and creative spirituality.

2.1. Radical Christo-centrism [8]

As we bear witness to Christ amidst the post-modern challenges of the multiplicity of choices between various pluralisms (including religious choices with Buddhist concepts and values), it is now more important to draw out the *sine qua non* essentials of our message. With information and communication overload, peoples need to hear more accurately what are the central points of our faith. (Perhaps the fewer essentials we have, the better access we will have to the busy and confused minds of our complex societies, including the Buddhist ones).

And there seems to be a simple message (thank God!): that people need to have a personal relationship with Jesus Christ as the Lord over their lives. One has just to share about Jesus of Nazareth, and how wonderful he *was* and *is*, and once a Buddhist decides to follow the Jesus being presented, she/he joins the family of God, regenerated and indwelt by the Holy Spirit.

> What distinguishes the true followers of Jesus is neither their creed nor their code of ethics, not their ceremonies nor their culture, but Christ. What is often mistakenly called "Christianity" is, in essence, neither a religion nor a system, but a person, Jesus of Nazareth. (Stott 1995, 346).

Evangelical Christo-centrism vis-à-vis other religions affirms the uniqueness of Christ as the only way to salvation, as revealed in Scriptures (John 5:39-40; 1 Cor. 8:5-6). The evangelistic message is that Jesus Christ is indeed the Creator God and Redeemer of the world. If he is not, we stand condemned as blasphemous and idolatrous. [9] Thus we consistently seek to invite people to submit to his lordship and adopt a Christ-centered worldview from whichever cultures and religions they come (Acts 4:33; 5:42; 8:35; 9:20; 1 Cor. 1:23; 2:2; cf. Col. 1:15-29). Evangelism is the offer of a personal *relationship* with God through Christ, not of a *religion*, not even of Christianity. [10] "It is not Christianity that saves, but Christ." [11] Hence every religious and cultural artifact, belief, or value (even in Christian traditions) must be evaluated in the light of the biblical revelation about the historical Jesus.

2.2. Dynamic Theologizing

Yet we must also add an important theological corollary to "radical Christo-centrism": doctrinal formulations should be relativized, and be opened to reformulations. [12] All Gospel versions are contextual, thus Jesus Christ must be presented in statements, stories and imageries [13] that best fit each person and culture. Evangelicals must be ready to formulate "fresh theological categories" as we try to evangelize Buddhists and people of other faiths. [14]

To Theravadan Buddhists, Jesus may be introduced as the *Maitreya* who has already come (cf. Thaiwatcharamas 1983). [15] To Mahayana Buddhists, he may be presented as the *dharma* that leads to the true *nirvana*, breaking the stronghold of *samsara* ruled by the law of *karma* (cf. Lim 1983, 187-193). To Tibetan Buddhists, he may be shown to "the lama of lamas," of a superior lama-hood than the Dalai Lama's tradition. The adoption of Buddhist concepts fits the use of the common Greco-Roman philosophical *logos* in John's gospel, and *mysterion* and *pleroma* in the Pauline epistles.[16] In some contexts, folk Buddhists may be shown Christ as the supreme God of their traditional animistic religion; for example in Sri Lanka, where they believe in *Sakra* who is the unique omniscient god, whose seat of stone warms up when a human is in trouble.[17] In all these situations, traditional usages are adopted, then infused with Christ-centered meanings. Moreover, most people, even in the West, and including Buddhists, do not only reason, think, and analyze facts and ideas (or do biblical hermeneutics) rationally, linearly, or logically. We need to develop a more functional concept of truth, beyond just the conceptual and propositional.[18]

> In Asia, the way one communicates truth cannot be divorced from the truth one communicates. ... If Christianity's truth claims are to be taken seriously by other religions, then Christians in Asia need to master social graces not only in behavioral patterns but also in communicational styles and attitudinal changes. (K. Tan 2000, 303-304).

Dynamic theologizing also means adopting a dialogic stance[19] (as non-confrontational as possible) in relating to people of other faiths.[20] Effective mission has always been dialogic, presenting one's truth claims and convictions for the consideration and acceptance of the other party(ies), as a common search for a "religion" that offers the best explanation for the whole experience of human life and world history. Without disregarding the differences of religions,[21] nor blurring the importance of seeking for truth, we must show respect for the other religion, and for its adherents as honest seekers for truth. It is like a pilgrim sharing with other pilgrims which "way, truth, and life" she/he has discovered and which she/he believes is good for all, with sensitivity to their beliefs and values and without condemning them for their ignorance or error.

Thus in actual evangelism, it is best that the witness introduces Jesus in such a way that fits into the Buddhist's situation and addresses the issues (health, family, work, religion, community, ethnicity, nation, and so forth) that she/he is concerned about. God gave us four Gospels, not one. Also, no two sermons in Acts are alike; and, specifically, the two messages preached to Gentile audiences were quite different (cf. Acts 14, 17). These seem to point to a "fulfillment theory" of other religions: the Christian faith offers complete truth in Jesus Christ, and other faiths (including Buddhism) offer partial truth (cf. Matt. 5:17).[22] God has not left himself without any witness among each people and culture of the world (Acts 14:17; cf. 10:34-35).[23]

It is just simple humility to recognize that we are human and not divine, with no absolute knowledge of the final truth. This can be called "provisional certitude": "All Christian beliefs are *our* beliefs, *human* beliefs and are as such always *provisional beliefs*. We assert that they are true; but we make this assertion provisionally" (Volf 1994, 103). This implies that the views of others (including Buddhists) are possibly true:

> The provisionality of our beliefs implies that truth and grace *may be* with the other. So there is nothing stubborn about our not moving to the position of the other, for we believe our position to be true. And there is nothing oppressive about believing that our position is true, for we grant that the positions of the other *may* be true (Volf 1994, 103).

We must beware that our power of "the iron logic of our proofs that we are absolutely right and others absolutely wrong" does not obscure God's power (cf. 2 Cor. 4:7-10), which is "nothing else but the 'life' of the crucified and resurrected Jesus Christ" (Volf 1994, 104).

2.3. Creative Spirituality

Another corollary of Christo-centrism is the need to evolve new spiritualities (religious practices and structures) that fit each culture, including Buddhist cultures. It is best that these expressions of faith be as indigenous as possible,[24] meaning that new Buddhist converts should be encouraged to form their own spiritual exercises and church structures that they feel most culturally comfortable with, without feeling the pressure to conform to the (Westernized) Christendom spiritualities of churches that are already among them. Are we ready to receive as fellow believers those from Buddhist-convert churches whose creeds,[25] rituals, practices, and organizations may be very different from our

"Christian heritage" (read: European-contextualized, Greek philosophy-based religiosities)?

One of the most successful attempts to develop Buddhist forms of spirituality is Tao Fong Shan, especially between 1930 and 1945, when it was reported to have brought 150 monks and nuns into the Christian faith. Through the vision and work of the Norwegian missionary Karl Ludvig Reichelt (1877-1952), a Christian ministry center was constructed with Buddhist architecture. It used Buddhist forms of meditation, teaching, and mission. [26] Its purpose has been to remove the Western trappings of Christianity, so that Christian theology can be interpreted in Chinese (Mahayana Buddhist, Taoist, and Confucianist) ways. Its ministries continue to this day, but seemingly with less evangelistic fervor. [27]

Moreover, in our quickly secularizing and urbanizing world, more and more religious practices (like public prayers and even incense-burning) have lost their religious significance. Modernity has provided an open neutral "civic space" (or "marketplace" or "public square") for freedom of religion and non-religion. Religious rituals and festivals no longer have as much religious significance as in their original forms. Many religious practices have just become mere *civil* or *cultural* artifacts for ethnic or national identity. Evangelical theologians in Asia have already been exploring the possibility that some forms of ancestral practices common in Buddhist cultures might be acceptable, since they serve civic functions (filial piety) rather than religious worship of gods (akin to the veneration of saints or memorials). [28]

It appears that the rapid church growth in Buddhist South Korea during the past three decades did not have to consciously work on (or against) Buddhism, for the rapid secularization of their society has diminished ties to their traditional religion. [29] But the lack of growth in the past few years [30] should challenge Korean Christians to find new spiritualities to address the needs of both the secularized and the folk Buddhist sectors of their society.

Dialogic Christology, therefore, contrasts with dogmatic Christology, which has a static understanding of the theological formulation and structural formation of the Christian faith. In actual evangelism, we seldom use technical theological language. In fact, for effective evangelism, it is best to avoid using it, instead using plain "street language" (read: new formulations). In defining biblical Christianity as "radically Christo-centric," we should be open to new ways of introducing Jesus to Buddhists, and to new spiritualities in which Buddhist converts can express their faith in Christ. This will enrich not only our knowledge of Jesus Christ, but also our understanding and expression of the multi-faceted riches (still many to be discovered) of biblical Christianity.[31]

3. Diaconal Ecclesiology

The third dimension of RC is the "cruciform of the body of Christ." To follow the "way of the cross," there needs to be a paradigm shift from the dominant ecclesiology of Christendom to that of "servant-church" in Buddhist contexts. This "diaconal ecclesiology" consists of at least three major aspects: ecclesial indigenization, ecclesiastical re-structuring and socio-political involvement. These are important because one of the biggest hindrances to mission in Buddhist lands has been the uncontextualized (foreign and strange) church forms and structures that prevail there.

3.1. Ecclesial Indigenization

For saturation evangelization to happen among Buddhists, the churches that will be formed should be, from the start, truly self-governing, self-supporting, and self-propagating.

By self-government is meant that the key leaders should be Buddhist converts. After all, they are the best evangelists and best contextualizers among their own people, at least in terms of identity, language, and cultural understanding. Missionaries or church planters should consider themselves "facilitators" or "catalysts" of church-planting movements among them, but leave as soon as possible, and let them take the lead. This plea for local leadership has been sounded in mission circles, especially since 1860, but hardly practiced (Allen 1962, 151; Newbigin 1978, 144; Peters 1977, 162; Parshall 1988, 179-181; Patterson 1988, 612). Hence today the call to "overhaul the missions system" still stands (Shenk 1999, 98-100). M. Tsering has called for local leadership for missions among Tibetan Buddhists since the 1980s.

Paul did not take long to appoint elders in each locality as quickly as possible, so he would be able to evangelize elsewhere (cf. Acts 14:23; Titus 1:5). He entrusted and authorized his converts to the Holy Spirit and the Word, even though he knew false teachings would rise from both inside and outside the Ephesian church (Acts 20:28-32). He did not have to stay long; he might hinder the development of spiritual gifts and the quick rise local leadership.

Great people movements have often been "not the result of foreign work in any direct way" (Smalley 1988, 501). Oftentimes they occur through the witness of someone who has been converted by the efforts of a foreign missionary. But the problem has always been "paternalism": it is hard to let go and let churches grow by themselves under the guidance of the Holy Spirit. For they will most probably develop spiritualities not to the missionary's liking (read: the latter's exported or transplanted denominational patterns).[32] And if the missionary has the association or cultural perception of being rich and powerful, then, all the more, she/he has to decrease her/his presence and leadership as soon as possible.

Self-support is also important for contextualization to develop, so that no dependency on foreign resources occurs. This calls for two key moves: First, there needs to be a *simple church structure* to start with, with minimum overhead costs. Hence the discovery in recent years of the idea of planting CPMs, rather than (transplanted) local churches, is a giant step in the right direction. The past practice of importing church structures, especially of church buildings, from one culture to another, has been one of the worst hindrances in saturation evangelism. How can we compete, and how much of our resources are we going to use up in order to parallel the Buddhist structures already in place (not to mention the secular and commercial buildings going up today)? Can't we dream that these Buddhist and secular properties *will be* ours, once our CPMs "win over" the populace, including the monks? (Are they not already God's, hence ours also by faith?)

The other key ingredient in self-support is the need for *economic development,* especially if mission is done among the poor. Local believers should be encouraged to stay in their professions and enterprises so that a secure local support base is established. One of the outstanding models is the Issaan Development Foundation ministry in Udon Thani, Thailand (Gustafson 1998). This also ensures that the local people will be truly self-governing, and become self-propagating with both local and foreign missions.

And "self-propagation" is needed to prove that the local Christian movement is indeed contextualized. It will have adopted local communication methods and decision-making processes so that saturation evangelism can be achieved. The emphasis will be on "total mobilization" of the Buddhist converts. After all, the best evangelization is done by "local evangelists, catechists and lay people speaking and acting the gospel" (Shenk 1999, 108). Mass movements to Christianity have often followed the communication patterns used by local people (Cf. Nida 1988; Hiebert 1988; Hesselgrave 1988, 408-409). This should vary among Buddhists in different tribal, peasant, and urban societies.

It will also follow the decision-making procedures of the particular culture; only then can "group by group" conversions and "group conversions" occur more often (McGavran 1985, 1955), including among Buddhist monks and in Buddhist monasteries,[33] and even "village conversions." Conversions are dynamic processes that include socio-cultural dimensions. Thus, following the decision-making patterns of the culture is a must for community or mass conversions and even for social movements (Kraft 1979, 328-344, 345-377).

3.2. Ecclesiastical Re-structuring

A corollary to the above is the need to transform church structures in Buddhist lands from centralized to decentralized, top-down to bottom-up, and hierarchical to democratic structures, even if these seem counter-cultural at first sight. They are actually necessary for "church multiplication through total mobilization" to occur. Saturation evangelism can occur only if there is a proliferation (in the form of networks) of simple and small reproducing "disciple-making groups," instead of a gradual church growth into a few mega-churches.

Following the underground house church movements in

restricted areas (including Buddhist-dominated Vietnam, Cambodia, and China), and the "home cell units" in growing megachurches in Korea and elsewhere, many sections of Christendom have discovered the importance of small groups in the "quantity through quality" growth of the church. In fact, Latin American theologians have developed a "missiological ecclesiology" that recognizes the important role of "basic Christian communities" in the Catholic churches and "cell groups" in Protestant and Pentecostal churches.[34] They see that evangelism is inherently incompatible with a Christendom ecclesiology: it "produces unevangelized Catholics" (Richard 1987, 114), and "Protestant Christendom ... produces unevangelized evangelicals" (Padilla 1999, 110). They see hope, not in elitist Christianity, but in the "grassroots ecclesial communities."

For Buddhist identity, there is no requirement for them to be loyal to only one monk, to frequent only one temple or monastery, or to visit and perform religious ceremonies every week in scheduled meetings. The local church structure we have inherited may merely be a product of Western Christian cultural development. After all, there was no "local church," there were only "house churches" in the New Testament, and in fact, for most of the first three centuries of the church! And the local "elders" of the "house churches in each city" were not ordained "full-time" clergy!

3.3. Socio-political involvement

Last, but not least, for saturation evangelism to win entire communities and people groups, RC requires socio-political action, to show Buddhists that we care for the people's welfare (not just the church's), while also connecting the local believers to community leaders. This is mainly to concretize the commitment of Christians to "incarnational missions," to be the "church of the poor" (see 1.3, above).

This includes "spiritual warfare," not just in the form of prayer rallies to repent of the people's specific sins and cast out evil territorial spirits, but also in the form of political marches—not to fight "flesh and blood" politicians but the evil "spiritual forces" that dominate the thinking and actions of socio-economico-political leaders of societies.[35] Even recent Buddhist movements recognize the importance of this dimension of their mission. May we find them to be our allies and comrades, in order for us to find another good common ground to seek God and truth (through dialogic friendship evangelism!)[36] Through this, the church becomes a reconciling community vis-à-vis the divisions of people amidst ethnic, religious, and other pluralities (Tan 2000, 299).

If there are existing church buildings in Buddhist lands, they should be transformed into community ministry centers, to serve the needs in their Buddhist neighborhood. Such "shining light" ministry through good works can lead to effective evangelism and transformation of the (Buddhist-dominant) community (cf. Matt. 5:14-16). In many increasingly violent inter-religious situations (especially in Sri Lanka, Nepal, and Myanmar), these acts of kindness can help establish multi-cultural, multi-ethnic and multi-religious "peace cells" to prevent conflicts from erupting, and develop appropriate rites for reconciliation and for healing of painful memories.

Conclusion:

This is what I believe to be a good representation of "missiology from the periphery," which should form the framework for evangelical missiology in evangelizing Buddhists and people of other faiths. May the church today follow in the excellent instances of RC in other contexts in mission history, especially those of the Celtics, Franciscans, Moravians, and early Methodists. May the Buddhist peoples receive Christ into their midst *en masse*, because his church dares to follow his mission of radical contextualization!

Notes

1 Lee (2000, 144) claims that his opinion was shared by others in the Think Tank of the Iguassu Consultation (cf. his fn. 35).

2 Escobar (2000, 112, cf. 112-114) depicted the crisis thus: "The idea that an accumulation of material resources is bound to produce certain effects has reflected itself in the constant preoccupation with augmenting the missionary force quantitatively, with-

out much debate about the quality of that missionary action. The suspicion of some Third World Christians is that they are being used as objects of a missionary action that seems to be directed to the main objective of enhancing the financial, informational and decision-making power of some centers of mission in the First World."

3 Trinitarian missiology was a theme in the Iguassu Consultation (cf. Escobar 2000, 114-120; Fernando 2000; etc.; e.g., Bonino 1995, 117-149; Bjork 1997, 117-134).

4 For examples, see Olson 1973 and Richardson 1974 (cf. Richardson 1981); also in African religions (A. Anderson 2001; Spear and Kimambo 1999).

5 Nida (1960, 226) puts this well: "All divine communication is essentially incarnational, for it comes not only in words, but in life. Even if a truth is given only in words, it has no real validity until it is translated into life. Only then does the Word of life become life to the receptor. The words are in a sense nothing in and of themselves. Even as wisdom is emptiness unless lived out in behavior, so the Word is void unless related to experience. In the incarnation of God in Jesus Christ, the Word (expression and revelation of the wisdom of God) became flesh. This same principle has been followed throughout the history of the church, for God has constantly chosen to use not only words but human beings as well to witness to His grace; not only the message, but the messenger; not only the Bible, but the church."

6 Harper (2001) suggests this for witnessing to cultists, too: relation-building before any truth encounter!

7 Hertig (2001, 175) cites the contrast as being between "love of power" and "power of love." I view this contrast as being between the "way of the world" and the "way of the cross."

8 Used in Escobar 2000 (p. 117).

9 For excellent critiques of the pluralist view that believes any faith can save, cf. Wright 2000, Fleming 1997, and Ramachandra 1999.

10 Seamands (2000, 64-65) gives a simple contrast between "gospel" and "religion."

11 Andrew Walls cited in Bediako 1994 (p. 53; cf. Ramachandra 1999, 116).

12 Kraft (1979) called for "Dynamic-Equivalent Transculturation of the Message" (pp. 276-290) and "Dynamic-Equivalent Theologizing" (291-312). Also cf. Fleming (1995, 160) on "transcontextual theologizing."

13 On use of narratives, see Steffen 1997. Pelikan (1985) shows that at least eighteen major imageries of Jesus have been used through history, such as the Rabbi (to the Jews), the Light to the Gentiles (of missionaries and apologists), the Cosmic Christ (of Christianized Platonic philosophers), the True Image (in Byzantine culture), the Bridegroom of the Soul (of mystics), the Mirror of the Eternal (of the Reformers), the Prince of Peace (of Anabaptists), and the list goes on.

14 Tan (2000, 300) observes, "In general, the Evangelical community's perspectives on Christianity's relations with non-Christian religions have gradually shifted from Barth's model of total discontinuity (Christ against religions), to Kraemer's model of radical discontinuity."

15 This formulation does not depend on the factuality of Thaiwatcharamas' article.

16 Also, Jesus Christ may be known as "the Ancestor" in Africa (Bediako 1994, 54) and "the Peace Child" among the Sawi tribe (Richardson 1974).

17 This is alleged to be mentioned by Buddha in some sutras, and in some "Jataka" stories (cf. Mendis 1990, 25).

18 Pieris (1993, 33-35) critiques "the Euro-ecclesiastical Christ of the official Church."

19 For examples, see K. Tan 2000 (pp. 302-303), Ramachandra 1999 (102-103), Seamands 2000 (101-105; cf. Dy 2001).

20 This has already been affirmed in the World Evangelical Fellowship Manila Declaration in July 1992. See Nicholls 1994 (pp. 26-27): "Christ as the Hope and Judge in Relation to Other Religions." (Also cf. Anderson 1970 and Berentsen 1985, 297-298).

21 Cf. clear contrasts between Buddha and Christ (Aagaard 1996, 10-12), between the bodhi tree and the cross (Seamands 2000, 173-183), and between reincarnation and resurrection (Aagaard 1996, 5-8). Also cf. Kung (1986) for exhaustive study on Theravada (pp. 289-360), Mahayana, Vajrayana, and Shaktist Tantrism (361-398), and Modern and Neo-Buddhisms (399-437).

22 Japanese evangelist Toyohiko Kagawa used the Japanese analogy of various pilgrim paths leading to the summit of Mt. Fuji: some religions become tired and stop at the third or fourth or sixth station; Buddhism (his former faith) reaches the ninth, but only Christianity leads to the top (Cited in Seamands 2000, 43).

23 Richardson (1981) enumerates many instances of "God in general revelation."

24 On "dynamic equivalent churchness," see Kraft 1979 (pp 315-323).

25 Davis (1993) documents a laudable attempt in creedal formulation for a Buddhist context at Bangkok Bible College, Thailand.

26 This is akin to the RC (called C-5 and C-6) in the C-1 to C-6 spectrum of spiritualities among Muslim converts (cf. the debate between Parshall and Travis in *Evangelical Missions Quarterly* in the late 1990's, reprinted in Parshall 2000, 90-113).

27 Its address: 33 Tao Fong Shan Road, Shatin, New Territories, Hongkong, S.A.R., People's Republic of China; website: www.tfscc.org; e-mail: tfsacad@asiaonline.net.

28 See Ro 1985, esp. the articles of Berentsen and McGavran (1985).

29 I think Japan, Taiwan, Hong Kong, and other similar quickly secularizing Buddhist contexts did not parallel Korean church growth, mainly because they did not have the ecclesiastical structure of the "home cell units" of the Koreans (see 3.1 and 3.2).

30 Hong (2001) reports that a 1995 survey lists Korean Buddhists as 23.1%, Protestants as 19.7%, and Roman Catholics as 6.6% of the population. A 1997 estimate shows there are 600,000 *musog-ins* (shamans), that is, eight times the number of Protestant ministers in Korea.

31 The WEF Manila Declaration states that "even in those areas where the biblical revelation directly speaks, it may be that our understanding is limited or faulty, and discussions with people of other faiths may have a role in correcting our misunderstanding" (Nicholls 1994, 26).

32 Cf. Smalley 1988 (pp. 500-501). On "dynamic equivalent leadership," see Kraft 1979 (323-327).

33 Seamands (2000, 40-41) narrates how Frank Laubach was able to win Muslim chiefs and their communities to the faith, and win Muslim priests as friends, in Mindanao in 1930s.

34 Padilla (1999) and Escobar (2000; cf. Guder 2000) critique "the cultural captivity of the institutional structures" of the Western church(es) that has hindered the exercise of authentic Christian mission.

35 For "liberation" prophetic perspectives in Buddhist contexts (without accepting their universalistic tendencies), see Song 1982 (pp. 108-126, 161-191), Pieris 1993 (44-46), Nemeshegyi 1993, and Balasuriya 1993.

36 K. Tan (2000, 304) calls evangelicals to work with other religious groups on social concern: "Such engagements with structural evils are not to be considered as 'second class' involvement within the mission of the church."

Bibliography on Contextualization for Buddhist Megasphere

Aagaard, Johannes. 1996. Buddha and Christ. *Spirituality in East and West*. 1 (March 1996).

Anderson, J.N.D. 1970. *Christianity and Comparative Religion*. Downers Grove: IVP.

Balasuriya, Tissa. 1993. The Christian Workers' Fellowship of Sri Lanka. *Any Room for Christ in Asia?*, ed. L. Boff and V. Elizondo. Maryknoll: Orbis. 121-130.

Bentley-Taylor, David, and Clark Offner. 1975. Buddhism. *The World's Religions*, ed. Norman Anderson. Leicester: IVP; Grand Rapids: Eerdmans.

Berentsen, Jan Martin. 1985. The Ancestral Rites–Barriers or Bridges. *Christian Alternatives to Ancestor Practices*, ed. Bong Rin Ro. Taichung: Asia Theological Association. 287-301.

Boff, Leonardo, and V. Elizondo, eds. 1993. *Any Room for Christ in Asia?* Maryknoll: Orbis.

Crawford, C. 1985. The Buddha's Thoughts on Thinking: Implications for Ecumenical Dialogue. *Religion in the Pacific Era*, eds. F. Flinn and T. Hendricks. New York: Paragon House Publications.

Davis, John. 1993. *Poles Apart? Contextualizing the Gospel.* Bangkok: OMF Publications.

———. 1997. *The Path to Enlightenment: Introducing Buddhism.* London: Hodder and Stoughton.

Dy, Ari C. 2001. The Great Beyond: Personal Eschatology for Chinese Filipino Catholics. *Tulay*, October 23, 2001: 10, 12.

Dye, T. Wayne. 1976. Toward a Cross-Cultural Definition of Sin. *Missiology*. 4 (1976):26-30.

Fleming, Dean. 1995. The Third Horizon: A Wesleyan Contribution to the Contextualization Debate. *Wesleyan Theological Journal*. 30.2 (Fall 1995):139-163.

———. 1997. Biblical Theological Foundations for a Response to Religious Pluralism.

Asbury Theological Journal. 52.2 (Fall 1997):43-61.

Flinn, F., and T. Hendricks, eds.. 1985. *Religion in the Pacific Era*. New York: Paragon House Publications.

Gustafson, James. 1998. The Integration of Development and Evangelism. *Missiology*. 26.2 (April 1998):131-142.

Hong, Young-gi. 2001. Modernity, Tradition and the Korean Church. *Journal of Asian Mission*. 3.2 (2001):185-211.

Kung, Hans, et al. 1986. *Christianity and the World Religions: Paths of Dialogue with Islam, Hinduism and Buddhism*. New York: Doubleday & Co., Inc.

Lim, David. 1983. Biblical Christianity in the Context of Buddhism. *Sharing Jesus in the Two Thirds World*, eds. V. Samuel and C. Sugden. Grand Rapids: Eerdmans. 175-203.

McGavran, Donald. 1985. Honoring Ancestors in Japan. *Christian Alternatives to Ancestor Practices*, ed. Bong Rin Ro. Taichung: Asia Theological Association. 303-318.

Mendis, Lalith. 1990. *Unashamed*. Colombo: Christian Professionals Forum.

Nemeshegyi, Peter. 1993. Being a Christian in Japan. *Any Room for Christ in Asia?*, eds. L. Boff and V. Elizondo. Maryknoll: Orbis. 110-120.

Nicholls, Bruce, ed. 1994. *The Unique Christ in our Pluralist World*. Grand Rapids: Baker.

Pieris, Alysius. 1993. Does Christ Have a Place in Asia? A Panoramic View. *Any Room for Christ in Asia?*, ed. L. Boff and V. Elizondo. Maryknoll: Orbis. 33-47.

Ramachandra, Vinoth. 1999. *Faiths in Conflict*. Leicester: IVP.

Ro, Bong Rin, ed. 1985. *Christian Alternatives to Ancestor Practices*. Taichung: Asia Theological Association.

——, and Mark Albrecht, eds. 1986. *God in Asian Contexts*. Taichung: Asia Theological Association.

Rubenstein, R. L. 1985. Religion and the Economic Pearl Harbor: A Preliminary Statement. *Religion in the Pacific Era*, ed. F. Flinn and T. Hendricks. New York: Paragon House Publications.

Ruiz, Daniel. 1998. The Boddhisatva of Compassion. *World Mission*. November, 1998:20-22.

Samantha, Stanley. 1991. *One Christ—Many Religions: Toward a Revised Christology*. Maryknoll: Orbis.

Seamands, John. 2000. *Tell It Well: Communicating the Gospel Across Cultures*. Chennai: Mission Educational Books.

Smith, Alex. 2001. *Buddhism Through Christian Eyes*. Littleton, CO: OMF International.

Song, Choan Seng. 1982. *The Compassionate God*. Maryknoll: Orbis/London: SCM.

Tan, Kang San. 2000. Evangelical Missiology from an East Asian Perspective: A Study on Christian Encounter with People of Other Faiths. *Global Missiology for the 21st Century: The Iguassu Dialogue*, ed. W. Taylor. Grand Rapids: Baker. 295-306.

Tan, Michael. 2001. Buddhism in the Philippines. *Today*. August 26, 2001:6.

Taylor, William, ed. 2002. *Global Missiology for the 21st Century: The Iguassu Dialogue*. Grand Rapids: Baker.

Thaiwatcharamas, Pracha. 1983. God and Christ in the Context of Buddhism. *Sharing Jesus in the Two Thirds World*, eds. V. Samuel and C. Sugden. Grand Rapids: Eerdmans, 204-216.

Tsering, Marku. n.d. *Sharing Christ in the Tibetan Buddhist World*. Upper Darby, PA: Tibet Press.

Volf, Miroslav. 1994. The Unique Christ in the Challenge of Modernity. *The Unique Christ in our Pluralist World*, ed. B. Nicholls. Grand Rapids: Baker. 96-106.

Weerasingha, Tissa. 1986. Buddhism Through Christian Eyes. *God in Asian Contexts*, eds. B. Ro and M. Albrecht. Taichung: Asia Theological Association. 145-164.

Wright, Chris. 2000. Christ and the Mosaic of Pluralisms. *Global Missiology for the 21st Century: The Iguassu Dialogue*, ed. W. Taylor. Grand Rapids: Baker. 71-99.

Supplementary References on Contextualization

Allen, Roland. 1962. *Missionary Methods: St. Paul's or Ours?* Grand Rapids: Eerdmans.

Anderson, Alan. 2001. Types and Butterflies: African Initiated Churches and European Typologies. *International Bulletin of Missionary Research*. 25.3 (July 2001):107-118.

Bediako, Kwame. 1994. The Unique Christ in the Plurality of Religions. *The Unique Christ in our Pluralist World*, ed. B. Nicholls. Grand Rapids: Baker. 47-56.

Bjork, David. 1997. *Unfamiliar Paths*. Pasadena: William Carey Library.

Boff, Leonardo. 1986. *Ecclesiogenesis*. Maryknoll: Orbis.

Bonino, Jose Miguez. 1995. *Faces of Latin American Protestantism*. Grand Rapids: Eerdmans.

Conn, Harvie. 1984. *Eternal Word and Changing Worlds.* Grand Rapids: Zondervan.

Escobar, Samuel. 2000. Evangelical Missiology: Peering into the Future at the 21st Century. *Global Missiology for the 21st Century: The Iguassu Dialogue*, ed. W. Taylor. Grand Rapids: Baker. 101-122.

Fernando, Ajith. 2000. Jesus: The Message and Model of Mission. *Global Missiology for the 21st Century: The Iguassu Dialogue*, ed. W. Taylor. Grand Rapids: Baker. 207-222.

Garrison, David. 2000. *Church Planting Movements*. Richmond, VA: International Mission Board of the Southern Baptist Convention.

Gerlach, L. P., and V. H. Vine. 1970. *People, Power, Change: Movements of Social Transformation.* New York: Bobbs-Merrill Co.

Guder, Darrell. 2000.*The Continuing Conversion of the Church.* Grand Rapids: Eerdmans.

Harper, Ann. 2001. The Iglesia Ni Cristo and Evangelical Christianity. *Journal of Asian Mission.* 3.1 (2001):101-119.

Hedlund, Roger. 2001. Previews of Christian Indigeneity in India. *Journal of Asian Mission.* 3.2 (2001):213-230.

Hertig, Paul. 2001. Re-positioning Center and Margin in Church and Society. *Journal of Asian Mission.* 3.2 (2001):167-183.

Hesselgrave, David. 1988. Worldview and Contextualization. *Perspectives*, eds. R. Winter and S. Hawthorne. Pasadena: William Carey Library. 398-410.

Hiebert, Paul. 1988. Social Structure and Church Growth. *Perspectives*, eds. R. Winter and S. Hawthorne. Pasadena: William Carey Library. 380-389.

Kraft, Charles. 1979. *Christianity in Cultures.* Maryknoll: Orbis.

Lee, David Tai-Wong. 2000. A Two-Thirds World Evaluation of Contemporary Evangelical Missiology. *Global Missiology for the 21st Century: The Iguassu Dialogue,* ed. W. Taylor. Grand Rapids: Baker. 133-148.

Love, Rick. 2000. *Muslims, Magic and the Kingdom of God.* Pasadena: William Carey Library.

McGavran, Donald. 1955. *Bridges of God.* London: World Dominion Press.

———. 1988. Today's Task, Opportunity and Imperative. *Perspectives*, eds. R. Winter and S. Hawthorne. Pasadena: William Carey Library. 541-554.

Newbigin, Lesslie. 1978. *The Open Secret.* London: SPCK.

Nida, Eugene. 1960. *Message and Mission.* New York: Harper.

———. 1988. Communication and Social Structure. *Perspectives*, eds. R. Winter and S. Hawthorne. Pasadena: William Carey Library. 428-443.

Olson, Bruce. 1973. *Bruchko.* Chicester: New Wine Press.

Padilla, C. Rene. 1999. The Future of Christianity in Latin America: Missiological Perspectives and Challenges. *International Bulletin of Missionary Research.* 23.3 (July 1999):105-112.

Parshall, Phil. 1988. God's Communicator in the '80's. *Perspectives*, eds. R. Winter and S. Hawthorne. Pasadena: William Carey Library. 473-481.

———, ed. 2000. *The Last Great Frontier.* Quezon City: Open Doors with Brother Andrew.

Patterson, George. 1988. The Spontaneous Multiplication of Churches. *Perspectives*, eds. R. Winter and S. Hawthorne. Pasadena: William Carey Library. 601-616.

Pelikan, Jaroslav. 1985. *Jesus through the Centuries*. New Haven: Yale University Press.

Peters, George. 1977. Issues Confronting Evangelical Missions. *Evangelical Missions Tomorrow*. Pasadena: William Carey Library.

Richard, H.L. 1999. *Following Jesus in the Hindu Context*. Pasadena: William Carey Library.

Richard, Pablo. 1987. *Death of Christendoms, Birth of the Church*. Maryknoll: Orbis.

Richardson, Don. 1974. *The Peace Child*. Glendale, CA: Regal.

——. 1981. *Eternity in their Hearts*. Ventura, CA: Regal.

Shenk, Wilbert. 1999. *Changing Frontiers of Mission*. Maryknoll: Orbis.

Smalley, William. 1988. Cultural Implications of an Indigenous Church. *Perspectives*, eds. R. Winter and S. Hawthorne. Pasadena: William Carey Library.

Spear, Thomas, and Isaias Kimambo, eds. 1999. *African Expressions of Christianity*. Athens, OH: Ohio University Press.

Steffen, Tom. 1997. Reaching Resistant People Through Intentional Narrative. Paper presented to the Evangelical Mission Society, Southwest Regional Conference, 4 April 1997. 12pp.

Stott, John. 1995. *Authentic Christianity*. Downers Grove: IVP.

Sunder Raj, Ebe. 2001. *National Debate on Conversion*. Chennai: Bharat Jyoti.

Wagner, C. Peter. 1988. The Fourth Dimension of Missions: Strategy. *Perspectives*, eds. R. Winter and S. Hawthorne. Pasadena: William Carey Library. 573-580.

Winter, Ralph, and Stephen Hawthorne, eds. 1988. *Perspectives on the World Christian Movement: A Reader*. Pasadena: William Carey Library.

Woodberry, Dudley. 1989. *Muslims and Christians on the Emmaus Road*. Monrovia: MARC.

Evangelism in the New Millenium:

An Integrated Model
of Evangelism to Buddhists
Using Theology, Anthropology,
and Religious Studies

Ubolwan Mejudhon

Tears and Triumph

I taught Buddhist philosophy in a Thai university before I became a Christian in 1971. In 1973, my husband and I were called to plant an indigenous church, the Muangthai Church. However, we used Western ways of approaching, witnessing, and nurturing Christians and non-Christians. The church slowly expanded. We found many split-level Christians among the believers. We also found that hundreds of those who prayed to accept Jesus did not follow Him.

During the years 1994 to 1998, my husband and I furthered our study at the E. Stanley Jones School of World Mission and Evangelism, Asbury Theological Seminary in Wilmore, Kentucky, in the United States. There we encountered an important turning point in our ministry, when we studied anthropology, religious studies, and contextualization. I learned to open up Thai culture, Thai belief systems, and Thai relationships, as well as using the principles and methods Christians have used to spread the gospel in the past.

I discovered that Thai Christianity seemed westernized. Carl E. Blanford commented about Christianity in Thailand as follows:

> Christianity has been introduced into Thailand by Westerners and is generally regarded as a "foreign religion." Its institutions are foreign. The architecture of its buildings is foreign. Its music is foreign. Its emphasis on individual conversion and the separation of its members from their original social relationships also cause people to regard it as foreign. This foreignness of Christianity as introduced and practiced in Thailand constitutes a difficult barrier for the present-day missionary to overcome (Blanford 1985, 84).

My study revealed the negative attitudes of missionaries toward Buddhism and Thai culture. Dr. Dan Beach Bradley arrived in Thailand on July 18, 1835. On September 24, 1935, he wrote in his diary:

> Lectured my people on the falsity of their religion and the many ways in which they sin against Jehovah. A good degree of seriousness manifested. The people stare when I tell them plainly the rottenness of their religious system, but they seem to say that what I say is probably but too true (Feltus 1936, 46).

The research of Philip H. Hughes (1989) also illustrated that the Thai way of understanding religion was much different from that of the missionaries. Moreover, I found that Thais accepted messengers before they accept messages. However, missionaries wanted the Thais to quickly receive the gospel message. Eugene A. Nida (1954, 251) mentions that, "It is not primarily the message but the messenger of Christianity that provides the greatest problems for the average non-Christian."

I, therefore, propose a new hypothesis, one I pretested in 1998. From January 1999 to January 2002, I tested this hypothesis in the Muangthai Church. The research findings are very encouraging.

In this paper, I will present the statement of the problem; the conceptual, practical, and theoretical framework; the data; and the methodology of research testing. I will conclude with the summary of research findings, which confirms my hypothesis given in the statement of the problem.

I personally believe that my theoretical framework can be most effectively used with Buddhists in Southeast Asia. However, I also believe the principles and methods should be applicable to most contexts in the new millennium, because this theoretical framework manifested itself in the life and work of our Lord Jesus.

Turn, Turn, Turn

There is a time for everything. For 200 years, Buddhists in Thailand have not widely accepted the gospel of Jesus. Thailand is less than one percent Christian and has become the headquarters of Buddhism. In the past, Christians have ignored the context of Buddhist belief and culture. We have not studied the personalities of Buddhists in each context. We have been ignorant of the ways in which Buddhists learn religion. We have also overlooked the ways Buddhists create deep relational bonding.

In this paper, I use Thailand as an example for learning how to witness to Buddhists. I would like to propose a more effective method for discipling Buddhists, one which comes from: (1) a better understanding of the personality of Buddhists in each context, (2) knowing how Buddhists learn religion, and (3) learning how Buddhists create deep relational bonding.

By discipling, I mean evangelizing, nurturing, and disciplining. However, in this paper I refer to it as evangelism. I believe this definition of discipling is congruent with biblical discipling. I supported this conclusion in my dissertation, "The Way of Meekness: Being Christian and Thai in the Thai Way" (1997, 321–340). A.H. Mathias Zahniser (1997, 23) also holds that God's discipling of individuals has already begun—before their spiritual birth.

In my dissertation, I examined the personalities of Thai Buddhists, their religious learning methods, and their ways of deep relational bonding. These research findings in 1997 broke fresh new ground for theories of discipling. I used these new theories to find new methodologies in discipling. I then pretested the theories and methodologies for one year in a local church in 1998. After that, I tested the theoretical framework and methodology for three years, from 1999 to 2002.

Having presented my introduction and stated the problem, I will now illustrate my theoretical framework, which is the criterion for measuring the effectiveness of my thesis. Next, I will elucidate the data collected from the local church as well as the methodology I used. At the end, I will exemplify a summary of the research findings. Now, we will go directly to the theoretical framework.

Theoretical Framework

I devote this part of the paper to the theoretical framework. My conceptual theoretical framework consists of three main parts: (1) the Thai way of meekness, the Komin model, as stated in my dissertation (1997); (2) the Thai way of meekness in religious discipling, mentioned in the same dissertation; and (3) Thai ways of relational bonding by Lauriston Sharp (1978) and my additional research findings (1997) concerning this matter.

Theoretical Framework of Thai Personality:

The Thai Way of Meekness, the Komin Model:

Psychology of the Thai People: Value and Behavior Patterns (1991) is the result of Komin's ten plus years of studying Thai values. Her empirical research reveals the Thai national character in the form of nine value clusters: (1) ego orientation, (2) grateful relationship orientation, (3) smooth interpersonal relationship orientation, (4) flexible and adjustment orientation, (5) religio-psychical orientation, (6) education and competence orientation, (7) interdependence orientation, (8) fun and pleasure orientation, and (9) achievement-task orientation. Anyone who violates these nine value clusters is considered to be "aggressive."

Komin presents the Thai as a people who have a strong self-identity and who use the Thai way of meekness to avoid confrontation in order to keep smooth relationships and to protect their identity. Komin's theory presents the way of Thai meekness as the avoidance mechanism that fends off unnecessary clashes. Thai meekness is not used out of fear, rather the Thai are first and foremost ego-oriented and characterized by the highest ego value. They are independent and self-esteem is a very high value for them. Moreover, the Thai emphasize relationships. Therefore, the Thai way of meekness functions socially through a strong self-identity, grateful relationships, smooth interpersonal relationships, flexibility and adjustment, interdependence, as well as fun and pleasure. It seems to me that the values mentioned above exhibit themselves also in the Thai religio-psychical orientation. Komin does not mention much about the Thai worldview. Her research findings of nine Thai national value clusters seem to point to the Thai worldview of "power and weakness." This worldview is exhibited by a strong self-identity as well as by the gentle and indirect ways of Thai social interaction.

Komin also presents Thai behavior patterns as follows: (1) Thais can react aggressively if their self-identity is violated; (2) Thais use indirect ways to soften a negative assertion in order to avoid public confrontation that challenges the inferior, the equal, and the superior; (3) Thais use reciprocity of kindness between givers and receivers; (4) Thais cherish a non-assertive, polite, humble personality, expressed through appearance, manners, and an interpersonal approach; (5) Thais have compromising and warm personalities, but are lax in principles; (6) Thais learn religion from ceremonies, rituals, and festivals; (7) Thais emphasize the forms of education more than the knowledge; (8) Thais cherish assimilation and communal cooperation; (9) Thais enjoy fun and pleasure, but are able to work hard, and (10) Thais work most successfully when they are able to balance hierarchy and relationship.

Komin's research seems to suggest that Thai society is structured around three core elements: hierarchy, relationship, and individualism. Moreover, she proposes that these Thai characteristics come from Thai culture and not from Buddhism, because Thai Muslims and Thai Christians demonstrate the same traits of meekness. However, since Buddhism first arrived in Thailand, it could have been the source of meekness in all three groups.

Her research also demonstrates that the Thai believe more in Buddhist folk religion than in the high religion. This assumption can be argued from the point of view of religious studies. Buddhism, Islam, Hinduism, Christianity, and traditional religions all emphasize the concept of meekness. Buddhism confirms the "mid-

dle way." Islam elucidates "submission to God." Hinduism emphasizes "unity and nonviolence." Christianity cherishes "love toward
God and humankind," and traditional religion suggests "harmony
with nature, supernatural beings, and powers." Therefore, it is
partly true that the Thai way of meekness comes from culture. The
additional factors of geography, history, and economics, in the
past provided the tranquility needed for the Thai way of meekness
to develop. Additionally, it is also probable that the syncretism of
the various religions mentioned above is also an important source
of the Thai way of meekness, because the mentality of a people is
affected by its worldview, religion, and mythology (Luzbetak 1988,
252).

Komin's research, concerning the Thai value system, which she
proposes as being in the form of nine value clusters, seems to suggest that the Thai worldview is focused on power and weakness. I,
therefore, proposed in my dissertation that the Thai personality
consisted of binary oppositions; in other words, power and weakness according to Levi-Strauss's theory of structuralism of culture
(Levi-Strauss 1953, 524–553).

Therefore, the structure of the characteristics of the Thai personality is presented below. The structure is a theoretical model for
evaluating data from the research testing.

Thais have a "both/and" worldview, structured as power and
weakness, which is presented by the center circle in figure 1. These
are the mental eyeglasses Thais use to see the world around them.
Closely related to this center worldview are arranged the nine value clusters, represented by the next concentric circle in Figure 1.
The Thai value system carries nine value clusters: (1) ego orientation, (2) grateful relationship orientation, (3) smooth interpersonal
relationship orientation, (4) flexibility and adjustment orientation,
(5) religio-psychical orientation, (6) education and competence
orientation, (7) interdependence orientation, (8) fun and pleasure
orientation, and (9) achievement-task orientation.

Moving out to the next concentric circle we come to Thai
behavior patterns. The purpose of practicing Thai behavior patterns is to keep the Thai's nine value clusters intact, especially the
self-identity cluster. The worldview of power and weakness influ-

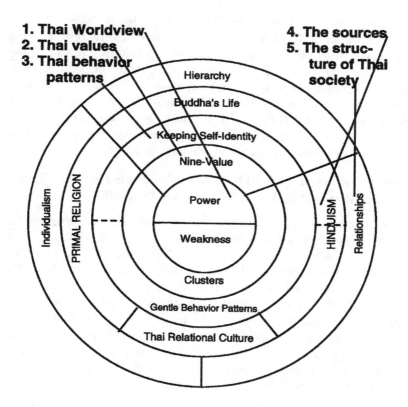

1. Thai Worldview
2. Thai values
3. Thai behavior
   patterns

4. The sources
5. The struc-
   ture of Thai
   society

Hierarchy

Buddha's Life

Keeping Self-Identity

Nine-Value

Power

Weakness

Clusters

Gentle Behavior Patterns

Thai Relational Culture

Individualism

PRIMAL RELIGION

HINDUISM

Relationships

Fig. 1 The Structure of the Characteristics of the
Thai Way of Meekness.

ences the Thai to use humble attitudes and gentle behavior patterns in Thai social interaction. However, when the Thai's self-
identity is violated, he or she reacts aggressively.

The next concentric circle in Figure 1 contains the sources of the
Thai way of meekness. Primal religion, Buddha's life model, Hinduism, and Thai relational culture have each made an impact on Thai
personality. The final circle represents Thai society, structured as it

is, by the elements of hierarchy, relationship, and individualism.

The theoretical framework for Thai personality reveals some important practical theories for discipling Thai Buddhists. Effective discipling is vulnerable, progressive, and cooperative. Discipling moves from where non-Christians are to where Christ is. These practical theories help keep the egos of Thai Buddhists intact. As a result, Thai Buddhists become more receptive to the gospel of Jesus Christ. Now we are ready for the theoretical framework for Thai Buddhist ways of religious learning.

Theoretical Framework of the Thai's Religious Learning: The Thai Way of Meekness in Religious Discipling:

I spent a year and a half researching Thai ways of religious discipling. I studied a Buddhist Jataka and modern Thai literature concerning Buddhist monks. I also conducted interviews with non-Christians. The research yielded an important theory about the ways the Thais learn religion. The research findings elucidate the Thai Buddhist way in religious discipling as follows: (1) religion is affective; (2) religion is applicable to the present felt needs; (3) religion is practical, solving life's problems; (4) religion emphasizes rituals, ceremonies, and festivals; (5) religion has integrative functions; (6) religion is concrete, experiential; (7) religion is bonding; and (8) religion does not force faith.

The theoretical framework of Thai Buddhists' ways of religious learning demonstrates the practical theories mentioned above. Effective discipling should be vulnerable, progressive, and cooperative. Powerful discipling moves from the familiar to the unfamiliar. These practical theories enhance the theoretical framework of Thai Buddhist religious learning. Now I will move directly to the theoretical framework of Thai Buddhist ways of deep relational bonding.

Theoretical Framework for Thai Buddhist Deep Relational Bonding:

Lauriston Sharp explains about Thai Buddhist ways of deep relational bonding in *Bang Chan: Social History of a Rural Community in Thailand* (1978). Sharp believes that the Thai kinship system selects potential kinsmen in three ways: (1) they must share some difficult experiences in the natural ways of living; (2) they must exchange services and favors to the extent that an investor in or reciprocator of services lays aside all conditions for ensuring that his gain; love, and respect dominate the relationship, and (3) they must accept a long-term commitment of fixed obligations beneath the easily contracted arrangement. Then two people, whatever their origin, become kinsmen.

My interview research (1997) illustrates some Thai ways of creating deep relational bonding: (1) participation in the communal activities, (2) sharing difficult experiences in the natural pattern of life, and (3) togetherness and long-term commitment. The theoretical framework for the Thai Buddhist way of deep relational bonding confirms the practical theories mentioned above. Effective discipling should be vulnerable, cooperative, progressive, and move from the familiar to the unfamiliar.

I believe these practical theories are congruent with Scripture. Reading the Scriptures from the perspective of a believer in a Third World country, I believe Jesus was vulnerable, progressive, and cooperative in his ways of discipling the apostles. Our Lord accepted people as they were. Then He moved them to where God wanted them to be. His attitude in witnessing poured first from his heart (Mark 6:34; Matt. 9:36; and Matt. 14:?). Jesus asked for help; He asked for water from a Samaritan woman. He borrowed a boat from Peter. Our Lord was vulnerable. Jesus allowed Nicodemus to take time to make a decision. Our Savior worked progressively. He cooperated with Andrew, as well as other disciples, in discipling Peter. His discipling behavior pattern was cooperative.

Dr. A.H. Mathias Zahniser emphasizes the important role of vulnerability in witnessing (Zahniser 1994). John Paul Fieg argues that the Thai concept of time is longer than that of westerners (Fieg 1989). Paul G. Hiebert's (1985) book *Anthropological Insights for Missionaries* states that Third World people cherish cooperation among people in groups. Their self-actualization and personal growth gives way to the best interest of their group. Moreover their identity comes from community. Lamin Sanneh (1993) agrees that familiarity breeds faith. Therefore, I present below the structure for my conceptual and practical framework.

The Task of Testing: Data

I have presented the introduction, the statement of problem, as well as my conceptual and practical theoretical framework. In this

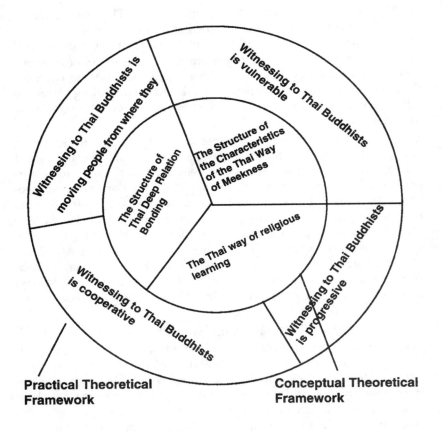

Fig. 2 Conceptual and Practical Theoretical Framework

section, I will support them with my research data. First, I would like to briefly explain the background of the Muangthai Church where I conducted the testing of my theoretical framework and methodology. I will explain who the participants were. Some were my Christian teacher's aids and some were non-Christians who had been brought to our church. I started the pretest of my theoretical framework in the Muangthai Church in 1998. I then launched the full research test concerning the Thai way of witnessing to Buddhists from 1999 to 2002.

The Muangthai Church, Bangkok, Thailand, is an indigenous church. It was started by six lay people in 1973. It was founded by Rev. Nantachai Mejudhon (who is now the pastor), myself, and three others. The church used Western ways of witnessing, teaching, and training from the very beginning until 1998. The church experienced a crisis during the years between 1994 and 1997 when Rev. Mejudhon furthered his studies in the USA. Attendance dropped and fewer people were enthusiastic about evangelism. Those who prayed to accept Christ did not attend the church. When I started my research pretesting, the attendance was around eighty people.

The data collection was conducted as follows: First, I chose three congregants to be participant-observers in my Sunday School class for non-Christians during 1999 and 2000. Two more lay people were chosen to be teachers among slum pre-adolescents between 1999 and 2001. All of them took over the classes in 2001. Second, I encouraged members of the Muangthai Church to invite people from their social networks to visit our church. The distribution of Christians and non-Christians who participated in this research is shown in Tables 1, 2, 3, and 4.

The Task of Testing: Bonding with People

The Muangthai church encouraged congregants to bond themselves with members of their social networks. The pastor educated members about the nine values of the Thai. Christians learned to re-engineer their values and behavior patterns to fit more within the Thai context. We learned to be Christian and Thai. As a result, significantly more non-Christians visited our church during regu-

Table 1 Distribution of Christian Participants: Teacher Aids

Sex Num.	Female	4	Male	1		
Age Num.	31-40	3	20-30	2		
Education Num.	Bachelor Degrees	3	High School	1	Primary School	1
Economics Num.	Upper Middle Class	1	Middle Class	2	Lower Middle Class	2
Jobs Num.	Professional	3	Laborer	1	Housewife	1
Years of believing Num.	20	1	15	3	5	1
Personality Num.	Meek	5	Aggressive			

lar worship services and Christian festivals, from January 1999 to January 2002.

Moreover the pastor educated the members concerning the biblical perspectives on social concern. The church property is next to a slum area in Bangkok. Two members, Pen and Pong, started to care for orphans and neglected slum children from our neighborhood. Both of them volunteered to do the job and they used their own money. Soon more members joined to support the work. The church became like a foster family to about twenty children. We did not force them to listen to the gospel or attend the church. However, they wanted to come because they were loved and forgiven, time and again, for their mischief. After a year of bonding, on January 2002, fourteen of them voluntarily committed their lives to Christ.

A record conversion of fourteen slum students confirms the validity of our theoretical framework. Among the twenty slum children taken care of by Pen and Pong, five boys were seemingly hopeless. They were orphans whose parents had either died of AIDS or had been murdered. Some of them sold drugs. They regularly skipped school. Their ages were between eight and twelve years old. Our church was their favorite playground. They ate dinner at

Table 2 Distribution of Christian Participants: Lay Evangelists From Jan. 1999–Jan. 2002

Sex	Female	Male			
Num.	21	11			
Age	15-20	21-30	31-40	41-50	51-65
Num.	2	8	10	8	4
Education	Doctoral Degrees	Master Degrees	Bachelor Degrees	High School	Middle School	Primary School
Num.	4	3	12	8	1	4

Economics	Upper Class	Middle Class	Lower Middle Class	Poor
Num.	6	7	14	5

Jobs	Professional	Business	Laborers	Jobless	Students
Num.	12	2	10	6	2

Years of believing	40	30	25	20	15	10	5	1
Num.	1	2	2	3	6	3	6	9

Number of Non-Christians invited per one Christian	15	8	5	4	3	2	1
Num.	2	1	2	1	4	2	9

*Between 1999 and 2001, seventy-five non-Christians attended the Muangthai Church's Sunday School for non-believers. Sixty people regularly attended. They completed the course. In Table 3, the distribution of regular seekers is presented.

Table 3 Distribution of Regular Seekers from Jan. 1999–Jan. 2002

Sex	Male	Female				
Num.	27	33				
Age	13-15	16-18	20-30	31-40	41-50	51-65
Num.	6	7	16	13	5	3
Education	Univ. Grad	High School Grad	Middle School Grad	Primary School Grad	No Education	
Num.	17	14	19	10		
Religions	Buddhists	Muslim	No Religion			
Num.	58	1	1			
Economics	Upper Class	Upper Middle Class	Middle Class	Lower Middle Class	Poor	
Num.	2	7	18	15	18	
Jobs	Professional People	Business People	Laborers	Jobless	Students	
Num.	12	10	5	10	23	

**Table 4 Distribution of Teaching, Learning, and Training
From Jan. 1999–Jan. 2002**

Groups	Time	Number of Non-Christians	Instructors	Number of Participant observers	Remarks
1	Jan. to July 1999	8	1	3	I am the instructor
2	August 1999– February 2000	10	1	3	
3	March 2000– September 2000	10	1	3	
4	October 2000– June 2001	12	1	5	
5	August 2001– January 2002	35	5	3	Previous Observers took over the class New observers joined the class.

the church with Pen and Pong, who were like their foster parents. We had problems with their vulgar language and violent fighting. However one boy, Bee, said, "I know teacher Pen still loves me." Every Friday they came to listen to storytelling. Pen and Pong gradually told them about Jesus according to a rough lesson plan. Many times, they adapted the lessons to help their audience better understand the gospel.

Many people reached out to these slum children. Sunday school teachers took them to a children's museum. A minister took them to stay overnight in his home when the government cut electricity to Bee's house. Three people tried to teach them English and help them with their homework. Other members taught them to draw pictures and play football. We also used them to play Thai folk music during the Christmas 2001 program. These youngsters freely moved in and out among us. Pen and Pong devoted themselves to them by taking them to run and play around in a public park each Saturday. They even taught the children how to take a bath using soap, at the church. These kids stayed with their relatives in the nearby slum. We began to feel hopeless, because we knew time was running out. Drug traffic was spreading in the slums. The wicked system of drug trafficking especially trapped students who skipped school.

On January 6, 2002, the "gang of five" attended our worship service for the first time with the other children. They sat through the Children's Day celebration. The pastor explained how precious children are by showing stars hidden in apples. In the afternoon, Pen and Pong, presented all the children with the gospel of Jesus. Realizing they did not have a father model, Pen presented Jesus as their Father and she gave them time to make a decision. Fourteen of them wanted to follow Jesus. The following evening, they came by themselves to confess their sins. Some great changes in behavior took place. The gang of five returned to school. They also regularly attended the church and the class to prepare for the baptismal service. Their violent natures were completely transformed. The church and non-Christians in our neighborhood have noticed the changes and are very happy.

This primary stage, mentioned above, validates the important roles of vulnerability, cooperation, and progression in bonding with non-Christians. Christians carefully help their friends move from the familiar Thai Buddhist context to the unfamiliar context of the gospel. This research testing confirms the validity of our theoretical framework.

The Task of Testing: Worship Services

After the primary stage of bonding, understanding the field of religious studies introduced many good changes in our Sunday worship services. The research findings from my dissertation concerning the Thai Buddhist way of learning religion indicated the need for many changes in the decorations of our sanctuary, worship songs, and the style of preaching. The Muangthai Church has made some experiments, which I will briefly explain below.

First, we found a Thai traditional music teacher in our midst. We also bought some Thai traditional musical instruments. Then some children, students, and adults paid a teacher to learn Sawong, an art which has been lost among Christian churches. We researched how to develop proper Thai tunes and songs that would open up Thai feelings. We also invented some Thai ways of reading scriptures. Moreover, we introduced a new way of giving a testimony. The one who gives the testimony dances to a Thai music tune and a singer chants the testimony.

Second, we tried our best to make each Sunday worship service festive. The sanctuary was decorated with sights, sounds, symbols, and fragrances. One Good Friday service, we arranged the tables and chairs in the form of a cross. On each table, we put a candle and a vase of white flowers. A full-sized wooden cross was put up in our sanctuary. Three big nails and a crown of thorns were passed around among the congregants. The preaching message was concretely near, now, new, and narrative to the audience's ears. After the service, the church gave each member a small bag of Thai potpourri, which was made at the royal palace. That night, many members mentioned how they had encountered Jesus' presence. Such an experience is very important because, as Peter McKenzie comments about encountering Jesus:

> Religion, including Christianity, is not philosophy, not world-
> view, not theology, but intercourse with the sacred. This inter-

> course is a twofold one. It comes to expression very clearly in
> the dialogues between the soul and Christ as they are found in
> the most beautiful and popular writings of the German mystics:
> *The Booklet of Eternal Wisdom* of Henry Suso and the *Imitation of
> Christ* of Thomas a Kempis (1988, 310).

Third, we added variety to the worship services. On the first and third week, we have different teams of youth lead the worship. On the second week, we have traditional worship services for elderly people. On the fourth week, we have worship services for young adults. Every two months, we have a special service focusing on the Thai way of worship. Our church also organized a church choir.

Fourth, the preachers tried to preach the Scripture at the deep level of attitudes and values, rather than at the behavior pattern level. Sermon delivery became more concrete, concise, and constructive. Listeners laughed and participated more while they listened to the Word of God. After worship services, Christians and non-Christians preferred to spend time discussing the applications of the sermons they had heard.

Fifth, we held evangelistic meetings during Christian festivals and some other Thai festivals. The most popular Christian festival is the Christmas celebration. Popular Thai festivals are Children's Day, Teacher's Day, the Chinese New Year, Valentine's Day, Mother's Day, the Thai New Year, and the King's Birthday. We rarely had "altar calls," but we encouraged seekers to attend Sunday School class. Our church aimed at progressive and cooperative witnessing. After seekers met Jesus Christ in Sunday School classes, the pastor gave altar calls for them to come forward. Then, new converts publicly confessed their determination to follow Christ.

An example of our Christmas 2000 outreach will demonstrate the effectiveness of our theoretical framework. During the Christmas 2000 celebration, we planned to use the Thai way of evangelism, using Victor Turner's (1969) book, *The Ritual Process: Structure and Anti-Structure* and William E. Paden's (1988) book, *Religious Worlds: The Comparative Study of Religion* as our guidelines for the program preparation. We, therefore, planned four important stages: 1) presenting the story of Christ's Nativity in a Thai Way; 2) inductive preaching for a verdict; 3) preparing a counseling team, and 4) having a love feast after the Christmas worship service. The committee tried to design ways in which we could repeatedly and artistically present the story of Christ's Nativity to non-Christians who were unfamiliar with the Christmas story. We also wanted to present the theme of Jesus' incarnation, explaining how He left heaven to live on earth. We also expected a lot of participation from the audience. As a result, we narrated the story through Thai traditional ways of dancing and singing which symbolize a high level of hierarchy. We, then, immediately used Thai folk dances and singing to repeat the narration. The folk ways symbolize a low level of hierarchy. Over 200 audience members participated in singing the folk songs. A lot of non-Christians celebrated the Christmas narration at the end of the program by walking forward and dancing a Thai folk dance. The program indirectly indicated that the high class met the low class in Jesus' birth.

Then the pastor inductively preached an evangelistic sermon. Ten non-Christians responded to the invitation. Most of them are now members in our church. During the love feast, the pastor interviewed non-Christians concerning the presentation of the Christmas narration and the sermon. The pastor could not find even one negative response. However, one Christian family was quite annoyed with the way we presented the Christmas story. Most non-Christians repeatedly commented that they clearly understood the gospel. One non-Christian who had attended our Christmas programs for the past ten years said, "This is the best Christmas program."

Research testing illustrates the validity of our conceptual and practical theoretical framework. The knowledge of religious studies improves our worship services. Vulnerability, progression, and cooperation play important roles in effective evangelism to Thai Buddhists. The presentation of Christmas 2000 confirms that Christians should lovingly and gently move non-Christians from their Thai Buddhist familiar context to the unfamiliar context of the gospel of Christ.

The Task of Testing: Presenting the Gospel

We now come to the very important part, presenting the content of the gospel to Thai Buddhists. During the past twenty-five years, the Muangthai Church has encountered two problems: (1) there are many split-level Christians who converted only at the level of behavior patterns, not at the worldview or value levels; and (2) there are those who prayed to accept Christ, but did not become Christ's believers. With the help of my theoretical framework, I planned the course and the methods of dialoguing about the content of the gospel.

The course I designed coincides with what Asbury Theological Seminary professors, Dr. Darrell Whiteman and Dr. J.T. Seamand, have presented. Dr. Whiteman (1994) spoke of culture and the gospel in his lecture at the E. Stanley Jones School of World Mission and Evangelism at Asbury Theological Seminary, U.S.A. as follows:

> Gospel traverses culture. Gospel judges and saves culture. Gospel dedicates, and sanctifies culture. Gospel beautifies culture. Gospel exorcises demons in culture.

Dr. J.T Seamand agreed that the gospel of "The Four Noble Truths" is the best way to witness to the Buddhists. He suggested:

> "Four Noble Truths" and "The Eight-fold Path." The Four Noble Truths are:
>
> a. Suffering is a fact of life.
>
> b. The cause of suffering is sin.
>
> c. The cure for sins is the suffering of Christ.
>
> d. The way of deliverance is through faith in Jesus Christ. (1981, 175)

Moreover, cultural anthropologists believe culture functions as an interrelated whole. Technology, economics, politics, kinship, and religion remain important institutions of culture. Stephen A. Grunlan and Marvin K. Mayers confirm the idea. They wrote:

> Culture is the integrated system of learned behavior patterns characteristic of the member of a society. Cultural anthropology deals with the sytem as a whole, how the parts fit and function within the whole, and how whole systems relate and compare. (1979, 56)

Therefore, during witnessing, any discussion about the topic of the suffering of human beings will always include concern about materialism, relationships, and idealism.

The course of presenting the gospel to Thai Buddhists consists of two steps:

1. The eradication of the old wicked parts of the worldview and values and the preservation of the good in the Thai Buddhist worldview and values.

2. The Presentation of the gospel context consisting of:

    a. The suffering of human-beings in materialism, relationships, and idealism

    b. The suffering of Jesus Christ as 100% man

    c. The cause of suffering: the sins of mankind

    d. The cure of suffering: Jesus Christ's death and resurrection as 100% God

    e. The call to reconciliation with Christ: faith in Jesus Christ

The method of teaching is comprised of seven important elements as follows:

1. Christians create a friendly and family-like atmosphere in the Sunday School class for non-Christians.

2. Non-Christians are welcomed to ask questions and criticize Christianity, Christians, and Christian churches. Teachers and teacher aids pay focused attention to the non-Christian's ideas.

3. Non-Christians are included in sharing their opinions concerning the topics being discussed. Arguing and debating are not encouraged on the part of Christians.

4. Christians usually give explanations after non-Christians give their opinions. Christians use illustrations, testimonies, and the Scriptures in answering questions or objections. Christians can simply say they cannot answer every question.

5. Christians end each session by encouraging non-Christians

to directly ask Jesus and read the Scriptures to find the answers on their own.

6. The course is not a fixed model. Teachers can adapt the content of the lesson plan according to the guidance of the Holy Spirit and the context of the non-Christians present.

7. Prayer is important for the effective witness of the gospel to Thai Buddhists. The church should pray for both teachers and non-Christians.

Some testimonies of those who became Christians in this class will exemplify the efficiency of the theoretical framework. I will record the conversion of two persons, Pung, and Sutkate.

Pung was a lady who was twenty years old. Her father had died of alcoholism. Pung ran away from home at fifteen. She had a young son, but she had broken up with her husband, who took her son away. At the point when she was deeply depressed, a Christian relative came to help. Pung attended our Sunday School class for seven months. She loved Christians, but she could not believe Jesus was God. One night, she prayed that God would help her know about her little son's situation. On the following day, she received a letter from her husband who had not communicated for about a year. He shared about their son's situation. God had answered her prayer. She knew He was real. Pung became a Christian. She witnessed to her younger sister. Her younger sister became a Christian. Moreover, now her older sister wants to be a Christian too.

Sutkate was an architect of Thai architecture. He lost one arm in an accident when he was eight years old. Sutkate asked many difficult questions in the Sunday School class. He had experienced having a Hindu idol answer his prayers as well as Jesus. He wondered why he should believe in Jesus as the one and only way. Christians tried to answer, but Sutkate was not satisfied. Therefore, Sutkate, sought answers on his own from the Bible. He also prayed directly to Jesus. Sutkate found the answers that satisfied his soul. He became a Christian within seven months. He now actively serves among slum orphans.

The record of the course of presenting the gospel content as well as the methods of dialoguing about the gospel confirms the efficiency of our theoretical framework. The roles of vulnerability, progression, cooperation, as well as, moving non-Christians from the familiar Buddhist context to the unfamiliar gospel context are obvious in dialog about the gospel with Thai Buddhists.

The task of testing illustrates positive results in the Muangthai Church. By January 2002, fifty-eight of sixty regular seekers became Christians. Only two men did not make decisions. They continue to attend our Sunday School class for non-Christians. The percentage of converts is 96.67. Between 1999 and 2001, there were seventy-five non-Christians who attended the Muangthai Church's Sunday School for non-believers. The percentage of converts among those who attended the class was 77.33. Average attendance at the church is now 150, which is 87.50% more than the 1997 attendance. We now have two Sunday School classes for non-Christians. Ten more congregants are being trained to be teachers and teacher aids. Baptismal classes have expanded to three.

Moreover, the test of our theoretical framework has also greatly affected our Sunday School curriculum. The church has produced 500 Sunday School lessons for children from two to fifteen using the conceptual and practical theoretical framework. We aim at preparing children to progressively and cooperatively absorb and encounter Jesus within three years as they learn the New Testament and the Old Testament. Children actively participate in their Sunday School classes. The church has also opened a training center for cross-cultural communication. We have trained about seventy missionaries. Many have reported the effectiveness of the theoretical framework we have taught, when applied to their ministry situations.

The Task of Testing: A Summary of Findings

At this point, the test demonstrates that the witness in the Sunday School class for non-believers and the witness among slum children confirm the effectiveness of our theoretical framework. Figure 2 illustrates the conceptual and practical theoretical framework.

As noted in the theoretical framework, Thais have a unique personality, and unique way of learning religion, as well as the uniqueness of the Thai way of deep relational bonding. Figure 2. is

Theoretical Framework

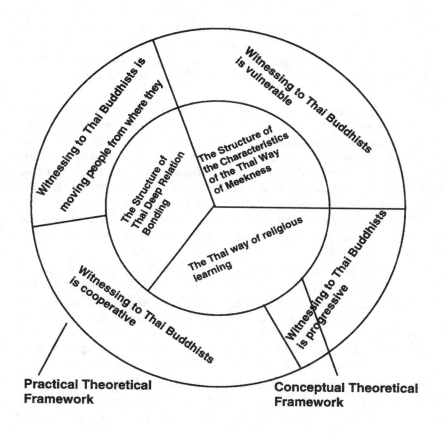

Fig. 2 Conceptual and Practical Theoretical Framework

our theoretical framework. The conceptual theoretical framework consists of: (1) the structure of characteristics of the Thai way of meekness as mentioned in figure 1; (2) the Thai way of religious learning, and (3) the structure of Thai deep relational bonding. Number 2 and number 3 were mentioned in detail in the discussion of the theoretical framework. The conceptual theoretical framework comes from anthropology and religious studies. The practical theoretical framework suggests that vulnerability, progression, and cooperation are all vital in witnessing to Thai Buddhists. Moreover, more Thai Buddhists will understand, as well as accept Christ and his gospel, if Christians gently help them move from the familiar Buddhist context to the unfamiliar context of the gospel.

The conceptual and practical theoretical framework exemplified themselves in the process of creating deep relational bonding with non-Christians, and in the process of improving worship services as well as in the process of witnessing the gospel. Moreover, the theoretical framework affected the children's Sunday School and our practice of social concern. We can create effective three-year Sunday School curriculum and lessons using this theoretical framework. The theoretical framework has helped us expand social and humanitarian work among our slum neighborhood. The church now fits better within its context.

I, therefore, confirm my statement of the problem, that there is a time for everything. For 200 years, Buddhists in Thailand did not widely accept the gospel of Jesus. Less than one percent of the population accepted Christ. Thailand became the headquarter of Buddhism. In the past, Christians ignored the context of Buddhists. We did not study the Buddhist personality in each context. We were ignorant of the ways Buddhists learn religion. We also overlooked the ways Buddhists create deep relational bonding.

In this paper, I have used Thailand as an example for learning how to witness to Buddhists. I have proposed a more effective way of discipling Thai Buddhists, which comes from: (1) a better understanding of the Thai Buddhist personality in each context, (2) knowing how Thai Buddhists learn religion, and (3) learning how Thai Buddhists create deep relational bonding. The task of testing demonstrated the validity of my solution to the stated problem.

References Cited and Bibliography

Blanford, Carl E. 1985. *Chinese Churches in Thailand.* Bankok: Suriyaban Publishing House.

Feltus, George H., ed. 1936. *Abstract of the Journal of Rev. Dan Beach Bradley: Medical Missionary in Siam 1835–1873.* Oberlin, OH: The Multigraph Department of Pilgrim Church.

Fieg, John Paul. 1989. *A Common Core: Thais and Americans* Yarmouth, ME: Intercultural Press Inc.

Grunlan, Stephen A. and Marvin k. Mayers. 1979. *Cultural Anthropology: A Christian Perspective.* Grand Rapids: Zondervan Corporation.

Hiebert, Paul G. 1985. *Anthropological Insights for Missionaries* Grand Rapids: Baker Book House.

Hughes, Philip H. 1989. *Proclamation and Response* Bankok: Payap University Archives.

Komin, Suntaree. 1991. *Psychology of the Thai People: Value and Behavior Patterns* Bankok: National Institute of Development Administration.

Lamin, Sanneh. 1993. *Translating the Message.* Maryknoll, NY: Orbis Books.

Levi-Strauss, Claude. 1953. Social Structure. *Anthropology Today.* Alfred L. Kroeber, ed., 524–553.

Luzbetak, Louis J. 1988. *The Church and Culture: New Perspectives in Missiological Anthropology* Maryknoll, NY: Orbis Books.

McKenzie, Peter. 1988. *The Christians: Their Beliefs and Practices.* Nashville: Abingdon Press.

Mejudhon, Ubolwan. 1997. *The Way of Meekness: Being Christian and Thai in the Thai Way* D. Miss. diss., Asbury Theological Seminary.

Nida, Eugene A. 1954. *Customs and Cultures: Anthropology for Christian Missions.* New York: Harper and Row.

Paden, William E. 1988. *Religious Worlds: The Comparative Study of Religion.* Boston: Beacon Press.

Seamand, J.T. 1981. *Tell It Well: Communicating the Gospel across Cultures.* Kansas City: Beacon Hill Press.

Sharp, Lauriston. 1978. *Bang Chan: Social History of a Rural Community in Thailand* Ithaca, NY: Cornell University Press.

Turner, Victor. 1969. *The Ritual Process: Structure and Anti-Structure* Rochester: Aldine De Gruyter.

Whiteman, Darrell. 1994. Lecture on Anthropology at the E. Stanley Jones School of World Mission and Evangelism, Asbury Theological Seminary, Wilmore, KY.

Zahniser, A.H. Mathias. 1994. Close Encounters of the Vulnerable Kind: Christian Dialogical Proclamation Among Muslims. *The Asbury Theological Journal,* 49 (1): 71–781.

———. 1997. *Symbol and Ceremony: Making Disciples across Cultures* Monrovia, CA: MARC.

Contextualizing
with Thai Folk Buddhists

Paul H. DeNeui

Introduction

Grandmother Somlee [1] was a healer. This small, frail woman had been endowed with spiritual powers that enabled her to find yah phii bawk, (spirit-delivered medicine). Through spiritual interaction, it was revealed to her where certain herbs and plants grew. By mixing these together into potions (also supernaturally revealed) she was able to cure ailments, prevent miscarriages and bring about healings in several cases. All of these "acquired skills" came to her, not from the study of books or from other human sources, but from the spiritual interaction she had with the spirit of her area's territorial power, called the Chao Phua, located in the city pillar shrine of her northeastern Thai province.

In a nearby village lived a man named Father Niran. He was a village elder and a well-known musician in his district. He had no formal training in music but knew how to play the Lao bamboo wind instrument locally called the kaen. This instrument is widely used throughout the Lao-speaking region of northeastern Thailand (known as Isaan [2]) at every good social event, to provide the musical entertainment that delights the hearts of these people. Father Niran, however, was not an entertainer. He did one thing with his playing, which was known as bpao phii faa, (calling up the sky spirits). This was a specific ceremony for the sick where he would play a lively tune into the ear of the ill to induce the spirit of the patient to revive and get up and dance. It could be elaborately lengthened depending upon the need. It was also the only tune Father Niran knew how to play.

121

Are Thai people truly Buddhists? The answer to this would depend upon whom you were asking. Certainly the average Thai would answer that, "to be Thai is to be Buddhist." But what is Thai Buddhism? Many missionaries have been surprised, upon their arrival in Thailand, to discover that despite what they have read in books,[3] Thai Buddhism as it is lived and practiced is actually a conglomeration of many religions and beliefs.[4] It is a syncretistic mix that is flexible, accommodating and dynamic. If the Thai are pure Buddhists then why the proliferation of spirit houses in front of many hotels, businesses, and homes? Why the profusion of the sale of amulets and charms—often by Buddhist monks themselves? Why are tattoos still popular for spiritual protection? What, in all of this, is Thai Buddhism and what is not?

The author has had the opportunity to spend fourteen years in the northeast region of Thailand, known as *Isaan*, working in a team ministry with *Isaan* believers, and has grown to deeply appreciate the cultural forms that are distinctive for this people group. This paper is submitted with the goal that it facilitate better communication of Jesus Christ to the Thai, through understanding their syncretistic worldview and through reviewing some contextualized practices that speak to the heart of the Thai Folk Buddhist.

What Is Thai Folk Buddhism?

An Historical Overview from Old Siam

The Thai people have a long history of cultural and religious accommodation. The earliest racial group known as the "Thai"[6] is thought to have come into existence around the sixth century B.C. along the southern border of China, east of the Mekong river (Gustafson 1970, 18). Some theorize that these early peoples were animistic,[7] though this is debated.[8] Archaeologists have recovered evidence of Buddhist inscriptions in both Chinese and Sanskrit in this region, dating from about the eleventh century A.D. This would establish the date of existence of Mahayana Buddhism[9] within the people group from this time (Gustafson 1970, 18). As the Thai people migrated south in the thirteenth century, they added the cultural and religious elements of the Mon-Khmer peoples they encountered, and adopted their animistic practices (HRAF 1956, 26).

The history of the modern Thai people is first documented by King Rama Khamhaeng (1283–1317 A.D.), the founder of the Sukhothai kingdom and inventor of the modern Thai alphabet. During the late thirteenth century, Theravada Buddhist monks from Ceylon settled in southern Thailand and their influence eventually caught the attention of the Sukhothai king (Gustafson 1970, 22). In 1292, Rama Khamhaeng, by this time a devoted follower of the Theravada sect, made an inscription proclaiming the official religion of the Sukhothai kingdom to be the Theravada form of Buddhism. At the same time, he continued his regular sojourns to the spirit of the hill located on the south side of the city of Sukhothai [10] (Gustafson 1970, 25). Animism, or primal religious practices, [11] and Theravada Buddhism existed comfortably together.

Later, along with animistic practices, Brahmanistic rituals from Indian Hinduism were also incorporated into Thai Buddhism. Today, Buddhist tradition and Brahman tradition use the same vocabulary; it is impossible to separate the two. "It is unthinkable in Thailand that a local *brahman* can be outside the Buddhist faith, or that his rites and those of the monk can be mutually exclusive" (Tambiah 1970, 256).

Following the Thai tradition of accommodation, animistic practices, Brahmanistic beliefs, and Buddhist foundations have all combined to make a complicated and sometimes contradictory conglomerate, one that can be labeled Thai Folk Buddhism. Attempts to diagram this integration can be seen in Appendix 1, done by Harvard University Anthropologist Dr. Stanley J. Tambiah. This brief paper does not allow for a thorough exploration of the interrelationship between the so-called "higher" religion of Buddhism and the so-called "lower" primal practices of supposedly pre-Buddhist animism. These issues have been dealt with extensively elsewhere. [12] The fact that Thai Folk Buddhism is syncretistic is problematic only for a devout few.

Most Thai people have a pragmatic view that whatever works for them in their area of Thailand is what is practiced. [13] While the external manifestations of Theravada Buddhism are highly visible around the country (temples, monks walking in the morning, celebration of holy days), in reality much of the actual practices follow animistic tradition. Animism, or primal religion, can be defined as:

> The belief that personal spiritual beings and impersonal spiritual forces have power over human affairs and, consequently, that human beings must discover what beings and forces are influencing them in order to determine future action and frequently, to manipulate their power (Van Rheenen 1991, 19).

Missiological Approaches to Thai Folk Buddhism

Early missiologists took an evolutionary view towards animism—that it was a "lower form of pre-logical primitive thought"—and believed it would soon be replaced by one of the "higher," formal religions, preferably Christianity (Hiebert et al. 1999, 76). The German missionary, Johannes Warneck, with his 1922 volume entitled *The Living Christ and Dying Heathenism* is an example. Describing his experiences among "animistic heathendom" in the Indian Archipelago, he strongly argued for the "spiritual superiority" of Christianity as viewed in terms of its "civilizing power." It was clear to him that the "dull eyes of the heathen (would recognize) the earthly blessings that accompany Christianity, and thereby learn to value the new religion" [14] (Warneck 1922, 18, 165). The reality, however, has proved to be different. Neither "higher religion" nor modern scientific discovery has caused animistic practices to diminish. Anthropologist Robert H. Lowie writes:

> (Science) is admittedly our best possible instrument for controlling physical environment and for formulating ideas of the material world. But it does not at all follow that it is soul-satisfying, or that it can serve as a basis for moral action ... What the normal human being wants is peace, security, [15] and relations. And he can never find these things in that dynamic, ever-growing, ever-disturbing thing that we have found science to be (Lehmen 1985, 23).

Much of traditional Christian missionary effort has followed a western rationalist approach and has thus divorced itself from addressing many of the issues that are between science and religion. This area has been labeled the "excluded middle" and has been well explained by Dr. Paul Hiebert (Hiebert 1994, 189-202). Religion has been, and continues to be, the place where many in the world find their sense of security. If, however, the traditional higher religions (as defined by the evolutionary understanding of religions) [16] fail to provide the sense of security needed, the adherents may return to primary religious practices (animism) in their attempt to have their deeper, urgent needs addressed.

Understanding the Thai Folk Buddhist Worldview

Pure Theravada Buddhism and its practices deal primarily with death. The making of merit in Buddhism is not primarily for those living today but for the future—either for the benefit of future reincarnations of the living or to benefit those already dead. Animistic practices, on the other hand, address the issues of the here and now. For the majority of both urban and rural Thai people,[17] a clear distinction would not be relevant to them. It is the practice of animism within their Buddhist context that provides a sense of security for the present, something that science and traditional western religious practices tend to ignore.[18] Animism is the means of dealing with what is important for living life today.

> Within Buddhism religious action is phrased in terms of the ideology of *bun* (merit)—when one gives gifts to the monks or the temple (*wat*)[19] one receives merit; but when one propitiates or placates *Chao Phua* (*territorial or regional spirits*) villagers explicitly consider the transaction as a *bargain*, an offering made to gain a particular favor, generally to remove an affliction caused by the *phii* (spirit) because of an offense committed (Tambiah 1970, 270).

How Does Folk Buddhism Help People?

> As a girl, worshipping at the city pillar, Somlee heard a voice that spoke to her. "If you worship me, I will give you power." As she was a poor, uneducated girl, this had great appeal. She decided to submit to this authority. She was given a promise of future abilities and eventually these came—but not for free. In the earliest years, the simple donation of a candle or joss stick at the city pillar was sufficient. As her powers in herbal remedies increased, however, the requirements to return the favor also increased proportionally. More expensive gifts were required to be offered to the spirit. If at any time she failed, Somlee would suffer severe headaches and chest pains. These symptoms became even stronger and more frequent as her popularity, power with medicine, and success increased. Her power came at a price.

> Father Niran could bpao phii faa (call the sky spirit) on the bamboo kaen and bring the sick back to health—but there were personal requirements for him. He presented offerings regularly to spirits, but for him there was added a dietary restriction: he could never eat any winged creature. No bird or fowl of any kind, neither domestic nor wild, could be in

his meals. Not even the fruit bats, a popular food source in Isaan, could he eat. If, even unknowingly, he broke this taboo, he would suffer from severe intestinal pain for several days. The spirit of the sky exacted this price from him as long as he continued to play its song on the kaen.

Folk Buddhism Promises Power—at a Price

Buddhism, with its system of regulations and rituals, can be understood in the traditional religious sense. Animistic practices, however, with their emphasis on the present, are more involved with their requirements to the spirit or "gods" [20] from which the appeal is made. The price is much higher for a deeper sense of either security or some form of power. It is not uncommon for those who "receive power through a revelation to also receive usually at least one and perhaps more life-long and onerous restrictions" [21] (Lehmann 1985, 21). Within animism, power does not come without a corresponding price.

The forms of these onerous restrictions vary from person to person but clearly there is a price that must be paid for assistance from the spirit world. The higher the involvement the greater the price required. Sometimes these restrictions are taboos, [22] as in the case of Niran.

A taboo ... is a ban or prohibition ... which restricts the human uses of things and people. Some of the taboos are said to avoid punishment or vengeance from gods, ghosts and others spirits. Some of them are supposed to produce automatically their dreaded effects. Crop failures, sickness, hunting accidents, famine, drought, epidemic (events in the physical realm), they may all result from breach of taboos (Douglas in Lehmann 1985, 64, 66).

In other cases the restrictions may involve lifestyle issues for the person who has been empowered. Very often there will be restrictions against sexual intercourse or immorality. The penalty for disobedience can vary in physical, emotional, or spiritual forms. In addition, individuals who have invited these special powers to dwell within them can themselves become a force for evil, known in Thai as *phii paub*.

Village theory is that a man or woman who is a *mau wicha*, an expert in the magical arts of love magic, or protective magic (such as making amulets that make the wearer bullet-proof), or control of epidemics (like cholera), is the person who is prone to harbor a *phii paub*, [23] if he acts immorally or contravenes taboos associated with his dangerous but potent art. Since his special powers derive from this secret knowledge of charms and spells, it is said that under certain conditions these spells themselves turn into *phii paub.* Typical circumstances that lead to this transformation are (1) if a *mau wicha* discontinues his practice; (2) if he uses spells immorally by causing diseases in people rather than curing them, or if he exploits his patients by charging excessive fees (the accusation here being that he himself sends disease in order to extract fees); (3) if he fails to respect and propitiate his teacher; or (4) if he breaks food taboos associated with his profession ... All controllers of magical powers (*mau wicha*) and all exorcists (*mau tham*) are said to have special food taboos associated with their practice ... Such powers have their use in society and must be kept available for those who need them. But, at the same time, such powers are in themselves dangerous; they are a double-edged sword, cutting both ways. He who dabbles in them in order to control spirits is in danger of becoming their victim or agent. Thus a man who learns to control disease through spells may himself sometimes send or cause disease; a man who gives love magic to dearest lovers may himself come to fornicate with village wives; the man who exorcises malevolent spirits may himself become a sorcerer sending spirits to possess his enemies (Tambiah 1970, 318-319).

The localization of spirit power in specific designations, such as the city pillar for Grandma Somlee, is very common throughout the country of Thailand. Like that found in the earlier Sukhothai kingdom of Rama Khamhaeng, the city pillar is the localization of a territorial spirit to whom the authorities and the locals look for protection and granting of favors. These were often constructed with human sacrifice (Terwiel 1976, 160ff). The most famous in Thailand is the Bangkok city pillar.

The *lak mueang* is the "pillar of the city" of Bangkok; because it is the foundation pillar of the country's capital city, it is a focal point for the country as a whole. The Bangkok pillar was installed in 1792 as the very beginning of the Chakkri dynasty. [24] The pillar is placed in the center of a shrine, where also reside the guardian deities of the capital. The *lak mueang* is not unique to Bangkok. Many of the provincial cities of Thailand have city pillars and shrines associated with them ... The guardian spirit associated with the pillar is believed to protect the locality or territory that constitutes the *mueang* (city). Today the pillar shrine at Bangkok is considered to be the foremost in the country. Hundreds of people flock to the shrine every day to ask for favors from the pillar and the deities and propitiate them with flowers, candlesticks, joss sticks, silk scarves, gold leaf, and food and drink for favors granted. The pillar is personified and referred to as *"Cao Phau,"* which, literally meaning honored father, and is the usual reference and address term for a guardian deity (Tambiah 1984, 244).

Folk Buddhism Counterfeits Christ

Throughout Thailand animistic practices within Folk Buddhism address some of the heart issues of Thai people by providing them with a source of power they believe will assist them in life. A careful study of what is actually happening will show that much of what is being "offered" is a very clever counterfeit to what is actually found in Jesus Christ. To cope with the many uncertainties of life, an appeal to the spirits provides an attempt to appease or in some way connect with those forces seen to be "in control."

> Though primitive religions do tend to help (people) to adjust to the universe by giving them some sense of control, thus eliminating certain elements of fear, they do not actually solve this problem of meeting life's crises. The trouble is that elemental fear of the immediate, primary danger is only transferred to a secondary agent of concern, namely, the spirits themselves, who cannot ultimately be trusted. Though fear demands a more highly charged response than does trust, nevertheless, in the ultimate analysis, the fear of largely irresponsible spirits is no competition to trust in a loving, heavenly Father (Nida 1959, 58).

Within pure Buddhism there is no god. Thai Folk Buddhists do refer to an ultimate power or being, who is known as *Pra Cao* (God). This term is rarely used other than as an exclamatory interjection in times of distress,[25] as in *"Pra Cao chuay!"* (literally, O God, help!) This does not indicate a relationship, merely an obscure awareness.

The language used within animism, however, is not coincidental. The spirit pillars are called *"Cao Phau"* ("honored father") and sometimes *"Cao Mee"* ("honored mother").[26] The assumption that these forces will care for the practitioner in a "parental," beneficent manner disguises the reality of spiritual enslavement. Initially the gods (or God), are perceived as far away, but the spirits are intimately close. They are Respected Father and Honored Mother who know and deal with the issues of daily life. Eventually, through increasing devotion, the follower begins to delegate an authority to the spirit so that for that individual it now becomes "a god."

> From the beginning there is an attempt by (humanity) to place himself in the right relationship to unseen powers, to deprecate their hostility and to secure their good will. With deliberate acts of worship we come to a personal approach to the spirits and often they are regarded as gods (Harris 1960, 14).

The promise of a presence upon which to rely has deep appeal within the human psyche. The spirit world demonstrates abilities that appeal (spirit of light) and makes promises that directly replace what Christ has offered. Animistic practices appear to guarantee (to the faithful) an ability to deal with life in ways that appear not to fail. Note the tactic that replaces Christ words, "I am with you always" (Matt. 28:20 NIV; Acts 18:10). Another type of hope and light counterfeit the source of light (John 8:12); the false servants masquerade as servants of righteousness (2 Cor. 11:14, 15). The appeal of a helper is there, but the reality is false.

Perhaps the main appeal from many animistic practices of Folk Buddhism is to somehow know more, experience more, or gain more control than that possessed by the average human being. In fact, for however brief or long the period, the goal with connecting to this "power source" is to somehow allow the follower to ultimately become *like God*. This is the most ancient strategy employed by satanic powers known in scripture (Gen. 3:5) and directly counterfeits the work of Christ who, being God, became human in order to allow all of humanity to experience the fullness of God in him (John 1:14; Col. 1:19, 20).

Spiritual powers continually seek and demand worship from their followers at an ever-increasing expense (Matt. 4:8, 9). This attempt to usurp what is due the Ultimate Creator Authority (Matt. 4:10) demands unquestioning obedience and is exacted through the use of fear and frequently even through physical force (see examples above). Unlike the True Reality, who came not to seek power or position (Phil. 2:4-8), spiritual forces hunger for followers with an insatiable desire to possess, attack, devour, and destroy (Gen. 4:7, I Peter 5:8). For more specific comparison of counterfeit forms of Christ by spirit powers, refer to Appendix 2,

"Claims of Christ and Counterfeit Claims" and Appendix 3, "Claims of Others About Christ and Counterfeit Claims."

What Do We Need to Learn from Thai Folk Buddhists?

Many well-intentioned missionaries go overseas with the idea of being the conveyors of the gospel message. In part, this is true. However, should we not acknowledge that God is already working within the Thai Folk Buddhist context before we as missionaries ever arrive? Do we not come as fellow seekers ourselves? How, therefore, can we, as fellow seekers, learn to be more sensitive and receptive to those areas where God is already present in the lives of Thai people? How can we communicate Christ in a society which says that, "to be Thai is to be Buddhist?"

Understanding Thai Folk Buddhism and its cultural context is an important starting place. There are several studies on contextualization from which we can learn much. [27] But what can be learned from Thai Folk Buddhists themselves? Four areas are suggested: 1) the need for a wholistic approach, 2) communication must involve all major signal systems, 3) a recognition that the major barriers to allowing Christ to fully enter into a culture are primarily social and not religious, and 4) an honest awareness of the realities of the spirit world. Each of these areas will be discussed further.

The Need for a Wholistic Approach.

Animists see themselves and their beliefs as part of the whole of life. The monistic worldview of the Thai Folk Buddhist sees no dichotomy between the community of the living, natural world and the supernatural spirit world. They do not compartmentalize their livea as would Western linear-thinking cultures. They would ask questions such as, how does Christ relate to the rest of life? Does he care about our rice crop? Will he be able to act on our behalf in a way that we now ask the spirits to do? Communication of the gospel with Folk Buddhists must integrate the physical, spiritual, and social aspects of life within the community, and not be done individually as is often done in evangelical approaches.

Individualistic thought forms are diametrically opposed to animistic perspectives. While individualists believe they can chart their own courses, animists believe that they are living in an interconnected world. They feel intimately connected to their *families*, some of whom are living and some of whom have already passed on to a spiritual realm. Animists also believe they are connected to the *spiritual world*. Gods, spirits, ancestors, and ghosts pervade the world, and their ambivalent yearnings affect the living. Animists frequently feel a connectedness with *nature* ... The animist believes that no person can live as an individual, separate and apart from his extended family, spiritual powers, nature or thoughts of other human beings. Animists live in an interconnected universe (Van Rheenen 1991, 131).

Communication Involves All Signal Systems

Every culture uses signal systems to communicate. The twelve basic systems used are described by Donald Smith as verbal, written, numeric, pictorial, audio, artifactual, kinesic, optical, tactile, spatial, temporal, and olfactory. These are in order of decreasing consciousness of use and increasing degree of believability. Eighty-three percent of the information we receive comes through seeing; eleven percent we receive through hearing; 1.5 percent from touch (tactile), one percent from taste and 3.5 percent from smell (Smith 1992, 162-3). The sensory systems—seeing, hearing (including speaking and music), touch, and olfactory—are discussed, as well as two more important signal systems, often overlooked by Western cross-cultural workers: the spatial and the temporal signal systems. These general categories can be reviewed in terms of evaluatory questions for any specific Thai Folk Buddhist context when seeking improved communication and understanding.

Seeing: Consider the perspective of the Thai Folk Buddhist when they hear about Jesus for the first time. What do they actually perceive? If a non-local is the communicator of the message, a wide range of messages will be sent which are unrelated to the intended message. Is the speaker selling something? Is the speaker trustworthy? How can the speaker help me with what I need?

When a Thai Folk Buddhist is invited to church, what does he or she see? Is the setting familiar enough to be comfortable to an outsider? Are there furnishings that speak of his or her culture, or are the furnishings foreign? If so, why? Are there other items present that clearly communicate to outsiders, or are they only "insider-friendly"? One Thai mother was greatly puzzled at her son's Christian wedding in a Western-style building. She considered each item decorating the sanctuary deeply symbolic for Christians, but upon asking was unable to find anyone able to give meaning to any of them! Western "decorations" may speak a message to Thai Folk Buddhist people of which most westernized Christians are unaware. While westerners have sometimes criticized folk religionists for practicing meaningless ritual, we need to consider our own forms and ask the same questions of ourselves.

Hearing: What language does Jesus speak? Can his words truly be understood by anyone? Consider what it means for a Thai Folk Buddhist to hear a Christian sermon.[28] Typically, a Thai would go to the Buddhist *wat* and listen to the sermon in order to make merit. The purpose of listening to chanting in Sanskrit is not to find meaning but for the transference of merit *through the hearing of the sounds*. The words themselves are considered sacred, powerful, and meritorious for the soul. What happens, in this case, when an individual with this mindset is placed in a "Christian" context? He or she sits on a pew in a church, listens to a "sermon" and doesn't necessarily understand the meaning of what was spoken. What is the effect? That person leaves thinking, "So what if I don't understand anything? I've just made merit the Christian way!" Interactive dialogue, still common in Thai culture, may allow more effective and natural communication of biblical knowledge with Thai Folk Buddhists.

What signifies the end of a prayer? Is there a term used within the culture that communicates to the worldview of the Thai Folk Buddhist that the prayer is now over? In fact, there is. Throughout all of Thailand the word, "*Saatu*" (meaning, "so be it") is used and clearly communicates the desire of the prayer. Followers of Jesus in Isaan churches use it today.

Music: What type of music speaks to the heart of the Thai Folk Buddhist? Some types of music are used to call up spirits and others to simply lend a joyous atmosphere to a social event. Do the instruments carry spiritual meaning? Can they be dedicated for the service of God? Writing new lyrics for traditional tunes has been done effectively. Even better is when local musicians are enabled to write new styles of music that still retain the cultural appeal and flavor, but are distinctively of the family of faith (King 1999, 59). The creative ability of God as expressed in his gifted local servants is not limited only to existing cultural tunes but can be expressed even more deeply through the encouraged production of new cultural music, with great appeal and usefulness.

Sense of Touch: How do people from Thai Folk Buddhist cultures touch each other? Are there culturally appropriate forms that indicate genuine closeness and can be used to communicate spiritual intimacy both with God and within the family of believers? Consider the string-tying ceremonies of northeastern Thai (Isaan) culture.[29] What does tying a blessing on the wrist of a believer, in the name of Jesus, communicate to someone from a Thai Folk Buddhist worldview? Several who have experienced such a ceremony have felt it was the first time they could be a Christian and still be a Thai. In a culture where physical touching is not shown in public this ceremony has been a deeply significant experience of God's grace for many.

Sense of Taste and Smell: What is the staple of life for the community involved? Is it possible to use this as the element for communion? In northeastern Thailand the staple food, glutinous sticky rice, is roasted into small loaves and used in celebrating the Lord's supper. The bitter red juice made from a local flower (krachiap daeng)[30] is used to represent the blood. According to Smith, the communication system which most profoundly speaks to the heart and is most believed is the olfactory! Is it any wonder that Christ commanded us to eat his body and drink his blood regularly to remember him?

Spatial: How do Thai Folk Buddhists normally use the space around them? How far apart or close together do people need to be to effectively communicate? Thai people normally relax while sitting closely together, barefoot, on straw mats. This is natural in house churches, however some churches that meet in buildings have also found this to be an inviting and natural spatial form that clearly speaks of fellowship to Thai people.

What is the body language used in communication? What is the physical posture which communicates prayer to a Thai Folk Buddhist? More and more Thai believers are using the commonly used greeting of the "wai" (palms raised together) in prayer. Such a form is used many times daily to show respect to a fellow human. Using a raised "wai" means even more to Thais when speaking with God, including reverence, honor, and submission.

Temporal: What is the attitude of the Thai Folk Buddhist towards time? Is there a feeling that time is limited and conversations should be rushed? One Thai Christian leader gave this testimony:

> I always knew that the Christian missionaries had something important to say. They left their homelands and the life style from their countries and spent lots of money to come all the way to Thailand. They spent lots of time and effort going to language classes and trying to learn our language. I knew they had a significant message to communicate but what I couldn't figure out was: *if it was so important why did they have to try and say it all in the first ten minutes?* [31]

Most Barriers Are Social Not Religious

Along with employing a wholistic approach, and using all the signal systems in communication, there is an urgent need to recognize that for most Thai Folk Buddhists the strongest barriers to Christ they experience are not religious but social. The so-called "religious tenets" of their faith are relative! If cultural barriers do not exist or can be minimized, then social barriers must next be examined. As mentioned above, are the methods of communicating Jesus Christ to Thai Folk Buddhists encouraging the bringing of people together into social community (a high cultural value in Thailand) or are they pulling people away from a sense of community towards a more westernized individualism? Often evangelical witness focuses on individual conversion. This is problematic when working in the Thai Folk Buddhist context in which, even today, many major decisions are decided in a group.

> Conversion theology is an inadequate model for converting animists for two reasons. First, conversion in animistic contexts fre-

quently is not individualistic ... Decisions to come to Christ might be made by a group of people interacting with each other and with God ... A lengthy discussion precedes any response to the gospel message. The individuals in the group significantly influence each other to accept or reject the Christian message. Second, and more significant, the content of the biblical message encompasses more than conversion. The message to the animist must present a God who sent his Son not only to bring salvation from sin (Luke 19:10) but also to destroy the works of Satan (I John 3:8) (Van Rheenen 1991, 131).

Once the new believer is part of a community of faith in Jesus Christ, how are social needs integrated into worship and community? A social sense of the need for ceremony is extremely important to Thai people. As Rev. Tongpan Phrommedda, a Thai Christian evangelist for forty years in his home region of Isaan (northeast region of Thailand), explained:

> You need to understand this part of Isaan culture. Ceremony is the traditional way in our culture to officially mark a new beginning. If there is no ceremony then there has been no new beginning. If we do a ceremony, then it means we have now received or started something new. These ceremonies address our cultural need to show that something has begun. They come from our cultural background and address the deep need we have as Isaan people to show "beginning" (Phrommedda in DeNeui 2001, 35).

Ceremony can take many forms and fills a different role than the two biblically commanded sacraments of baptism and communion. However, the importance of regular communion in a sacramental society cannot be overstated. Several churches in Thailand celebrate communion weekly at every worship service; anything less would be to abuse by omission one of the strongest symbolic social activities in which the follower of Jesus can participate.

> The Animist is a member of a sacramental society. At his many praying-places he often takes part in ceremonies which involve a common meal and food shared with spirits. It is pathetic to find that so often, when a man becomes a Christian and has renounced spirit-worship, he is only able to attend a service of Holy Communion two or three times a year ... The Animist has a genius for sacramental worship, and everything should be done to see that it find its fullest expression in the Christian rite (Harris 1960, 61-62).

Recognising the Reality of Power in the Spirit World

Perhaps what Thai Folk Buddhism can best teach cross-cultural workers, who seek to follow and communicate Christ, is the recognition of the reality of the power found in the spirit world. 1 Corinthians 4:20 says, "For the kingdom of God is not just a matter of fancy talk; it is living by God's power" (NLT). It was because of a need for power that many sought out animistic practices in the first place. What is the attitude of the cross-cultural worker to be?

It is easy to go to either extreme. Many westerners come from a perspective that the realities of the spirit world are trivial, and either deny their existence or rationalize them away. Others focus on them too much. The scripture gives guidelines that these realities should not be ignored.

> Ephesians 6:10-20 warns us that we must be alert to discern spiritual reality behind human facades. Ephesians 6:12 says, "For our struggle is not against flesh and blood (human beings), but against the rulers, against the authorities, against the powers of this dark world and against the spiritual forces of evil in the heavenly realms." Verses 18-20 identify one of the most effective weapons to use in spiritual warfare: intercessory prayer.
>
> Studying these passages leads to an important principle regarding spiritual warfare: *Physical situations may well be caused, controlled, or instigated by spiritual beings.*
>
> You can see that discernment is necessary in spiritual warfare, and that one must avoid the twofold spiritual warfare problem. Maintaining dynamic balance between the two extremes takes discernment. A leader must heed two cautions concerning the spiritual warfare process item. Don't *underestimate* and don't *overestimate* the spiritual warfare behind every situation. God will give the necessary discernment as the leader is open to learn (NIV, Clinton 1998, 112).

There are many excellent resources in this area, which can be read and reviewed [32] but none will compare to a personal understanding that God has empowered each of his servants to the task to which he calls him or her. This includes not only natural abilities and acquired skills but also spiritual gifts including word gifts, gifts demonstrating love, and gifts demonstrating power (Clinton and Clinton 1998, 40). We are unfaithful to his calling if any of these areas are ignored. There are many folk religionists who remain enslaved to spirit powers, even within churches all throughout the world, because issues of power have never been fully addressed.

Father Niran became a follower of Jesus and led many in his village to also follow Jesus. Upon his conversion, however, he no longer played the kaen*. He seemed unable to learn any new tunes upon this indigenous musical instrument, which was used in the weekly worship of Jesus in his Thai village. He continued to be unable to eat meat of any winged creature or simply refused to. When he did, he still complained of severe intestinal discomfort. Finally, when his wife demanded that he become a Buddhist monk for three days in order to fulfill a vow she had made, he agreed—much to the chagrin of his local fellowship. Afterwards, his feelings of shame kept him from rejoining the church and he continued to show enslavement to spirit forces.*

Conclusion

Animistic practices have existed long before Bible times. Animism flourished in the days of the early church and many of the believers came from an animistic tradition. Michael Green asks what attracted the ordinary Gentiles to Christianity in the early church and concludes that "perhaps the greatest single factor which appealed to the man in the street was deliverance from demons, from Fate, from magic" (Green 1970, 123). These same practices, dressed in modern garb, continue in our day and show no sign of demise. Have we learned yet how to communicate Christ to people of an animistic worldview?

Many efforts to bring Christ to the Thai Folk Buddhist worldview show that God's Spirit is working throughout the kingdom of Thailand and all over the world. Today there is a need for a measuring tool to use in deciphering how far contextualization of the gospel in the church has truly progressed.

May God give us willingness to be effective servants, willing to learn from our Thai Folk Buddhist friends and neighbors and to experience his grace in wisdom and in power.

Grandma Somlee was in the midst of her most vivid nightmare. Crushing pressure upon her chest convinced her that angry spirits had come to squeeze the life breath from her. Just as she felt all must end she saw a white light and heard a voice, which said, calmly, "Do not be afraid. I am coming to you." She had no idea who it was. The next week two Thai believers came to her from the direction of the white light and began to talk. She accepted their message of freedom through Jesus Christ. That night her nightmare returned again but at the peak of her physical pain she cried out, "Jesus, Help me!" The pressure and pain was released immediately. When she woke the next day she had no further memory of the medicinal recipes that had formerly employed and enslaved her. She purged her yard of any remnants of the herbal plants much to the ridicule of neighbors. Later she told them, "The spirits were always hungry and never satisfied but God always wants to give. Now I am free."

"Take a firm stand against the Devil, and be strong in your faith, Remember that your Christian brothers and sisters all over the world are going through the same kind of suffering you are."
1 Peter 5:9 *NLT*

Notes

1 Though the actual names of the people in these stories have been changed, the author personally knew these individuals and their stories are true.

2 Isaan is the Thai word for the language, people, and geographic area of northeast Thailand. It is a distinct people group of approximately twenty million people. Among themselves, Isaan people refer to each other, their language, and culture as "Lao." Isaan people are culturally linked with the lowland Lao across the Mekong River.

3 Kosuke Koyama in his book, *Waterbuffalo Theology*, describes "Thai Buddhism as, perhaps, the purest form of Buddhism practiced in the world today" (Koyama 1974, 129).

4 "Brahmanical" rites, spirit cults and Buddhist rites ... form an interrelated set, with different values being attached to them in a single religious field (Tambiah 1984, 381).

5 "The guardian spirits ... have village as well as regional significance, and the cult associated with them comprises a ritual complex that has an important place in the totality of religious behavior of the villagers. It is the phenomenon that some writers have called 'animism' and which, with pseudo-historical conjecture, they have identified as pre-Buddhist. Moreover, they have variously treated it both as incompatible with, and as combining with, Buddhism. In actual fact its relationship to Buddhism is not simple but complex, involving opposition, complementarity, linkage, and hierarchy" (Tambiah 1970, 263).

6 The name "Thai" means "free." This expressed desire for independence was shown early in their history as they migrated southward to escape conditions that might have led to them becoming vassals to the Chinese (Gustafson 1970, 18).

7 The term "animism" was originated by Edward B. Tylor in 1873 in Religion in Primitive Cultures and defined as, "the doctrine of Spiritual Beings. This includes

the belief in souls and in a future state, in controlling deities and subordinate spirits, ... resulting in some kind of active worship" (Van Rheenen 1991, 19).

8 This is based on what Tambiah labels, "pseudo-historical conjecture (which) they have identified as pre-Buddhist" (Tambiah 1970, 263).

9 The history of the Mahayana tradition of Buddhism in China is dealt with in other literature.

10 The *Manansila* inscription now kept in the Chapel of the Emerald Buddha in Bangkok reads, "To the south of the city of Sukhothai ... there are monasteries and sanctuaries wherein monks reside; ... there is a spring by the hill; there is the spirit of the hill, greater than all the others spirits. Whichever monarch rules ... Sukhothai, if he renders proper respect and due offerings thereto, then this state is stable and prosperous; if however, he renders improper respect and offerings the spirit neither protects nor respects him; and the state comes to calamity" (Gustafson 1970, 26).

11 Animism is considered a pejorative term among anthropologists today. The preferred term is "primal religion."

12 The relationship between Buddhism, Brahmanism, and animism is covered in detail in Tamiah's work, *Buddhism and the Spirit Cults of Northeast Thailand.* Thai syncretism is covered in Gustafson's *Syncretistic Rural Thai Buddhism.*

13 Worldwide, the response to the Christian message has been one of pragmatism. Dr. Kraft shared that during his early experience as a missionary in Nigeria he noted Christian church leaders still continued their visits to the village shaman when they encountered problems. Upon inquiring he was told, "Oh, we believe in Jesus, but we go to the shaman because things happen faster" (Private conversation November 15, 2001).

14 "A kindred fact in the divine leading, which cannot fail to open up the way for the Gospel among the indifferent heathen, is the superiority of the white race that brings them the gospel. That race takes a dominant position everywhere in the heathen world" (Warneck 1922, 165).

15 Elementary to human beings around the world is the need for security. After Sept. 11, 2001, one of the first actions taken by the president of the United States was to establish "The Office of Homeland Security." For most people, however, a sense of personal security is not found in weapons technology or military strength.

16 To summarize, the evolutionary theory of religion basically states that religions evolve from simple animistic beliefs and practices to the complex religions of the present. This is attributed to the growth of human rationality (Hiebert et al. 1999, 17).

17 Refer to Hard's article "Does Animism Die in the City?" for an interesting Korean equivalent (Hard 1989, 45).

18 The "excluded middle" concept deals with these issues in detail (Hiebert 1994, 189-202).

19 *Wat* is the Thai word for temple.

20 An in-depth treatment of the demonology of Thai gods is found in Attagara (1967, 39-95). A good summary is found in Hiebert et al. (1999, 56-57).

21 Lowie illustrates, "One old man of my acquaintance (among the Plains Indians) had not ridden a horse since the day of his vision thirty-years earlier, for the spirit had forbidden him to do so. He trudged on foot. Another Indian had been for-

bidden to eat eggs and was a constant nuisance because he would not eat anything unless he personally supervised its preparation, lest the cook slip in an egg without his knowledge. And a third was forbidden to touch salmon, one of the Crows' few delicacies; on one occasion he ate a mixture of prepared fish without knowing there was salmon there and attributed the following eleven years of rheumatism to his unwitting breaking of his taboo" (Lehmann 1958, 21).

22 Other documentation of taboo restrictions is listed. "Wanthong (a northeastern Thai village medium in Udon Thani province) observed certain food taboos which are required by his divining work"(Tambiah 1970, 272). Also see note 18 above.

23 Description of *phii paub* (a haunting spirit) found in Tambiah 1970, 321.

24 Chakkri is the name of the present reigning dynasty of Thailand. The present monarch, His Majesty Bumiphol Adulyadeh is ninth in the Chakkri dynasty and known as Rama the 9th.

25 In a moment of surprise, Thai youth think it comical to call out in English what they hear in western movies, "Oh my God!"

26 "Cao Mee" (Honored Mother), at the south end of the Bung Kaen Nakorn park in the city district of Khon Kaen province, is an example of a female pillar spirit.

27 In his book, Poles Apart, Dr. John Davis, gives four cautions for those doing contextualization. These are: no idolatry, no immorality, no injustice and no individualism (Davis 1998, 21-22). Dr. Paul Hiebert outlines four steps in a process he terms "critical contextualization." Step 1 Phenomenological Analysis—Learn from people what they do & why, Step 2 Ontological Reflections—test the truth from scripture & objective reality (life), Step 3 Critical Evaluation—Make decisions based on truth in #2, Step 4 Missiological Transformations, Result: Critical contextualization. These steps allow for a critical way to understand worldview, communicate understandably and allow for transformation (Hiebert et al. 1999, 22).

28 For Western missionaries, there is a great need to rediscover the breadth included in the meaning of the Greek word *kerygma* (usually translated in the English Bible "preach" or "proclaim"). The unfortunate generalisation that this term refers specifically to monologue preaching style is a misrepresentation of the text. Most of the uses of the word "preach" found in the New Testament can be better translated with the word "communicate" (Kraft 1991, 28).

29 A thorough reporting of the use and role of the string-tying ceremonies for propitiation of the *khwan* (life-spirit) and possible contextualized usages within the church has been done by Stephen K. Bailey in *Worldview Themes in Lao Khwan Rituals* (Bailey 2000).

30 Krachiap daeng, commonly known in English as Roselle or Jamaican Sorrel, is *Hibiscus sabdariffa*. The dried red calyx of the flower is boiled to make juice, wine, and food coloring and is said to have curative powers.

31 Dr. Nanthachai Mejudhon at the Isaan Congress, October 2000, Khon Kaen, Thailand.

32 Refer to Anderson 1990 and Kraft 1992. There are several other helps available on this topic.

Appendix 1: Tambiah's Overview of Thai Folk Buddhism

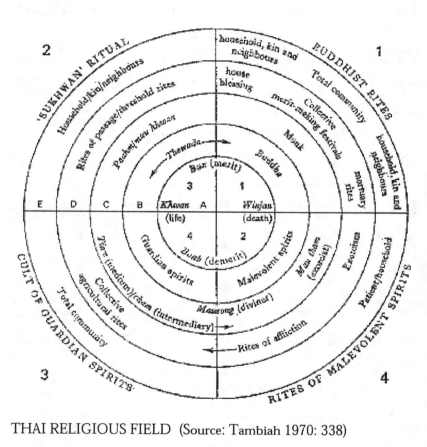

THAI RELIGIOUS FIELD (Source: Tambiah 1970: 338)

A. Primary religious concepts and fields of socio-religious interest

B. Supernatural personifications relating to A

C. Ritual specialists associated with B

D. Rites conducted by C

E. Scale of social participation in D

Appendix 2: Christ's Claims and the Counterfeit Claims

Verse	Jesus' Claims	Comments	Animism's Claims
Matthew 8:3	I am willing to act, to heal	Christ desires to benefit us	Spirits need persuading
Matthew 9:2	Your sins are forgiven	Deals with heart issues	Appears to deal w/ issues
Matthew 9:28	Do you believe I am able to do this?	Christ can do the miraculous	Spirits can do miracles
Matthew 11:29	I'm gentle, humble in heart	Side by side with us in life	Easily offended, above us
Matthew 28:20	I am with you always (also in Acts 18:10)	An ever-present source of help	Presence comes and goes
Mark 14:61, 62	I am the Christ, son of Most High God	Full authority revealed	Unknown source or position
Luke 23:43	I assure you: Today you will be with me in paradise	Assures us that he is able to take us to heaven with him	Appears able to help lead us to heaven
John 6:35, 51	I am the bread of life, the living bread	Source and sustainer of life	Appearance of sustaining life
John 8:12	I am the light of the world, light of life	Those who are in Jesus are not in darkness	Appearance of light
John 8:23	I am from above	Christ comes from heaven	From lower realm
John 8:49	I am not demon-possessed	Empowered by God, omnipresent	Empowered by father of demons
John 8:58	Before Abraham was, I am	Always existed	Unknown origin
John 9:5	I am the light of the world	A light in the last times	Appearance of light
John 10: 7, 8	I am the gate ... whoever enters through me is saved.	Takes us in and moves us on to salvation	Appears to be only hope, only way to get help
John 10:11, 14	I am the good shepherd	Beneficent on our behalf	Assists those who pay
John 10:30	I and the Father are one	Christ is one with God	Unknown linkages
John 11:25	I am the resurrection and the life; he who believes in me	As source of life, he is able to give life to others.	Helps as long as attended to, necessary but not "good"
John 13:13, 14	I am teacher, Lord, and servant	He gave us an example	Not a servant but to be served and then will help
John 14:6	I am the way, truth, the life	Only one, unique	One of many
John 14:20	I am in my Father, you are in me and I am in you	We become one in God through Christ	Spirits dwell in people but not one with them
John 14:21	I love those who obey me	Basis of relationship is love	Basis of relationship is slavery
John 15:1, 5	I am the vine, the true vine	Christ is the source	Appearance of source
Rev. 1:17, 18	I am the First and the Last (also 21:6)	Beginning and End	One of many, not unique
Rev. 2:23	I search hearts and minds	Knows us better than we know ourselves	Perceives but doesn't read minds or hearts
Rev. 22:16	I am the Root, David's offspring, Morning Star	Tied to a history of promise	Linked with a history of curse and destruction.

Source: (Day 1988, 182)

Appendix 3: Claims of Others about Christ and the Counterfeit Claim s

Verse	Scriptural Claims About Christ	Comments	Claims of Animism
Luke 24:6	He is not dead, he is risen	Victorious over death	Victory over present problems
John 5:21	He gives life	Life is in his control	Apparent control over life
John 1:14	He became one of us	God made flesh	Flesh appearing god-like
John 9:35-37	He is the Son of Man	All we have to do is confess	Appeasement available at price. No personal change.
Acts 4:11	He is the stone the builders rejected	Didn't appear as people thought he should	Sought out, not rejected
Acts 17:27	He is not far from any of us	Close, readily available	Available at a price, distant
2 Cor. 5:17	In Christ one is a new creation	Process begins w/ relationship	Not a relationship, nothing new, deeper enslavement
2 Cor. 12:10	He's strong when we're weak	He is intimately involved	Strong when we ask for help
Eph. 5:23	Christ is Head of the Church, Savior	He has supremacy over all	Unknown hierarchy of spirits
Col. 1:17	In Him all things hold together	Compassionate, understanding	Holds fate and future
Col. 1:18	He is the firstborn from the dead	Wants to interceded for us	Appearance of supremacy
Heb. 2:18	He is able to help those being tempted	Takes care of everything	Able to help the powerless
Heb. 7:25	He is able to save completely	He did it all for us	Able to save specifically
Heb. 8:6	He is mediator		Requires a medium
1 Peter 1:16	He is holy, therefore be holy like him	Hope of transformation	Pays debt, does not purify Need to repay repeatedly
1 John 1:7	Blood of Jesus purifies us from all sin	Hope of transformation	Pays debt, does not purify Need to repay repeatedly
1 John 1:9	He is faithful and just to forgive	He sought us out	May or may not forgive
1 John 2:2	He is the atoning sacrifice for us the whole world	He did what we cannot	We must make sacrifice, one by one
1 John 2:29	He is righteous and makes us same	Desires our best for us and helps us et there	Helps but doesn't make us right
1 John 3: 1, 2	When we see him we'll be like him	Able to transform	No one wants to see or be like spirits
1 John 4:10	He loved us first and sent his son for us	He initiated the relationship	People must seek out the spirits
Rev. 17:14	He is King of Kings and Lord of Lords He will defeat all foes	Ultimate authority Ultimate victory	Ultimate enemy, ultimate losers

References and Bibliography

Anderson, Neil. 1990. *The Bondage Breaker*. Eugene, Or: Harvest House.

Attagara, Kingkeo. 1967. *The Folk Religion of Ban Nai, a Hamlet in Central Thailand*. Ann Arbor, MI: University Microfilms, Inc.

Bailey, Stephen K. 2000. Worldview Themes in Lao Khwan Rituals. Pasadena, CA: Tutorial Paper for Fuller Theological Seminary, unpublished.

Brown, Peter. 1981. *The Cult of the Saints*. Chicago: University of Chicago Press.

Burns, Douglas M. 1970. *The Acharns (Meditation Teachers) of Northeast Thailand*. Bangkok: Thaikasem Press.

Clinton, J. Robert. 1998. *The Making of a Leader*. Colorado Springs, CO: NavPress.

Davis, John R. 1998. *Poles Apart: Contextualizing the Gospel in Asia*. Bangalore: Asia Theological Association.

Day, Terence Patrick. 1987. *Great Tradition and Little Tradition in Theravada Buddhist Studies*. Lewiston, NY: The Edwin Mellen Press.

De Neui, Paul H. 2001. *Voices from Asia: Communicating Contextualization through Story*. Pasadena, CA: Fuller Theological Seminary, unpublished.

Green, Michael. 1970. *Evangelism in the Early Church*. Grand Rapids, MI.: William B. Eerdmans Publishing Company.

Griswold, A.B. 1968. What Is a Buddha Image? *Thai Culture, New Series*. Fine Arts Department, Bangkok, No. 19 (B.E. 2511).

Gustafson, James W. 1970. *Syncretistic Rural Thai Buddhism*. Pasadena, CA: Fuller Seminary MA thesis, unpublished.

Hard, Theodore. 1989 Does Animism Die in the City? *Urban Mission*. 6 (Ja 1989):45-46.

Harris, W.T. and E.G. Parrinder. 1960. *The Christian Approach to the Animist*. London: Edinburgh House Press.

Hiebert, Paul G. 1994. *Anthropological Reflections on Missiological Issues*. Grand Rapids, MI: Baker Books.

Hiebert, Paul G, R. Daniel Shaw and Tite Tienou. 1999. *Understanding Folk Religion: A Christian Response to Popular Beliefs and Practices*. Grand Rapids, MI: Baker Books.

Heinze, Ruth-Inge. 1982. *Tham Khwan: How to Contain the Essence of Life*. Singapore: Singapore University Press.

HRAF. 1956. *Thailand*. Subcontractor's Monograph. New Have, HRAF Press.

King, Roberta. 1999. *A Time to Sing: A Manual for the African Church*. Nairobi: Evangel Publishing House.

Kraft, Charles H. 1991. *Communication Theory for Christian Witness*. Maryknoll, NY: Orbis.

——. 1992. *Defeating Dark Angels: Breaking Demonic Oppression in the Believer's Life*. Ann Arbor, MI: Servant Publications.

Koyama, Kosuke. 1974. *Waterbuffalo Theology*. Maryknoll, NY: Orbis Books.

Law, Bimala Churn. 1987. *The Buddhist Conception of Spirits*. Delhi, India: Indological Book House.

Lehmann, Arthur C., and James E. Myers. 1985. *Magic, Witchcraft and Religion: An Anthropological Study of the Supernatural*. Mountain View, CA: Mayfield Publishing Co.

Moreau, A. Scott. 1999. *Evangelical Dictionary of World Missions*. Grand Rapids, MI: Baker Books.

Nida, Eugene A. and William A. Smalley. 1959. *Introducing Animism*. New York: Friendship Press.

Notton, Camille. 1933. *The Cult of the Emerald Buddha*. Bangkok: Bangkok Times Press.

Rajadhon, Phya Anuman. 1963. *Thai Traditional Salutations*. Bangkok: Fine Arts Dept.

Rajjayakavi, Venerable Phra (Buddhadasa Bhikkhu). 1962. *Dhamma–the World Saviour*. Bangkok: Choom Noom Chang Printing.

Raksutti, Somlii. 1999. *Tomnan Nitaan Phii Isaan (Collection of Isaan Ghost Tales)*. Thai language. Bangkok: Pattanasuksaa Printers.

Rommen, Edward, ed. 1995. *Spiritual Power and Missions: Raising the Issues.* Pasadena, CA: William Carey Library.

Segaller, Denis. 1982. *More Thai Ways*. Bangkok: Post Books.

Sitompul, Adelbert A.. 1983. Nature and the Natural in Asian Thinking—Asian Animism and Primal Religion. *East Asia Journal of Theology*. 1 (1983):15-27.

Smith, Alex G. 2001. *Buddhism: Through Christian Eyes*. Littleton, CO: OMF International.

Smith, Bardwell L. 1973. *Tradition and Change in Theravada Buddhism: Essays on Ceylon and Thailand in the 19th and 20th Centuries*. Leiden: E.J. Brill.

Smith, Donald K. 1992. *Creating Understanding*. Grand Rapids, MI: Zondervan.

Sugirtharajah, R. S., ed. 1994. Frontiers in Asian Christian Theology: Emerging Trends. Maryknoll, NY: Orbis Books.

Tambiah, Stanley Jeyaraja. 1970. *Buddhism and the Spirit Cults in North-East Thailand*. Cambridge: Cambridge University Press.

——. 1976. *World Conqueror and World Renouncer: A Study of Buddhism and Polity in Thailand against a Historical Background*. Cambridge: Cambridge University Press.

——. 1984. *The Buddhist Saints of the Forest and the Cult of Amulets: A Study in Charisma, Hagiography, Sectarianism, and Millennial Buddhism*. London: Cambridge University Press.

Terwiel, B.J. 1976. The Origins and Meaning of the Thai "City Pillar." *Journal of the*

Siam Society. Vol. 66, Pt. 2, July 1976: 159-71.

Tilak S. John. 1983. Nature and the Natural in Asian Thinking: Asian Animism and Primal Religion, the Response and the Reaction to the Paper Read by Dr. A.A. Sitompul. *East Asia Journal of Theology.* 1 (1983): 28-30.

Unger, Merrill F. 1970. *Demons in the World Today: A Study of Occultism in the Light of God's Word.* Wheaton, IL: Tyndale House Publishers.

Van Rheenen, Gailyn. 1991. *Communicating Christ in Animistic Contexts.* Pasadena, CA: William Carey Library.

Warneck, Johannes Gustav. 1922. *The Living Christ and Dying Heathenism: The Experiences of a Missionary in Animistic Heathendom.* New York: Revell Company.

——. 1960. *Demon Experiences in Many Lands.* Chicago: Moody Press.

Wright, Michael A. 1968. Some Observations on Thai Animism. *Practical Anthropology* Vol 15 (Ja-F): 1-7.

Communication Strategies
for Christian Witness among the Lao

Stephen Bailey

Introduction

This article discusses a model of communicating the gospel among lowland Lao in the Lao People's Democratic Republic (Lao PDR). Given the limited response to the gospel after more than one hundred years of Christian witness, it is critical for expatriate and Lao Christians to take stock of the dynamics of communication in the Lao PDR. In addressing this problem, I have four objectives. First, I review some basic characteristics of the social context of the Lao PDR and the history of Christian witness among lowland Lao. Second, I consider the primary communicational model that Christians have used in witness among the lowland Lao people in the past. Third, I describe Lao world-view themes in order to discern what they say about Lao social relations. Finally, I suggest strategies for communicating the gospel in Lao society, which I believe hold promise for more effective witness. Given the similarities between the major cultural blocks of Southeast Asia, these strategies may also have implications for Christian witness outside of the Lao context. [1]

Overview of Christian Witness in Lao Society

The social context of Lao society has been, and continues to be, marked by political, economic, and physical vulnerability. Throughout history, neighboring countries have used Laos as a buffer state to keep opposing, expansionist visions at bay, or they have sought to annex portions of Laos to serve the same purpose.[2] Today the Lao PDR finds itself balancing its "special relationship" with Vietnam against the growing influence of China in Southeast Asia, their economic linkage with Thailand, and their fledging membership in ASEAN.

Roughly eighty-five percent of the Lao population are subsistence farmers. The topography and climate make it possible to farm paddy and upland rice as the staple food. But floods and insufficient rain often result in inadequate supplies of rice. Foreign rice grants have been necessary numerous times in recent years.[3] Kitchen gardens and food products gathered from the forest, supplement the diet, but the rapid depletion of forests and wildlife are adding to the difficulty presented by bad harvests.

Any description of the Lao PDR notes the general poverty. The annual per capita income is roughly $350 US, and more than half the gross domestic product comes from subsistence farming (*Asia 1998 Yearbook* 1998, 12-13). Although some medical workers in the country suggest there is evidence of insufficient nutrition among children, the poverty in Laos is not normally characterized by hunger.[4]

Laos has been dependent on foreign aid since the early days of French colonial rule (Stuart-Fox 1986, 105). Today, more than sixteen percent of the gross domestic product comes from foreign aid (*Asia 1998 Yearbook* 1998, 12-13; Lintner 2001).[5] Beyond this, dozens of government, international, and non-government aid agencies operate in the country. The Lao government mandates that even small non-government agencies spend over $100,000 US on direct project expenses. There are literally dozens of foreign aid agencies working in the Lao PDR today.

The poverty of the Lao people is more acutely felt in the areas of health and education. Traditionally health care was provided by one of several kinds of traditional healers. Today the Ministry of Public Health, with assistance from international aid agencies, is extending Western medical systems throughout the country.

Despite these efforts, the "life expectancy at birth for men and women in Laos was estimated in 1988 at forty-nine years, the same as in Cambodia but at least ten years lower than in any other Southeast Asian nation" (United States Library of Congress 1994).[6]

As the above overview shows, vulnerability has been a key characteristic of the social, political, and economic situation in Lao society for a long time. This context translates itself into a social system built on interdependence and allegiance to the social body, making Christian witness extremely difficult.

Almost half a century ago, William Smalley, former missionary to Laos, anthropologist and linguist, and editor of *Practical Anthropology*, wrote the following.

> Apparently the gospel has never been made to seem relevant to the Lao. I feel deeply that a careful study should be made of the communication of the gospel in relation to the Lao culture ... How can the Good News be made to seem good—to be something that people will really want—in this culture which does not, on the whole, see other needs than those met by its normal experience? Here the problem is not primarily one of language mastery. The missionaries are not worse than the average, and some are much better than the average.... The communication problems here are cultural ones (1956, 56-57).

For those who have traveled to Laos, or have had the privilege to live there as foreign guests, few have escaped falling in love with the ready hospitality of the people, recognized and referred to by the Lao themselves with the phrase, *namchay*.[7] They value a relaxed and even-tempered attitude toward life that they refer to with the phrase chayy_n 'cool heart'. They love *muan* 'to have a good time', and are quick to forgive offenses with the frequently repeated words, baw p_n yang 'it was nothing'. This unflappable style has served the Lao well during centuries of war and cyclical poverty. Many foreign powers have occupied Laos but few have been able to effect significant change on Lao society. Christian missionary efforts have not faired much better in their efforts to communicate the transformational message of the gospel.

The first missionary effort in Laos was attempted in 1642 by Jesuit missionary, Jean de Leria. He stayed there five years before pressure from Buddhist monks forced him to leave (Roffe 1975). In 1771, a Vietnamese catechist brought the gospel to the city of Thakaek, which has historically had a large Vietnamese population (Latourette 1939, 295-297). Later, in 1878, Catholic fathers tried again in northeastern Laos but the mission came to a tragic end with the martyrdom of twelve priests in 1884 and five more in 1889 (Roffe 1975). The most successful Catholic efforts occurred later in southern Laos.

The first Protestant missionary to Laos was Presbyterian Daniel McGilvary, who made several trips to northern Laos from Chiang Mai, Thailand between 1872 and 1898 (Andrianoff 1991). In 1902, Gabriel Contesse and Maurice Willy began the work of the Swiss Brethren in southern Laos (Andrianoff 2002). Later, in the early 1950s, Christian Mission in Many Lands and the Overseas Missionary Fellowship (OMF) entered southern Laos to work in cooperation with the Swiss (Oppel 1984). [8]

The first resident Protestant missionary in northern Laos, G. Edward Roffe, was sent by the Christian and Missionary Alliance (C&MA) in 1930. In the 1960s, small contingents from Missionary Aviation Fellowship, the Southern Baptists, World Vision, the Mennonite Central Committee (MCC), the Far East Broadcasting Company and Asian Christian Service arrived (Oppel 1984). [9]

Just before the communist takeover in 1975, all foreign missionaries left Laos. The exception was MCC, the only western mission that continued its presence into the post-liberation era. MCC continues to do community development projects in the Lao PDR today. [10] At the time of "liberation" both the northern and southern churches were self-governing and had worked together cooperatively for many years. The total number of Protestant Christians in the south was about 2,000 (Oppel 1984) and in the north the number was about 7,000 (C&MA 1973). [11] The ethnic breakdown of the Church was, at the time, roughly sixty percent highland Hmong from the north, fifteen percent lowland Lao, and twenty percent midland Lao Khamu, with various other people groups making up the remainder.

The Protestant, Lao Evangelical Church (LEC) was formed in the 1950s. It was a merger between the northern Protestant churches, planted by C&MA missionaries between 1930 and 1975; and the southern Protestant churches, planted by missionaries under the

Swiss Mission Évangélique (between 1902 and 1975), the OMF, and the American Brethren.

Christian witness among the lowland Lao began and first bore fruit in southern Laos before World War II. Southern Lao have been relatively more responsive than Lao in the north, but there may have been social factors for this. First, many of these early converts were social outcasts, making conversion a more attractive option than normal. [12] Second, in northern Laos, Christianity was associated with the French in Vientiane, and in the northern provinces with the Hmong, a group that the Lao generally look down on.

Today the LEC reports more than 40,000 members, but these numbers are difficult to verify since travel and communication between many provinces remains difficult. More than half of the LEC is made up of Khamu people (midland Lao). The Hmong (upland Lao) represent roughly another thirty-five percent of the church. There are several small, Protestant church gatherings not associated with the LEC such as the Seventh Day Adventist Church, a church associated with a Lutheran mission; some small gatherings associated with Campus Crusade for Christ; and several groups that connect themselves to the sending churches of various Asian missionaries.

Some property belonging to the Catholic community (mostly in the form of schools) was confiscated by the communist government after it took control in 1975. After 1990, some Catholic churches were refurbished, and a new education and training home for village girls opened in Vientiane municipality. [13] As of 1995, the Catholic Church was organized into four vicariates, overseen by three bishops. There were sixteen other ordained priests, seven of whom were ordained after 1975. Government pressure on the Church, however, continues to hamper many Catholic efforts. There are roughly 35,000 Catholics, with the largest group in the church being midland Lao, followed in number by the lowland Lao. Several young men are being trained for the priesthood and there is a vital youth ministry in Vientiane.

After more than one hundred years of missionary witness among lowland Lao people, it is unlikely that there are more than

7,000 Protestant Lao believers in the Lao PDR. This translates into .2 percent of the lowland population in Laos. With the exception perhaps of Savannakhet, Lao Christians have made little impact on Lao society. In many cases, there simply has been no opportunity for the majority of Lao to hear the gospel. But even when they have heard the gospel, very few Lao have converted. Many who do convert, return to their traditional beliefs after a period of time. Lao Christians themselves seem unable to reverse this situation.

Among the problems confronting Christian witness in Laos is the fact that Christianity is largely seen as the religion of Western foreigners. Those who convert are seen as people who have chosen a foreign identity over their Lao identity. "To be Lao is to be Buddhist, and to practice and respect the traditions and customs of the ancestors," is a deeply held belief by the Lao People's Revolutionary Party, government officials, and the population at large. Since at least 1994, this attitude has translated into widespread and systematic persecution of Christians (United States State Department 2001). What appears curious at first is that most non-Christian Lao voice approval of the teachings of Christianity while being clearly opposed to the conversion of Lao to the Christian Church. This apparent contradiction is at the heart of the communicational problem I address below.

A Primary Communicational Model from the Past

In looking at this situation, it is not difficult to discern that Christian witness in Laos has been confronted with a high level of spiritual hardness. Among the general population, Lao Buddhism is more oriented towards the care of ancestral, guardian, and nature spirits than it is toward the moral metaphysics of the Buddha. Many people are engaged in contracts (*baphii*) with spirits for the things they need in their daily lives. Many also live in some level of fear of these capricious spirits. The Lao give offerings to the spirits as often as they feed the monks who come begging in the morning. A great number of concentrated prayer and power ministries are needed to address this situation.

From another vantage point, the situation suggests that the history of missions among the Lao calls for a more thoroughly contextualized gospel. Have the Lao really heard the gospel in a form they can understand? Perhaps if missionaries communicated the gospel more within the cultural assumptions and forms of the Lao it would make a greater impact. From my perspective, the churches in the city of Vientiane would certainly benefit from such an effort. For example, it is standard practice for the Lao to remove their shoes before entering a home or place of worship. Worship is also typically done while sitting on the floor. But in two Vientiane churches, worshipers keep their shoes on in the sanctuary and sit on western style pews.

While the Church can always benefit from more concerted prayer, it should be recognized that there has been a significant prayer effort for Laos for some time now. [14] Furthermore, prayer and power ministries already play significant roles in the life of the Lao Evangelical Church. In Vientiane all three local churches give considerable time to prayer and healing ministries. Testimonies to God's direct and powerful intervention in the lives of Christians for healing, provision, deliverance from the fear of spirits, and other needs are the norm among Protestants.

Looking at past efforts to contextualize the gospel is more complicated. There are two levels to contextualization: a level of form, and a level of meaning. In regard to the latter, I am convinced that the gospel is always contexualized in terms of meaning by local populations, whether local church leaders and/or missionaries give permission or not. [15] People interpret the meaning of the gospel within the framework of their personal history and identity. How the Lao interpret the meaning of the gospel often has more to do with the perceived intentions of Christians than with the content of the gospel. I'll return to this later.

In terms of the use of local forms to convey the meaning of the gospel, the Lao have made periodic steps they are not fully at ease with. Cultural forms often mark the boundaries of a group's identity, and Lao Christians often feel caught between wanting to be Lao while not wanting to mark their identity with allegiance to traditional religious rituals.

I know of at least three forms that the LEC in Vientiane has attempted to use in order to contextualize the communication of the gospel. First, in a rather unconscious way, the Lao have created a ritual they call the 'Thanking God Ritual' *Phithi Khawbkhun Phrachao*. This ritual mirrors a common type of household ritual known as *suukhwan*. It is performed to bring blessing to a person by calling their *khwan* (life essence). Lao Christians do not call their *khwan*, but in a similar way they use the "Thanking God Ritual" to mark blessing in their lives. A second traditional ritual, known as *soma*, has been incorporated into Christian wedding ceremonies. In this ritual young people seek the forgiveness and blessing of their parents or someone who has played the role of parent in their lives. Third, one LEC church in Vientiane now follows the traditional custom of taking off shoes before entering the place of worship and sitting on the floor rather than on pews. It is notable that all three of these forms entered into the worship life of the Protestant Church after the communist "liberation" of Laos and the departure of Western missionaries.

Even with these efforts, the majority of Christians in Laos are Khamu or Hmong. Thank the Lord for the growth of the church among these wonderful people! But we are still left wondering why the gospel is not impacting the lowland Lao.

From the beginning of Christian witness in Laos, a decision to give allegiance to Jesus has meant that converts cut off or seriously strain their relationships with key people in their lives by refusing to participate in the Lao religious ritual system. In the process, Lao identity has been replaced with membership in the small subculture of Christians. This small Christian community has their own specialized Christian language and ritual system. As in many Muslim, Hindu, and Buddhist communities, people who place their faith in Christ often face social death. At the same time, the small Christian community appears to have little to offer the rest of Lao society and is clearly linked to foreigners.

Christianity appears to be linked to foreigners in several ways. First, it is an imported faith that came with Westerners. Second, there are many foreigners who attend worship in the Vientiane churches and speak of their faith in their places of work. Third, the Lao are warned in the media that there are foreigners in Laos seeking to convert people to their religion using unethical means (e.g.

providing economic incentives). Fourth, the LEC and the Catholic communities are able to carry out projects that obviously go beyond the financial strength of their local communities. The conclusion of many is that the financial strength of these Christian communities is supported by foreign Christians. Fifth, many of the forms used in church life are foreign imports. I have already mentioned the wearing of shoes and sitting in pews. Perhaps even more telling is the breaking of bread, *khaoch*, during the communion service. *Khaochii* in the Lao mind is clearly linked to the colonial past and is understood to be the food of Western foreigners. For the Lao, rice is the stuff of life, not bread. Sixth, Lao Christians often use Lao words in ways that non-Christians do not understand.

The witness of local and expatriate Christians in Laos has not been without any effect. It has certainly been done with sincerity and, in some cases, even with sacrifice. My purpose here is not to criticize what has been done but to suggest that besides power ministries and contextualization of the cognitive content of the gospel, there is another issue that needs to be considered in Christian witness.

When Christian witness has been successful in Laos it has not been primarily because of power—there is no shortage of power in traditional Lao religion—or because of good contextualization of forms and meaning. I believe the key to the communication of the gospel among lowland Lao is communication that engages Lao in terms of the structure of Lao relationships. This kind of communication taps into the issue of identity, which is so vulnerable in the context of the Lao PDR.

Charles Kraft suggests three levels of encounter in Christian witness (Kraft 1999). First, there is the encounter with the power of the gospel. Second, there is an encounter with the truth of the gospel. Third, there is the encounter of relationship with and allegiance to Jesus as Lord.

Our first response to a lack of response to the gospel has tended to be prayer. This is appropriate and we should continue in these efforts. Our second response has often been to look for new ways to contextualize the content of the gospel. Contexualization has been concerned with translating the truth of the gospel accurately into the meaning systems of other cultures in order to achieve dynamic equivalence in meaning (Nida 1990; Kraft 1979). Clearly there is more work to be done in Laos in this area, but I suggest that this task will be done best with Lao Christians in the lead. Yet I wonder, along with Kraft, if the contextualization of the content of the gospel is as crucial as missionaries once thought. Particularly in traditional societies, but perhaps around the world, the <u>contextualization of relationships</u> is proving to be a more crucial task.

> God started with a Covenant, not with a book of doctrine. And Jesus came that the world might be saved through relationship, not through theology, as important as it is to think biblically. Theology then, is intended to serve relationship. ... Contextualization of relationship, then, has to become a major focus of our teaching, writing and witnessing. We need to learn what the contextualization of relationships is all about (Kraft 1999, 8).

I turn now to a description of the Lao worldview. Worldviews are a model *of* and *for* social relations (Geertz 1973). In other words, I assume that the core assumptions and psychological images that pattern the perception and interpretation of the world for Lao people also shape, and are shaped by, the structure of their society.

The Lao Worldview and Social Structure

The worldview of the Lao can be described in terms of six worldview themes. These themes represent the core assumptions about the world that all Lao share to one extent or another. Table 1 describes these assumptions for each category. What is important about these assumptions is what they reveal about social relations and how the structure of these relations impact communication.

I will use Mary Douglas' grid and group theory to relate these assumptions to. In her theory she compares societies in terms of two social dynamics.

["Group," she defines as] "the experience of a bounded social unit." It measures the degree of influence that the group has on the behavior of a member of the group.

"Grid refers to rules which relate one person to others on an ego-centered basis" (Douglas 1970, viii). In other words, grid measures, by comparison, the degree to which society structures the interpersonal relations of people in the group.

In Lao society it is possible to observe that group influence on individual behavior is quite strong in comparison to group influence in North American society. More particularly, the influence is experienced somewhat differently, depending on what level of Lao society you refer to. At the level of the household, the group influence is quite strong. Important decisions are always made in consultation with the members of one's household. Furthermore, households are oriented toward mothers, since they normally inherit the household property. Mothers are symbols of morality, because they tend to seek the welfare of the household group more consistently than others. A man generally lives with his wife's parents for the first few years of marriage.

At the level of the village, group influence is high but not as high as in the household. Villages are largely made up of households related through maternal kinship ties. At the level of society larger than the village (what the Lao call *muang*), the influence of the group drops off, but is still significant when compared to North American society.

The high value placed on the group reveals a deep need for each member of society to play a role in seeking the well-being of the group. Given the very vulnerable social context in the Lao PDR, this is not surprising. Survival in the Lao PDR has historically demanded a high level of social interdependence.

The level of grid is highest in the opposite direction. The highest level of structure and ritual in relationships is found at the level of the muang. It decreases at the level of the village and decreases further at the level of the household. Nevertheless, relationships at every level depend upon a relatively high degree of structure. It is of particular interest to communicators to understand what this structure looks like and how it operates.

Lao relationships are structured in terms of three basic categories. First, people always relate to one another in terms of an older to younger model. This is a kind of patron–client model that is defined first by the relative age of each person and then by factors such as education, wealth, and political power. This category is the fundamental building block for all Lao relationships. It is

Table 1
LAO WORLDVIEW THEMES

Worldview Theme Area	Orientation
Person-Group	Self as part of a web of household relationships structured in terms of older and younger obligations, male and female groups and ritual specialists and lay people, within a *muang* power complex.
Time, Space, Matter	They are animated by spiritual beings and structured in terms of auspicious and inauspicious directions and times. They can be manipulated to manage the impact of karma, spirits, and gods on human success and failure.
Causality	The quality of social relations with the living, the ancestors, and the gods greatly impact human history. Moral and amoral power can be used to change life circumstances.
Human Nature	People naturally make mistakes so they should be instructed on how to relate correctly to those who are older and younger. Society is a mirror of the sacred. People are not equal. Holiness is behaving properly in regard to the status of others. Sin is not behaving properly in regard to the status of others.
Meeting Human Needs	Needs and resources are assigned based on status in society. The primary strategies for increasing resources above needs is through alliances of mutual interest, established by token gift giving and final payment of the largest share to the older person in the relationship. Experts play a key role in managing natural and spiritual resources.
Preferences	Balance and harmony are highly valued and envy is avoided to protect institutionalized inequalities. Blame is diffused and rarely attributed to the social system. Instead, blame is attributed to non-integrated groups and individuals.

reflected in the worldview assumption regarding high and low space. The head is sacred. The feet are profane. North is auspicious. South is inauspicious. Mountains are good places for Buddhist temples, and valleys are not.

The second basic category in Lao social structure is that of gender. Women find their deepest friendships with other women and men with men. The value for friendship that we see in North American marriages is not as high in Lao society. Men have ritual knowledge and have better karma than women. Women are a threat to the spiritual power of men and are not allowed to touch monks or the ritual objects that belong to men. Significantly, a primary reason for men to become monks is to make merit on behalf of their mothers.

Finally, Lao society is structured in terms of those who have ritual knowledge and those who do not. There is a clear and important distinction between clergy (ritual specialist) and layperson. Religion and society are expressed ritually and while all Lao know how to act in each ritual, only some Lao (males) have learned the skills of actually conducting and empowering rituals.

What does all this say about communicating the gospel?

Strategies for Communicating the Gospel

There are many points at which engagement with the gospel of Jesus Christ will challenge the worldview of lowland Lao people. This engagement has cognitive implications regarding truth. It also has normative demands for the Lao context. But the cognitive and normative implications of the gospel must be discerned and decided on by the Lao Christian community under the guidance of the Holy Spirit. I suggest that this is not the primary task of missionaries.

The primary missionary task is to communicate the gospel in a way that allows the Lao to engage Jesus relationally. The intention of Christian witness is to bring people into relationship with Jesus. This can only be done effectively when missionaries themselves engage Lao people. Once people have engaged Christ relationally, the cognitive implications of the gospel will be interpreted based on the quality of relationships Christians have with non-Christians. This is the incarnation of the gospel.

An incarnational model of Christian witness means that relational issues shape the informational truth issues of the gospel for each context. In contrast, the struggle to do contextualization well is often motivated by the desire to define the gospel in terms of transcendental truth statements. Since all our knowledge is bound up in our culture, these supposedly transcendental truths are actually reflections on what missionaries have found to be crucial for their own identity and context. The gospel does not call for objectivity in interpretation. It calls us to interpret our context in terms of our relationship with Jesus Christ and the ethic of His kingdom.

Jesus lived in a particular time and place. He lived on behalf of others and died on the cross on behalf of others. His life and death established the vision of the kingdom of God. When Christ died on our behalf, he not only offered us freedom from the sin and a means to be in relationship with the Creator but he also established a new way for us relate to one another. From that point on the kingdom ethic declared that disciples of Jesus were to live on behalf of others. This vision, in like manner, establishes the interpretive key for the meaning of the cross in each context.

The missionary task is to bring people into relationship with the Creator through a relationship with Jesus. This is a social message and can only be communicated in the midst of social relations. In Lao society missionaries must incarnate Jesus following the social structure of the society. One of the key issues in this regard is to communicate in such a way that it protects and enhances the welfare of the household group and respects the older to younger pattern of relationships. It cannot be communicated by opting out of the social system altogether as has been the primary pattern for communicating the gospel in the past.

Communicating within the Group

The dominant issue (especially in the village) in Lao society is the interdependence of the social group. Individuals have freedom to choose their own path as long as they act in ways that do not endanger the well-being of those in their household, village, and nation. The influence of the group is strongest at the level of the household, where maternal kinship ties and obligation are strongest. Consequently, the first communicational strategy is to communicate within the structure of the interdependent social group, giving special attention to the household.

Communication of the gospel within the household should be done within relationships that allow Christians to relate in ways that have been transformed by the ethic of the kingdom of God. In the Lao context this means living on behalf of others in ways that recall the moral power of mothers and monks. Mothers and monks are important symbols of living selfless lives on behalf of others. Mothers and monks are the primary ones who enable people to experience *khwamsuk* (happiness, well being). Here, the vision of the Lao captured in the word *khwamsuk* overlaps with the vision of the kingdom of God.

Christians must mark their relationships with others by living on behalf of others. In this way, the non-verbal message of the gospel will be found more acceptable because it will affirm the group in morally powerful ways. Christian lives should even affirm the well-being of the group beyond normal expectations. Of course the worldview of non-Christian Lao will lead them to conclude that the intention of this kind of communication is to address and affirm the traditional moral quality of mothers and monks within the Buddhist context. This highlights the need for non-verbal communication to be supplemented by verbal communication.

Communicating the gospel within the group demands that the whole household unit be taken into account and that witness not result in disenfranchised individuals. Very often, young people have converted to Christianity as individuals, without the consent or input of their households. While it can be acknowledged that removing an individual for a time from their normal social group often opens them up to new ideas and ways of living, the failure to take into account the household group often results in a short lived faith. The pattern in these cases has been for households to ostracize, persecute, or even abandon young converts. At the age of marriage, many of these young converts marry other Christians who are also cut off from their household network, or they leave their Christian faith to return to the household's care and provision. While the household unit should be the main focus, special attention should be given to the heads of the household.

Pastors Nantachai and Ubolwan Mejudhon have modeled a household approach in Bangkok, Thailand where the social context is similar to that of Laos. Upon meeting a young person interested in the gospel, they ask for an opportunity to be introduced to the members of their household, especially the parents and elders. At this meeting they go out of their way to recognize the authority of the household structure in the young person's life and explain who they are. They also make sure that what the young person hears is the same as what all the members of the household have an opportunity to hear. Furthermore, they are careful not to dominate the time of young converts with church activities. Instead they instruct these new converts to take every opportunity to fulfill their obligations to their household. If a time comes when the new convert is ready to be baptized, the church then invites the young person's family to the service to participate in the service by presenting the newly-baptized Christian with his or her first Bible (Mejudhon and Mejudhon 2000).

Christians can also communicate within the group through a Christian witness characterized by hospitality. This should be a hospitality that works toward the integration of every person who attends the local church. Lao villagers traditionally deal with the danger they feel from outsiders by encouraging outsiders to come in and take a role as an insider. Christians should do the same by finding ways to include non-Christians in their worship.

Societies that are high group want to protect their boundaries. The gospel critiques this tendency. The boundaries of the local church need to be porous. Every effort should be made to include others in Christian worship. Non-Christians should be invited to read the scriptures, lead the singing, and assist in the preparations for common meals. It may also be appropriate to invite non-Christians to the Lord's supper if they are willing to recognize the Lord's death in the *Eucharist* ritual.[16] While Christians may balk at this suggestion, it should be remembered that non-Christians practice this kind of hospitality as a matter of course. Social integration of interested non-Christians within the Christian household of faith is a key to communicating the faith in Lao society.

Another means of communicating from within the group is to model local churches on the Lao household. The kinship relationships of the household, the sense of moral obligation to one another, and the priority for the well-being of the kin group are all appropriate models for relationships in local Lao churches. Institutional models of the church that reflect hierarchy and relationships of authority without kin-based relations will recall the amoral use of power (force) at the *muang* level of social experience. In cases where local churches are plagued by competition for control of foreign resources, they are already reflecting the *muang* power system.

Communicating the gospel within the group structure of Lao society also suggests the possibility of a "churchless" model of Christianity. Herbert Hoefer has made an argument for this model in the Hindu society of India (Hoefer 1991). He shares the advice he received from a Brahmin believer in Christ, whose ministry is to visit the *Jesu Bhaktas* (believers in Jesus who remain part of the Hindu community).

> His first advice is, "If anyone asks, tell them you are a Hindu."
> It is acceptable to worship the god of your choice as a Hindu.
> The statement also indicates that you have identified yourself
> with the culture, history, traditions, and cause of the nation. Sec-
> ondly, he advises Jesu Bhaktas never to go to a church. He
> warns that they will usually come after you immediately,
> embarrassing both you and your family. This will cause unnec-
> essary misunderstanding and opposition with your family.
> Thirdly, he advises avoiding going into full-time "church
> work." Rather, one should stay within one's family and fulfill
> one's social responsibilities. One's primary call and opportunity
> is to be a witness there (Hoefer 1999, 37).

Communicating within the Structure

Christian witness within the household group will require communication that follows the structure of Lao relationships. This strategy requires structuring communication to flow in terms of older to younger relationships, male and female groupings, and through the use of ritual.

Patron–Client Communication

Communication will be best when it flows within the structure of older to younger relationships. Missionaries will need to be concerned not only for the communication of information but also for the social obligations involved in the communicational relationship. For the most part, Christian witness should flow from the older one in the relationship to the younger one. But older communicators will need to be aware of and live up to the social responsibility to provide advice and security for those who are younger. They should not be surprised when the younger one converts rather quickly. But neither should they be surprised if these younger converts abandon the faith just as quickly, should the older one in the relationship not provide the kind of care expected of them. For foreign missionaries this creates a problem of establishing expectations they cannot live up to in the long-term.

One method of dealing with this is to connect converts to Lao Christian "older brothers and sisters" within the household of faith who can live up to these expectations. Another, more critical strategy, however, is to teach the younger one to look to God as the one who can provide for all his or her needs.

At the same time, converts should be instructed to continue to give their allegiance to the household to which they belong. Living up to their obligations in the household is important because 1) the scriptures teach us to honor our fathers and mothers so that things will go well with us (Eph. 6:2), 2) it will be a means of avoiding persecution for the wrong reasons, and 3) it will be a means of winning some social space necessary for further Christian witness.

Christian witness that flows from the younger one in a relationship to the older one is also possible. Ubolwan Mejudhon suggests that younger people in a relationship engage their older brother or sister in witness through meekness (1997). Witness in this context requires time and even more careful attention to fulfilling social obligations. [17] In this context witness begins by demonstrating obedience and loyalty. It requires that witness be primarily in non-verbal and non-confrontational formats. All Lao realize that older people know better than younger people, especially in the area of religious knowledge. It is likely that the older one in the relationship will counsel the younger one to abandon their Christian faith and return to the traditional religious rituals. In these cases polemic refusals will be unproductive. Younger Christians should prayerfully discern with the counsel of other brothers and sisters what parts of the ritual system they can participate in, and at what level. Participation in the ritual system at some level, even if at a low level, coupled with apologies and extra efforts in fulfilling other obligations will win tolerance. This is especially true if the younger party shows loyalty in spite of small returns from the relationship. Some level of ritual participation is crucial in this context because it demonstrates respect and honor for those involved.

Male and Female Communication

Communication in Lao society is best when it is between people of the same gender. This recognizes the male-female classification of Lao social relations. This is probably true around the world but it is stressed in the social context of Laos to a larger degree than in some other societies. This is especially true with married adults since friendships are strongest between married women and between married men. Unmarried young men and women, on the other hand, are often found socializing together (in groups, not alone). Communication can flow from an unmarried male to an unmarried female as long as it is done in a group setting. A man and woman are not allowed to speak alone unless it is public knowledge that they intend to be married.

Ritual Communication

Communication will be best when ritual shapes the media of communication. The emphasis on order in Lao relationships gives ritual a crucial place in the maintenance and transformation of relationships. This emphasis on ritual requires that communication often be shaped in a formalized code. Communication in Laos is often more concerned with *how* (relationally) something is said than in *what* (content) is said. Speeches generally follow an expected pattern. Meetings open and end with ritual words. Even humor follows a strict structure. Formalized communication can be a means of integrating the members of group and clarifying roles.

The communication of the gospel needs to be done in terms of ritualized language whether it is done in storytelling, the manipulation of symbolic objects, or in stylized speech.

Christians should also carefully consider when traditional rituals can be used, when traditional rituals can be used in altered form, and when there is a need to create new rituals. One of the most stressful times for converts to Christianity in Laos is when they are asked to participate with their household in *khwan* or Buddhist rituals. Protestant Christians are consistently instructed not to participate in traditional rituals. While I believe that this is a way of clearly marking their allegiance to Christ, on a social level it cuts off opportunities for further witness that would naturally be there through household relationships. Failing to participate in traditional Lao rituals communicates that a person has opted out of the group. The implication is that the person no longer feels obligated to the needs of the group.

Many Christians obey the instruction of the Protestant churches and end up cutting themselves off, or seriously straining their relationships. Other Christians find the prospect of social death more than they can accept and end up participating in rituals spiritually and socially unprepared. Afterwards, there is a good deal of remorse and they are careful to not let other Christians know about their participation. Another group of Lao Christians are experimenting with ways to participate in traditional rituals in a way that satisfies social obligations to the household and yet identifies them as Christians. Can a Lao person participate in traditional rituals in ways that demonstrate the proper respect to the structure of the household, village, and nation, while communicating their exclusive allegiance to Jesus Christ? I believe they can. Lao Christians need to prayerfully discern this path.

A key to participation is the ability to identify roles in the ritual performance that allow Christians to meaningfully participate and identify themselves as Christians. For example, when a Christian's non-Christian brother is being ordained as a monk it is a serious issue to completely refuse to participate. A young man's ordination is a rite of passage to full adulthood. Men are referred to as 'raw' *dib* before they are ordained and receive titles (e.g. *Tit*) after-wards, depending upon the level of ordination they attain before they remove their robe and return to secular life. According to some Lao Christians, the very lowest level of participation, but an appropriate one, would be to assist with the cost of the ceremony, the preparation for the feast, and to attend the ritual as an observer.

Attendance at *khwan* rituals can be done in a similar way. In my own experiments in this regard, I have found there are normal-ly ways to meaningfully participate. For instance, at the end of a *suukhwan* ritual everyone is given an opportunity to verbally bless the recipient. I do this with a short Christian prayer of blessing in Jesus' name, while I follow the custom of tying cotton string around the person's wrist. This tends to communicate my inten-tion to respect and bless the individual and their household, there-by establishing a solid basis for relationship and further com-munication.

Low-level participation in traditional Lao rituals raises the issue of spiritual power and dual allegiance. Given the social context, I believe Christians can and should participate in Lao rituals in low-level ways as a means of providing a witness to the gospel. But relig-ious rituals should not be participated in without careful considera-tion of the spiritual powers involved.[18] It should also be remem-bered that the power of Christ is stronger than any spiritual power that may be present, and that the power Christ used is available to his disciples (Luke 10:19). Paul Hiebert writes, "we must avoid two extremes: a denial of the reality of Satan and the spiritual battle within and around us in which we are engaged and an undue fas-cination with, and fear of, Satan and his hosts" (1994, 214).

There are two crucial issues involved here. First, prayer for spiritual protection and discernment should precede and accom-pany any participation in traditional Lao religious rituals. Second, believers should be firm in their faith in the presence and power of Christ for the situation. Without this kind of faith Christians would do better to refrain from some levels of participation. In any event, it should be recognized that ritual is a key factor in establishing, maintaining, and transforming relationships in Lao society.

For better or for worse, the media is very often the meaning that Lao people attribute to the message that Christians deliver. Strong kinship (household) level relationships are the most effective media for communication of the gospel to Lao people. The gospel is a relational message that requires covenant between humans and the Creator, and covenant keeping with each other. Spiritual power and cognitive truth will also be involved in communicating the gospel to the Lao. How the power and truth of the gospel are interpreted, however, depends upon how our Christian witness engages others relationally.

Notes

1 This article summarizes the major findings of my dissertation (Bailey 2002).

2 See Toye (1968) and Stuart-Fox (1996 and 1998) for discussions on Laos as a buffer state, and on the history of attempts to annex portions of Laos.

3 See Chamberlain, Alton and Crisfield (1995, 49) for statistics on rice production shortages from 1991 to 1995.

4 Jesuit missionary Father Leria, who arrived in Laos in 1642, observed that the Lao typically had more than enough to eat (Stuart-Fox 1998, 95). "Although nutrition appears to be marginal in the general population, health surveys are of varying quality. Some data indicate that stunting—low height for age—in the under-five population ranged from two to thirty-five percent, while wasting—low weight for height—probably does not exceed ten percent of the under-five population" (United States Library of Congress 1994).

5 Bi-lateral aid promised for the period 1997–2000 was a total of $1.2 billion US. Of this amount, $640 million US were outright grants (UNDP 1997). The total GDP in 1998 was 1.76 billion US (*Asia 1998 Yearbook* 1998, 12).

6 "Whereas the infant mortality rate for Vientiane was about fifty per 1,000, in some remote rural areas it was estimated to be as high as 350 per 1,000 live births; that is, thirty-five percent of all children died before the age of one" (United States Library of Congress 1994).

7 "Laos" is pronounced "Lao" by the Lao people. The final "s" is not pronounced. The term "Laotian" has been falling out of usage in literature, in favor of the term, "Lao." It might also be helpful to know that Vientiane is pronounced, "Viang Chan." There is no English equivalent for the word *nam chay*. Kerr defines it as, "spirit, will, agreement" (1972, 692).

8 Some Christian Brethren missionaries began work in southern Laos in 1951 (Andrianoff 2001). OMF began in 1954.

9 MAF and FEBC staff worked under the Christian and Missionary Alliance (Andrianoff 2002).

10 MCC entered Laos in early 1975. Because of the political situation, in August they

were asked by church leaders not to attend the LEC worship services. They did maintain a loose communication with the LEC during that time and continue good relationships with them today.

11 This figure from the *Annual Report* of the C&MA in 1973 reflects statistics reported by missionaries on the church in Laos from 1972. It is the last report provided by the C&MA mission in Laos.

12 Some of the early converts to Christianity in southern Laos were lepers. Others were people accused of being possessed by an evil spirit known as *phii pawb* (*The Call* 1946).

13 Vientiane municipality is the capital of the Lao PDR and has a population today of about 524,000 persons (Institute for Cultural Research 1999, 25).

14 *The Mekong Prayer Fellowship* newsletter has been published with the purpose of generating prayer support since the early 1980s. There are now several web-based prayer networks that include Laos. The AD 2000 Prayer movement also organized prayer for Laos.

15 See Lamin Sanneh's account of the impact of the gospel on Muslim Africans, and the impact of Islam in Africa on the meaning of the gospel in Africa (1989).

16 The teaching of Jesus in Matthew 13:26-29 suggests that the Church should not be concerned with sorting out who are the real believers. This task seems to be one that Christ will accomplish upon his return.

17 I was personally involved in witnessing to a Lao couple who were older than myself biologically and in terms of social status. I began my relationship with them in 1990 and although I worked closely with them nearly every day I was there, it was not until 2001 that they were baptized.

18 See Kraft's chapter on "Elements of Ministry," in *Christianity with Power* (1989, 147-163) for helpful guidance in power-oriented ministry.

References

Andrianoff, David. 1991. Daniel McGilvary and Early Protestant Missionary Outreach into Laos. Unpublished manuscript.

——. 2002. Personal correspondence. E-mail message dated February 2, 2002.

Far Eastern Economic Review. 1998. *Asia 1998 Yearbook*. Hong Kong: Review Publishing Company Ltd.

Bailey, Stephen. 2002. Communication Strategies for Christian Witness among the Lowland Lao Informed by Worldview Themes in Khwan Rituals. Doctoral diss., Pasadena, CA: Fuller Theological Seminary.

Chamberlain, James R., Charles Alton, and Arthur G. Crisfield. 1995. Indigenous peoples profile: Lao People's Democratic Republic. 2 Vols. Unpublished report prepared for the Word Bank by Care International, Vientiane, Lao PDR.

Christian and Missionary Alliance (C&MA). 1973. *Annual Report*. New York: Christian and Missionary Alliance.

Douglas, Mary. 1970. *Natural Symbols*. New York: Pantheon Books.

Geertz, Clifford. 1973. *The Interpretation of Cultures*. New York: Basic Books.

Hiebert, Paul. 1994. *Anthropological Reflections on Missiological Issues* Grand Rapids, MI: Baker Books.

Hoefer, Herbert. 1991. *Churchless Christianity*. *Madras*: Gurulul Lutheran Theological College and Research Institute.

——. 1999. Follow-up Reflections on Churchless Christianity. *Mission Frontiers* 21(3-4). Pasadena, CA: US Center for World Mission, 36-41

Institute for Cultural Research. 1999. *Vientiane Social Survey Project 1997–1998*. Ministry of Information and Culture, Government of the Lao PDR.

Kerr, Allen D. 1972. *Lao-English Dictionary*. 2 vols. Washington D.C.: The Catholic University of America Press.

Kraft, Charles. 1979. *Christianity in Culture: A Study in Dynamic Biblical Theologizing in Cross-cultural Perspective*. Maryknoll, NY: Orbis Books.

——. 1989. *Christianity with Power: Your Worldview and Your Experience of the Supernatural*. Ann Arbor, Michigan: Servant Publications.

——. 1999. Contextualization in Three Dimensions. Inauguration lecture: Chair of Global Mission. October 20. Pasadena, CA: Fuller Theological Seminary.

Lao Christian Services. 1987. *Life after Liberation* Nakhon Sawan, Thailand: Lao Christian Services.

Latourette, Kenneth S. 1939. *A History of the Expansion of Christianity: Three Centuries of Advance.* NY: Harper & Brothers Pub.

Lintner, Bertil. 2001. Laos: Gifts from Above. *Far Eastern Economic Review* August 30. Hong Kong, China: Dow Jones & Company, 51.

Mejudhon, Nantachai and Ubolwan Mejudhon. 2000. Contextualization workshop. Lao Day of Prayer, November 3, 2000. Bangkok, Thailand.

Mejudhon, Ubolwan. 1997. The Way of Meekness: Being Christian and Thai in the Thai way. Dissertation thesis, Asbury Theological Seminary.

Nida, Eugene. 1990. *Message and Mission.* (1st Edition 1960) Pasadena, CA: William Carey Library.

Oppel, Lolyd. 1984. Laos: Church and State Report. Unpublished manuscript.

Roffe, G. Edward. 1975. Laos in *The Church in Asia,* ed. Donald Hoke, 391-408. Chicago: Moody Press.

Sanneh, Lamin. 1989. *Translating the Message: The Missionary Impact on Culture.* Maryknoll, NY: Orbis Books.

Smalley, William. 1956. The Gospel and the Cultures of Laos. *Practical Anthropology.* 3(3). Bangkok, Thailand: Bangkok Publishing & Printing Service, 47-57.

Stuart-Fox, Martin. 1986. *Laos: Politics, Economics and Society.* Boulder, CO: Lynne Rienner.

———. 1996. *Buddhist Kingdom, Marxist State: The Making of Modern Laos.* Bangkok, Thailand: White Lotus.

———. 1998. *The Lao Kingdom of Lan Xang: Rise and Decline.* Bangkok: White Lotus Press.

Toye, Hugh. *Laos: Buffer State or Battleground.* London: Oxford University Press.

United States Library of Congress. 1994. Laos. Online. http://memory.loc.gov/cgi-bin/query/r?frd/cstdy:@field(DOCID+la0078 [cited March 2, 2000].

United States State Department. 2001. Laos: International religious freedom report. Online. http://www.state.gov/g/drl/rls/irf/2001/5607.htm [cited November 11, 2001].

Anätman as a Metaphor for Japan

The Challenge of a Buddhist Non-Self Culture for Missions

Mark Dominey

Introduction

The Search for Japanese Identity in the Twenty-first Century

Who are the Japanese? This is a question that the Japanese themselves have been struggling to answer, particularly since the Emperor, in his infamous Imperial Rescript (Jan. 1, 1946), denied his divinity and announced that his relationship to the people should not "depend upon mere legends and myths," especially the "false conception that the Emperor is divine and that the Japanese people are superior to other races and fated to rule the world" (Mullins et al, 1993, 103). This came as such a shock that some people promptly committed suicide. It did more violence to their worldview than they could apparently endure.

Over half a century later, Japan has changed dramatically. But with these changes questions of national or personal identity have also become a serious matter of discussion. This phenomenon has been expressed in a whole genre of literature formed in Japan and popularly called *Nihonjinron*, which literally means "Theory of the Japanese." *Nihonjinron* is essentially Japan's modern attempt to redefine who they are as a people. Much of the tone of such writings stresses what is "unique" about the Japanese and extols their culture in contrast to the West's, at times appearing more prescriptive than descriptive. Some even borders on racist diatribe. Nevertheless, missiologists concerned with Japan should consider carefully what this people group is saying about itself and what they value, what they think, and why.

For many Westerners, too, Japan holds a longstanding attraction as an exotic yet accessible culture, differing so significantly from their own society that at times it appears as a kind of mirror opposite of the West. Beginning with Ruth Benedict's now notorious anthropological study (which she completed in 1946, never having done fieldwork in Japan due to the war), Japan has received close attention of Western (or Western-trained Japanese) scholars in the postwar era and Japan Studies is now a mature discipline. Not many people groups have been the subject of so many comparative studies by cultural anthropologists (e.g., Lebra, Smith, Befu), sociologists (Nakane, McVeigh, Davis, Miller & Kanazawa), social anthropologists (Hendry), or social psychologists (Caudill; Doi; De Vos). What have they discovered?

One characteristic, which has fascinated Westerners the most and has predominated in the above descriptive studies, is the strong group orientation of Japanese society. More than just the penchant for office workers to do a daily calisthenics routine *en masse* and in synch to a nationwide radio broadcast, or busloads of Japanese tourists descending upon an unsuspecting restaurant, each ordering exactly the same meal, Japanese social behavior follows fairly strict rules emphasizing conformity in ritualized behavior, and makes sharp distinctions (*kejime*) in differentiating one's "ingroup" (*uchi*) from the "out-group" (*soto*). What is perhaps most perplexing to Westerners is how the status of the individual, one's personal sense of identity, is not fixed and independent in Japan, but normally defined by one's relationship to others *within a group*. Consequently, to some observers the Japanese at times seem as nearly lacking an autonomous sense of Self, willfully suppressing personal expression (*enryo*) and succumbing to social pressure to conform to group behavior beyond reason (i.e., workaholism). Although this social phenomenon has sometimes been stereotyped as "groupthink" or even "herd mentality," more serious scholarly research has produced various models of the Japanese sense of Self in relation to society. To wit, the Japanese Self has been described as "relational," "interdependent," "collective," "sociocentric," in addition to "group-oriented." Moreover, there is now Bachnik's "shifting Self" theory (Bachnik 1992, 152-172), Kuwayama's "reference other orientation" (1992, 121-151), Lebra's "three-dimensional Self" (interactional, inner, and boundless) and Doi's "two-tiered Self" (see Rosenburger 1992 for these and others). Needless to say, the nature of the Japanese Self, or even the question of whether one exists, is an important topic in Japan Studies originating in the West.

Missiologists generally recognize the Japanese as one of the world's most resistant people groups, and the thought of a church-planting movement (CPM) occurring in Japan still seems remote to many. There are many opinions as to why the Japanese are resistant and sociocultural factors have often been considered as significantly problematic (e.g., Dyer 1982, Clark 1985, Eyler 1996). This paper considers the comparatively weak autonomy of the individual in Japan (using the Buddhist concept of *anātman* as a metaphor) as recognized by sociologists, cultural anthropologists, ethnopsychologists, as well as other indigenous *Nihonjinron* writings and relates it to the missionary task. Several questions are thus raised: How can the indigenous (group) decision-making process be best accommodated in our evangelistic efforts? What is the role of peer pressure in conversion? Should individual autonomy be fostered as part of evangelism or pre-evangelism? Is the Buddhist doctrine of *anātman* (Non-Self) to blame for weak individual autonomy in Japan? Or is it due more to non-religious sociocultural factors? Is there a need for a theological response (indigenous or missionary formulated) to this problem of identity in Japan? How does this problem relate to contextualization of the gospel?

Self Identity in Japan as Seen in the Social Sciences

Japanese Social Consciousness and Worldview Shift

Some of the more prominent and widely accepted components of an ethnology of the Japanese include their high value of *harmony*, emphasis on *hierarchy* and *groupism*, as well as strong social pressures towards *conformity* and *uniformity*. Comparative studies with the West often point out the relatively weak role of individual autonomy in Japan, a role which is related to each one of the above characteristics and is itself another notable feature. That the Japanese have an arguably weak sense of Self is surely one reason that individual identity remains so elusive and why the *Nihonjinron* genre thrives. Thus, *Nihonjinron* literature has been thoroughly analyzed by Stanford anthropology professor emeritus Befu Harumi (2001), who sees it as an attempt to develop a new worldview and maintains that it has developed specifically due to what he considers as a weakness in Japanese identity.

Emic *Nihonjinron* theories can be seen as a reaction to modernism and a rapidly changing society. Befu explains, "It is often asked why *Nihonjinron* maintains such a strong hold in Japanese society....I submit that it is the absence of any alternative worldview, cultural model, or ideology that people might consider and propose in place of *Nihonjinron* that allows this outmoded worldview to persist in spite of the wide and even widening gap between the reality of the Japanese society and the imagery supported in *Nihonjinron*" (2001, 103). Befu criticizes his native land as mostly composed of a "vast majority of relatively apolitical, inert though educated people who are willing to be manipulated by the government...through such means as control of education" and predicts that *Nihonjinron* will continue to fill the void of identity "unless—and this is a big 'unless'—a rival civil religion can emerge to claim the hearts of the majority of the Japanese. So far, none is on the horizon" (2001, 122). Befu's frank analysis may seem shockingly un-Japanese (he obviously has been living in the West for some decades). However, his perception of growing angst in Japan needs to be considered.

Building his case on the works of Japanese who write in the *Nihonjinron* genre, one missiologist (Lee 1999) also makes the strong case that Japan is in the throws of a cultural identity crisis. He contrasts this with the Western view of an inviolable personal Self, which is unconnected and autonomous, uncompromising and therefore constantly in conflict—basically the opposite of the Japanese view. Christian change agents should take notice that anthropologists such as Befu and missiologists such as Lee are declaring that the Japanese are currently in search of a new worldview, but have been unfortunately offered no satisfying alternative except *Nihonjinron*. Many people seem hampered by their weak identity, ever reluctant to appear as at odds with national consensus, and remain very susceptible to the influence of the domestic mass media.

Indeed, Befu characterizes this *Nihonjinron* thinking as a de facto new religion. This is reminiscent of Yamamoto Shichihei (using the pen name "Isaiah Ben Dasan") who first articulated this notion in one of the earliest *Nihonjinron* bestsellers (Ben Dasan 1972), where he called the religion of the Japanese *Nihonkyö* ("Japan-religion" or "Nihonism"), which is essentially syncretistic religion and a heavy mix of *Nihonjinron* ideas. Yamamoto saw this "religion" as all absorbing: any foreign faith, even Christianity, will eventually be syncretized into *Nihonkyö* so that the result will merely be the "Christian sect" of Nihonism. Needless to say, most Japanese still define themselves as Buddhists when pressed, though their worldview is demonstrably not entirely Buddhistic, though certainly syncretistic.

Group Conformity and Japan's Hierarchical Structure

The Japanese live and move and have their being in groups. Indeed, the late Tokyo University professor of Buddhism, Nakamura Hajime, whose expertise in philosophy extended from Indian and Chinese thought to his native Japan, has said that the most distinctive feature of the Japanese people is the groupism which he described as *the tendency to emphasize a limited social nexus*. Significantly, "consciousness of the individual as an entity appears always in the wider sphere of consciousness of social relationships" (1964, 409). In other words, the Japanese both relate in groups, but also define themselves by groups. Stated more strongly, *individual consciousness does not really develop apart from one's role in a group context*.

At the same time, the internal structure of every group and the whole of society is *hierarchical*. Awareness of rank is deeply rooted in Japanese social behavior (this might be called a kind of self-awareness). Still, "ranking order not only regulates social behavior but also curbs the open expression of thought" (Nakane 1970, 33), yet it also, ironically, determines the actual grammatical form of the Japanese language employed. One cannot underestimate the significance of this sociolinguistic feature as well. Hierarchy and the nature of relationships in Japan are always indicated in the form of the language used (i.e., a completely different form of the language is used depending on whether one is talking *up* or *down* to a person). This is a constant reminder that *no two people are really equals among the Japanese.* [1] It also tends to make explicit whether different persons are members of the same group or not. As a rule, the more polite people are, the greater social distance exists between them, and the less of their true selves will be revealed in interaction.

The Japanese sense of Self has long been considered underdeveloped by intellectual observers. One ethnopsychologist specializing in Japanese issues found that until the postwar baby boom years, "the highest morality within Japanese society was in an identification of oneself as a family member rather than as a person with individual desires and goals. Even given the present-day conscious desire to find oneself as an entity, many Japanese experience a continuing inner incapacity to realize *jibun*, or a real sense of themselves as something apart from social role expectations" (De Vos 1973b). Nakamura wrote of the same generation: "In spite of the various Western modern thoughts introduced after the Meiji Restoration, the individual as a social entity has not come to be fully grasped by the general public. While the Japanese are keenly conscious of their membership in their small, closed nexus, they are *hardly fully aware of themselves as individuals,* or as social beings, to the extent the Western peoples are" (1964, 415, emphasis mine). One can detect many changes in the generations that have followed, but more recent researchers (Rosenberger 1992, Miller and Kanazawa 2000, Befu 2001) still see the lack of self-expression as a problem.

Japan's hierarchical structure, identity through groupism, and typical patterns of behavior have been thoroughly analyzed by sociologists such as Nakane Chie (1970) and cultural anthropologists such as Takie Sugiyama Lebra (1976). Nakane's work examined individual identity within the hierarchy and the primary group affiliation and explained that Japanese stress situational position, in what she called a particular *frame*, rather than a universal *attribute*. Consequently, people identify themselves primarily, not by profession (e.g., "an engineer"), but by primary group (*"Mitsubishi"*). Likewise, for example, it is not nearly as significant that a man holds a Ph.D. as that he graduated from a particular famous university. Identity is based more upon with whom one is affiliated than with any personal characteristic or accomplishment.

Nakane further shows that the power and influence of a group not only affects an individual's actions, but also his thinking, such that "Individual autonomy is minimized." However, this is not necessarily the bane it would appear to be for Westerners. "There are those who perceive this as a danger, an encroachment on their dignity as individuals; on the other hand, others feel safer in total-group consciousness. There seems little doubt that the latter group is the majority....With group consciousness so highly developed there is almost no social life outside the particular group on which an individual's major economic life depends" (Nakane 1970, 10). Such thinking and behavior are observed among any Japanese social groups (housewives, students), not just salarymen.

Contextual Personas and the Dual Self-Consciousness

The writings of Japanese psychiatrist Doi Takeo have contributed significantly to an understanding of the Japanese psyche, especially in his theory that dependency relationships (*amae*) are normative in Japan from infancy through adulthood. In considerable contrast to the West, Doi shows how Japanese children are nurtured to become *dependent* rather than *independent*. In Japan this is valued as healthy (though in the West it might be negatively labeled as "spoiling" or even "codependency"). In Doi's analysis, ultimately *"Amae* is a dependency need which manifests itself in a longing to merge with others" (1986, 160). Normally, it will be a junior member who "depends upon" the benevolence of a senior member of the same ingroup who takes an indulging (*amayakasu*) role. There might be some basis for this in Confucianism, which stresses the role of superiors to inspire loyalty through benevolence. At any rate, virtually all Japanese have been involved in these types of relationships at some time.

Central to Doi's *amae* thesis is the concept of ingroup (*uchi*) and outside group (soto) distinction mentioned above and the related modes of personal expression: the private or concealed "behind" (*ura*) and the public, outgroup oriented "front" (*omote*). He further relates his dependency model to *a dual self-consciousness* where the individual's persona adapts to both his primary "ingroup" and the public "out-group." Lebra (1976) has developed these concepts most completely in her analysis of Japanese behavior patterns. Put simply, the Japanese act in a restrained manner, suppressing their true selves in public (that is, outside of their inner circles), but are more open and honest when in the company of their closest relationships, such as family, friends, or group of affiliation. It is well-known in Japan that true feelings and opinions (called *honne*) are not normally expressed in the ritualized public setting, where conflict is avoided and harmony valued, even if it means adopting a "stance" or "surface" position (called *tatemae*) which is contradictory to one's real feelings. This switch in a person's behavior, the positions one takes, or the opinions one expresses is determined by *external* factors following sociocultural rules.

Again, these modes of relating are not unambiguous for the Japanese; they are deliberate (if not always entirely conscious) because the actual form of the Japanese language used (informal or one of the polite forms) usually changes depending upon whether one is addressing ingroup or out-group audience. Typically, concomitant to this change in language form is a ritual change in behavior. In short, Japanese not only *speak* differently, they *act* differently and take on a *different persona* depending on whether they are in company with family, friends, coworkers, superiors, or strangers. Part of the problem for foreign missions in Japan is in developing appropriate status and relationships so that honest communication can really take place. It is difficult if not impossible to become an intimate ingroup member with most people.

When taken to extremes, the dissonance between the superficial *tatemae/omote* façade and the *honne/ura* 'suppressed thought life' can at times result in a kind of dishonesty or even moral compromise, though it is generally thought of as good social tact. Doi admits, "The urge to eliminate ambivalence for a higher integrity is generally weak among the Japanese," though he maintains that the distinction between public and private selves "does not have the purpose of deliberately deceiving others" (Doi 1986; 152-153). Nevertheless he also recognizes that there are instances where people are praised for not having *ura/omote* [hidden motives] and it is here that "we feel a certain pain when we have to use *omote* and *ura*" (1986, 153). Doi admits it is strange that "it does not matter if they appear from the outside to contradict each other," but explains, "When one's standpoint is that of *omote, omote* is everything. It is as if *ura* does not exist, and it can be ignored" (1986, 152). Here we see the sublimation of the ego, because that is what *ura* is. Still, Hendry offers a dissenting view: "These different 'faces' are reflected in different speech forms used on different occasions, and none of them negates the existence of a complete Self using them all. Just as *tatemae* is distinguished from *honne*, one's real feelings or intention, behaviour in the group context may be distinguished from the individual who is acting out a role as member of the group" (1987, 50).

Self Expression in Japanese Contexts

How do the Japanese express themselves? This is a large topic that can only briefly be examined here. Some principles can be observed. Social convention based on Confucianism leads to a tendency in which the most senior member of a group typically becomes the leader, who is deferred to and allowed to monopolize the conversation while juniors have the passive role of listener. "Generally there is no development of dialectic style in Japanese conversation" according to Nakane (1970, 34). She even suggests a reason for why her people are weak in logical reasoning: "The premises underlying thesis-antithesis are parity and confrontation [the *opposites* of hierarchy and harmony] on an equal footing which will develop into or permit the possibility of synthesis. Because of the lack of a discipline for relationships between equals, the Japanese do not practice these three basic steps of reasoning and must overcome great odds in order to advance or cultivate any issue brought under discussion" (1970, 35).[2]

Self expression can be evaluated through discourse analysis. Barnlund did a comparative study and determined that the total "area" of the Self, accessible to others through communication, is significantly smaller in Japan than in the United States. Moreover, "There were more than a few, especially among the Japanese sample, whose average level of self expression was not near 100 [on a scale of 200], but closer to 0, who on *nearly all topics* and with *nearly all people* reported they 'Have told the person nothing about this aspect of myself'" (1975, 78-81). Americans, on the other hand, "reveal themselves more completely on the most superficially explored topics than do the Japanese on all but the safest and most completely explored topics of conversation" (1975, 89).

Barnlund found that "the extent to which the inner self is disclosed affects the accuracy with which self is perceived" (1975, 148). This raises the question of whether discouraging expression of thoughts and feelings reduces opportunities to actualize the Self. He asks further: Is expression of the Self essential to growth of the Self? This is relative and hard to answer. America is not the standard by which Japan is to be judged. Barnlund says yes, and raises concern about the health of Japanese society, while arguing that development of self-expression is necessary for psychological maturity.[3]

The Development of the Japanese Psyche

How do the Japanese learn this manner of relating? The socialization of Japanese children that makes them obedient members conforming to the group-based culture has been of considerable interest to researchers. An argument can be made that this process begins with early child rearing practices. Americans tend to view children as born totally *dependent,* and the socialization process is aimed at promoting *independence* as the ultimate goal of maturity. Japanese, however, view children as born *independent,* and the socialization process is aimed at drawing a child into a social group, where *dependency* will continue (Doi 1973; Lebra 1976). Thus, part of the socialization process is to foster a sense of *group dependence.*

One may argue that the reason Americans and Japanese take

such radically different approaches is because these characteristics will ultimately aid them in their respective societies. But even studies of infant behavior show very marked differences in Japanese babies (quieter and less expression) compared to American babies (more happy and vocal), which Caudill and Weinstein argue (1986, 201-246) results from different parenting strategies: Japanese mothers constantly soothe and quiet small children, strapping them to themselves while working, and sleeping with them at night. Americans let children cry themselves to sleep in another room, but encourage more expression and exploration.

Furthermore, this emphasis can also be seen in early schooling practices. Peak (1991) has reported that Japanese preschool teachers consider that nonparticipation in group activities is the most serious behavioral problem a preschooler can have. Whereas American philosophy of education considers developing a child's self-esteem to be crucial, though secondary to academic performance, Japanese goals for education normally include socialization to group life as primary. Fostering a group identity and a sense of psychological group dependence is an explicit part of the national school curriculum. Moreover, the transition from home to pre-school life has been found by social anthropologists to be perhaps the most crucial period in development of Japanese identity (Hendry, 1986), as well as the foundational process of socialization (Peak, 1991). Peak's work focused on how the dual self-consciousness is developed in Japanese children and concludes that it occurs as part of socialization process that begins in the pre-school years. [4]

Lewis (1995) has found much that is praiseworthy in the Japanese early education system, such as effective use of small groups and managing of misbehavior through peer groups, in spite of the typically large class sizes (35-40 students). Still, she faults it for suppressing individual self-expression. Its greatest shortcoming, however, is in the severe form it takes in the higher grades, which causes the education expert to lament: "Why does child-centered early education give way, at junior high, to monotonous lectures and authoritarian control?" Rohlen (1983) has shown how Japanese adolescents are further "socialized" by the Ministry of Education to the point that discussion and questioning are not encouraged.

"Making students stand to answer, furthermore, is hardly the way to induce open discussions" (1983, 245). Needless to say, the exam-based system emphasizes rote learning of facts much more than thinking or questioning. Some critics have openly wondered if the real goal of the Ministry's education system is not actually in producing a compliant work force, socialized to not challenge authority, leading them to accept severe working conditions, and never question taboos such as Japan's wartime responsibility. Nevertheless, Miller and Kanazawa maintain that it is accurate to conclude that children are socialized to be dependent on social groups because the Japanese social structure is designed to reward that behavior in adults (2000, 25).

McVeigh makes an interesting case that school uniforms actually symbolize social standardization, for "regulated attire makes the individual more uniform ('one form')" which is useful to superiors as "barometers of an individual's commitment." As such, it is a "visible expression of a moral system" (2000, 80-81). That uniforms are all embracing can be shown by the simple fact that even on Sundays, days off, and summer holidays, many students still prefer their school uniforms. This uniform matter of dress can be somewhat disconcerting for Westerners socialized to recognize people as individuals with distinct personalities expressed through clothing. Indeed, one Japanese male office worker interviewed disliked the idea of women workers wearing ordinary clothing because inevitably "I end up calling them by their names" (McVeigh 2000, 122). But many Japanese genuinely prefer this uniformity. They *like* looking the same because it expresses what they value: *belonging to a group*. To wit, the motto for one school's handbook on clothing regulations ironically reads, "Clothes express one's heart, so let's obey the clothing regulations" [*sic*]! (McVeigh 2000, 62). Nevertheless, students often do bend clothing regulations to show some degree of individuality.

Miller and Kanazawa have studied how social order is produced and maintained in Japan, especially via social psychological processes, which occur in small groups. They point out that while Japan and the United States are at opposite ends of a table of statistics, comparing the homicide rate in over ten countries, they are also at the opposite ends of a scale for number of Nobel prizes won, a fact which they argue is not unrelated. Social order exists to the degree that individuals follow rules; Japan is a rule-following society par excellence. Why?

The above researchers believe that the answer is not found in either Buddhism or Confucianism, but in informal social control methods, which permeate society and especially the education system. Behavioral conformity at the society level is less a product of individual decisions than it is a product of the social structure, but the authors maintain that it is also an unintended consequence of conformity at a small-group level. They show that the closed nature of Japanese small groups ultimately leads to distrust towards others and that the social conditions furthermore "strongly influence the way religious organizations have developed in Japan, and explain why the Japanese religious landscape is so different from that of the West" (Miller and Kanazawa 2000, 11).

Japanese Religiosity and Self-Consciousness

Buddhism in Its Japanese Historical Context

Strictly speaking, Buddhism does not believe in the objective reality of any event, so it ultimately holds the question of historicity as meaningless. Nevertheless, Prince Shōtoku is credited with officially adopting Buddhism as the court religion in the sixth century. Perhaps equally significant, he promulgated Japan's first constitution in 604 A.D., which gives us insight into the ancient value system of the people. His Seventeen Article Constitution (De Barry 1958, 48-51), begins in Article One by declaring, "*Harmony is to be valued* and an avoidance of wanton opposition to be honored" [emphasis mine]. Article Two then officially commands the subjects to reverence the "three treasures" of Buddhism. It is quite clear from this that maintaining social harmony was already a supreme value at the time of the arrival of Buddhism. Article Ten is particularly revealing: "Let us cease from wrath...for all men have hearts, and each heart has its own leanings." Although this appears to be recognition of individuality, it goes on to rhetorically ask, "How can any one lay down a rule by which to distinguish right from wrong?" and concludes, *"let us follow the multitude and act like them."* Article Fifteen further orders subjects "To turn away from that which is private, and to set our faces towards that which is public" with the purpose of acting "harmoniously with others." Although scholars take these passages to be essentially Confucian exhortations to seek common good, avoid corruption, and serve the Emperor, nearly 1400 years later, the Japanese could easily be described as maintaining these same values of *harmony* and *conformity*.

Although Buddhism entered Japan in the sixth century, it was essentially a religion for the elite of the court until its thirteenth century heyday. However, while at first the temples were the repositories of ancestor memorials, by 686 Emperor Temmu had ordered family altars (*butsudan*) to be erected in every home. As it became a way of life among the masses, who were unschooled in its finer doctrines, Buddhism developed into a cult of the dead, in which rituals containing Buddhist prayers and incantations were used to guard and protect the living by pacifying the spirits of the dead.

The early schools (Nara sects such as Kegon) soon competed with the more magical and esoteric Tendai and Shingon sects founded in the eighth century. But from the twelfth century onward there was tremendous development in Japanese Buddhism with the simultaneous founding of Zen sects, and then the emergence of Amidism in the Jōdo (Pure Land) school of Hōnen (1133-1212) and the Jōdo Shin school of Shinran (1173-1263). It was also during this time that the construction of great temples and images commenced. The Pure Land sects have eclipsed even Zen in terms of popularity, mainly due to their greatly simplified practices. However, there were those who opposed such teaching and real unity has never been achieved. Nichiren (1222-1282) in particular, vehemently denounced the new sects as utterly false and promptly founded his own ultranationalistic sect based on the Lotus Sutra. What is significant is to realize that Buddhism in Japan began to take shape as an indigenous system.[5]

The Ban on Christianity and Emergence of the Funeral Cult

After Jesuits came to Japan in the sixteenth century, the xenophobic Tokugawa regime (1600–1868) eventually reacted and not only banned Christianity, but sent the country into a policy of national seclusion. As part of the official persecution of Christianity, every household by law was forced to belong formally to a temple and sect (*danka seido*). This was purely a political rather than religious ploy, but through this attempt to destroy Christianity, the neighborhood Buddhist temples became legally linked to families and the modern funerary cult developed. By law, every year families had to appear at the temple to renounce Christianity. Needless to say, since all funerals (and memorial days) were required to be performed by the temples, they became the most pervasive activity. This not only enriched each temple, but also multiplied them into a virtual funeral industry, which remains to this day and is the most pervasive feature of Japanese Buddhism.

Affiliation to a temple was always through the household and "there was little overt conception of personal, chosen individual faith, especially after the formalization of this temple-household system" (Reader 1993, 142). This historical development also helps explain the trend towards syncretism or dual religiosity among the Japanese. When the country was opened again to foreign intercourse after the Meiji Restoration, the official "non-Christian certificates" formerly issued by the temples were no longer necessary, leaving only the funeral and memorial services as the functions of the temples, at a time when militaristic state Shintö began to be taught as the officially approved worldview and Buddhism became more syncretized.

As a result of the Shöwa Emperor's rescript, renouncing his divinity, "the Japanese people's traditional world of meaning and their understanding of history, which counted the sacred traditions of the ancient Shinto myths as historical facts, could no longer be preserved" (Kitagawa 1987, 281). But besides this radical and sudden damage to their worldview, a new civil code in 1947 effectively abolished the traditional system of interlocking households (*ie seido*) as a legal institution. This, in turn, weakened the Buddhist parish system, and consequently, "individuals were no longer bound by the established religious affiliation of their households." In short, they were freed from both state Shintö and Buddhism officially, and given an "American" democratic constitution, but they were offered no new religious alternative or worldview.

The Japanese and Mahāyāna Doctrine of Nonexistence of Self

What role has Buddhism played in the development of a Japanese view of Self? One needs to distinguish between philosophical Buddhism, as it is known among the religious elite in the various schools popular in Japan, and the religious notions of the average Japanese layperson, who would have a very hard time articulating the differences. Still, it is undeniable that Buddhism has influenced culture, to the extent that the Buddhist word for "Non-Self" (Sanskrit *anātman,* or *muga* in Japanese) is known even to children.

Mahāyāna Buddhism certainly contains the most developed doctrine of *anātman.* Indeed, one authority on Mahāyāna Buddhism has stated, "in the light of the doctrine of no-Self the Mahāyānist attitude is that if the other traditions talk of human beings, as with the Buddha, as though they inherently exist or have any ultimate importance, so this itself is an indication of spiritual backwardness" (Williams 1989, 32).

According to orthodox Buddhism, nothing is objectively real and nothing has independent existence as a thing in itself. All particular entities are described by such terms as *muga* and *kü* (Sk. *ßünyatä,* "void" or "non-existent"). Callaway rightly concludes, "Here is to be seen one of the most crucial differences between Buddhism and Christianity. *Muga* is a key doctrine of Buddhism. According to the doctrine there is no real individuality. Men exist only in the realm of *zokutai* [i.e., a worldly state of ignorance]; in the realm of *shintai* [ultimate reality] they are identical with *shinnyo* ["True Thusness"]. Since *shinnyo* itself is impersonal, it follows that men, its passing expressions, are likewise essentially impersonal. There is no place in the framework of Buddhist thought for the concept of individual personalities who can voluntarily enter into loving fellowship with one another" (1957, 189-190). In contrast, in his discourse on the individual in Mahāyāna thought, Japanese Buddhist apologist Ueda writes, "Our true self is the basic substance of the universe, and, when we know the true self, we not only unite with the good of mankind, but we merge with the basic substance of the universe and spiritually unite with the divine mind." He adds, "the logic of the relationship between the individual and the world is grasped as the relationship in which 'the one enters the many and the many enter the one'" (1967, 170-171).

Hori (1967, 201-227) has detailed the appearance of individual self-consciousness in historical Japanese Buddhist thought, especially examining Hönen and Shinran. But he notes that Confucianism and the emphasis on filial piety, ancestor worship, and *on* [obligation to repay a favor] debt in human relationships has further strengthened the concept of the individual, but *always in relationship to others*. Nakamura states that "the Japanese mind was affected by the views of the Kegon [*Buddha-avataṃsaka*] Sūtra more than we realize. And the problem of 'proving the existence of others'—a problem which Dharmakīrti, Indian logician and philosopher, was interested in—was never given attention either in China or Japan" (1964, 412).[6]

In spite of its location within the Mahäyäna branch and being the repository of the most developed schools of Buddhist thought, Japanese Buddhism, as it is popularly known, can surely be characterized as the most simplified and least troublesome path to buddhahood. This is not merely because of Mahäyäna's reliance on *tariki* (salvation through the merciful efforts of boddhisatvas), but the path of austerities has been whittled down by successive schools of thought to such an extent that most Japanese priests now marry, many eat meat, and (in the case of the Jödo Shin sect) it is popularly believed that one merely has to declare, "*Namu Amida Butsu!*" ("Praise be to Amithabha!") a *single time* (as opposed to the more constant chanting found in other sects such as Nichiren) in order to assure oneself of future buddhahood. For most, enlightenment is not attainable in this life, but is guaranteed after death on the basis of the rites performed by the descendents. To the dismay of some schools of Buddhist thought, "becoming a Buddha" (*hotoke ni naru*) in Japan is absolutely synonymous with death. But even then there is no real "extinguishing" (Jp. *nehan*, Sk. *nirvääa*) of the individual, but a continued existence as a buddha with a unique funerary name (*kaimyö*) signifying enlightenment.

This is in contrast to Buddhist "common knowledge" in other lands, such as Therevada in Thailand, where only devout monks have the hope of enlightenment (leading to a situation where almost every male becomes a monk for a brief time, and women pray to be reborn as a men)! But in Japan, anybody and everybody is assumed to become a buddha upon death. Moreover, although many people claim to believe in reincarnation, when it suggests past lives, one will search in vain for a Japanese who sees rebirth as a real *future* possibility. No matter how rank a life an individual may have led, all people—including yakuza gangsters and politicians—have essentially the same funeral rites and all are thought to end up in the same blissful state after death. Indeed, in his exhaustive study of Japanese ancestor worship, anthropologist Robert J. Smith rightly has lamented, "it is difficult to find much evidence that the Japanese really think of their ancestors as ever being in hell" (Smith 1974, 51).

In reality, Japanese Buddhism could be called Buddhist heresy. Indeed, Watanabe (1968) has critiqued Japanese Buddhism as being 1) nationalistic, 2) magical, 3) overly concerned with ceremonies for the dead, 4) compromising, and 5) formalistic, having forgotten its true nature. Buddhist scholar Nakamura Hajime goes further to state that the Japanese were not converted to Buddhism; they converted Buddhism to their own "tribalism" (1964, 528)!

Although the Buddhist doctrine of *anātman* may not be directly responsible for the weak view of Self in Japan, which is more the result of socialization and culture that likely predates Buddhism, an effusion of this dogma denying individual existence over the centuries certainly has done nothing to strengthen the role of the individual in society and has most probably exacerbated what was already latent in the social structure.

Indeed, one can argue that the concept of the individual as the basic unit of society has never been accepted in Japan, which still maintains a family registration system. Nakamura, who wrote as both an authority on Buddhist philosophy and Japanese intellectual development said, "it was natural that the individual as a free and independent agent should not have been conceived by the Japanese till modern times" (1964, 431). Moreover, "The Japanese in general did not develop a clear-cut concept of the human individual *qua* individual as an objective unit like an inanimate thing, but the individual is always found existing in a network of human relationships" (Nakamura 1967, 182).

Buddhist teachings deny the existence of the individual Self, ultimately in order to overcome *personal* suffering. But the Japanese penchant for sublimating personal desires seems to be more in order to maintain harmony (perhaps to avoid *social* suffering). Christians, on the other hand, are called to deny themselves—to give up selfish ambitions—in order to follow Christ, which sometimes leads to *embracing suffering* through an act of identification with the Savior.

Some Missiological Reflection

Japan as a Non-Self Culture?

How important are these issues for our Christian mission? Is Buddhist Non-Self doctrine a significant factor in the Japanese identity? On one hand, it is obvious that the majority of Japanese are not actively pursuing a religious awakening in Zen, consciously and deeply meditating on the Buddhist philosophical notion of Non-Self, nor even engaging in other less strenuous Buddhist practices (except as social obligations or peer group affiliation demands it, such as one's participation in a funeral). On the other hand, whether due to such diverse issues as childrearing practices, the high social and institutional pressures to conformity, discrete cultural conditioning, or even by the deep influence of the Buddhist doctrine of *anätman* in the historical background of the people for over a thousand years, the Japanese concept of individuality remains comparatively weak. I believe this can be considered a significant factor affecting the responsiveness of the nation to the Christian message.

I have argued that one major aspect of Japanese resistance is related to an identity based on others. At worst this becomes *extreme conformity*, which stifles individual expression, opposes the individual straying from group norms, and certainly makes religious conversion to Christianity difficult. To quote a popular maxim known all too well by the Japanese, "The nail that sticks out gets hammered down" (*deru kugi wa utareru*).

Even if it is not consciously embraced as one of the supreme truths of Buddhism, the *practice* of *muga*, as a way of life appears to be a latent feature in Japanese culture. Lebra, in an essay concerning selfhood in Japanese, writes: "Lacking a dogma to serve as the ultimate value standard, the Japanese make moral judgments in accordance with the presence or absence of...pure, sincere motives. Purity boils down to egolessness (*muga*)" (1976, 162).

Interestingly enough, few Japanese today would actually deny their self-existence, if asked, though they continue to identify themselves as Buddhists. Indeed, what few religious notions they could articulate, and are most likely to hold the strongest, such as the responsibility towards ancestor rites, could even be used to argue for the idea of continual *personal* existence.[7] The concept of Non-Self *itself* remains difficult to accept, though not many are willing to go so far as to call it definitely false, if it means renouncing the whole superstructure of Buddhism. That would be tantamount to *extinguishing their identity* as Japanese. Rather, they imagine this difficult doctrine to be something that one could be awakened to only after long and intense meditation—or better— not in this life, but conveniently after death when they presumably will become a buddha *themselves*. If judged by the strict standards of orthodox Buddhism, Japan is surely a nation of secular Buddhists.[8] They remain confused yet unwilling to shed the traditional belief system, unless perhaps their peer group or the power of an Alternative compels them to do so.

The Ultimate Affiliation of the Japanese

The difficulty of evangelistic work in Japan is reflected by statistics in church attendance, which remains at less than half of one percent, and church growth that does not even keep up with Japan's slow population growth. Western missionaries have a tendency to blame the Japanese for being "resistant" due to their "closed" culture. Others blame the devil ("territorial spirits"), some even blame the language (if not a lack of study).

How has the Japanese church responded to its people's struggle for self-identity, the unhealthier aspects of "groupthink," and modernization? First, they have largely ignored the problem. Second, they have tolerated compromise (especially in the war years). Third, some have drifted into heresy (see Davis 1992; Yagi 1997,

83-111; Odagaki 1997 113-140; or Mullins 1998 for examples). Fourth, some have been reactionary (e.g., Yamamoto's critique of "Self-Love" [self-esteem] Ben-Dasan 1997). It would be better to develop an indigenous and Biblical theological response, particularly focusing on the believer's identity in Christ.

To say that any Japanese individual does not have a "self"—if this means they do not have a God-given soul—would be both absurd and Biblically untenable. However, to say that the Japanese way of thinking about themselves is influenced by Buddhistic culture, social conventions, and sin to such an extent that each individual has a distorted or incomplete view of themselves (in addition to healthy views which may differ from Western notions), is certain. All people need the revelation of God, regeneration by His Spirit, as well as sanctification and a renewed mind to overcome whatever deception is present. The ultimate loyalty for a Christian is the truth of God; but for Japan, it has always been elsewhere, whether family, company, the Ministry of Education, social group, idols, or the Emperor. This is where the problem lies.

Japan is also not a monolith in spite of some cultural tendencies, such as the individual's deference and conformity to the group. Each individual is unique, in spite of shared characteristics. Even the popular but erroneous belief in Japan that there four personality types, each linked to blood type, is evidence that the Japanese recognize serious differences among individuals. Although this emic view is demonstrably false, it is probably no more so than pronouncements of "herd mentality."

The temptation to follow others into sin, a reluctance to stand against the crowd and for God, or a refusal to admit personal guilt are problems common to all peoples, not only the Japanese. Indeed, one could easily write at length about both the benefits of groupistic cultures, as well as the sinfulness of individualistic ones. The word "selfish" surely has negative implications in the West, just as it does in Japan.

However, the problems resulting from an identity based in others needs to be addressed by the church in Japan. Missiologically speaking, it is a significant issue. Robert Lee has perhaps gone furthest in his analysis of the situation: "For Christians concerned with the contextualization of the gospel in Japan, the problem of the individuation of the self remains a major issue" (1999, 14). He views the problem of Japanese cultural identity from a larger perspective, finding at its core a direct link from every individual and group ultimately to the cult of the emperor. This parallels the work of others, such as Nakamura who spoke of the "commitment to the symbolic head of the social nexus." Lee builds a case that "issues of modernization, the emperor system, national identity, and self-identity are inseparably linked" (1999, 23).

For Christians, this continues to present the same dual identity problem that Uchimura Kanzö faced when he made his famous statement: "I love two J's and no third; one is Jesus, and the other is Japan. I do not know which I love more, Jesus or Japan." [9] Lee and others see Uchimura's dilemma as archetypal of all Japanese Christians today. During the war years, many Japanese Christians clearly sided with the Emperor as they compromised in their faith and obeyed the national laws requiring idolatrous worship. Lee calls this a matter of *ultimate affiliation* and further declares, "For Christians in Japan, the Japanese emperor system has become the 'inescapable missiological issue'," because most Japanese "have not been able to come to terms with these issues in an unambiguous way" (Lee 1999, 17-18). Although one can argue that only a minority of Japanese are really interested in the Emperor, who is basically a symbolic figurehead, Lee has raised a very appropriate issue: *What is the ultimate affiliation of this people group who are so in search of an identity?*

Lee's assessment is that Western approaches have been lacking and complicate Japanese missiological studies because "too much of the theology in Japan today is derived from a western theology that is also the end product of a long cultural history, one that led to the development of a highly individuated, autonomous centered self" (1999, 31). He suggests that theology derived from this Western environment will not match Japan's real needs, and so calls for a more indigenous theology.

At the same time he proposes that the church *encourage more individualism*, cautioning that as modernization continues and traditional society gives way to more individualism in the youngest generations, the church has given an inadequate missiological response, even denouncing social change that is actually for the better, risking its relevancy. "It would be better for the church to accept or encourage greater individuation and freedom from the traditional social nexus and respond with evangelism that calls for greater (voluntary) reintegration within an alternative, new social order" (Lee 1999, 42-43). Ironically, it sounds as if Harvard-educated Lee is both calling for an *indigenous Japanese* theology and at the same time longing for what could be termed a greater *Westernization* of society—more freedom and raising the consciousness of individuals. But who can fault him? One has to really wonder if the Japanese church can respond well to the problems he raises without the help of the Western missiologists and plenty of objective input.

The Japanese seem to feel that existence, apart from others in a group, is not real existence, because in Japan, personal identity is very much determined by group affiliation. One more problem for Japanese churches to consider is how believers change their affiliation from society *to the church*. Far too many churches in Japan seem to be nothing more than closed social groups and it does not take long before believers relate closely only to church people. This is in keeping with sociological rules of society, but the community of those "called out" of this world must derive their identity, not from the church or peers, but from Christ alone. And then they must reach the world with the gospel.

Towards Earning the Right to Be Heard in Japan

Although our power to preach comes from God (Acts 1:8; cf., John 16:8), it is not power *per se* that delivers anyone from bondage to deception; it is truth that sets men free (John 8:32). The only foolproof method of converting secular Buddhists in Japan to Christianity is simple: *preach the gospel to them*, for that alone is "the power of God for salvation to everyone who believes" (Rom. 1:16 NASB). However, because faith comes from *hearing* (with understanding, Rom. 10:17), it is of utmost importance to preach in such a way that the message is heard accurately. In Japan this is more likely to occur as a process over time, rather than via a one-time presentation. But even before any presentation can be made, the evangelist must normally earn the right to be heard by developing a certain degree of trust and respect.

Among other cultural and linguistic problems, missiologists should consider carefully the implications of Japanese identity as it relates to the gospel message itself, as well as how it affects an individual's decision-making process. For many Japanese, social relationships and belongingness tend to be more important than truth *per se*. Individuals are *not* free agents; relationships within a group context appear as the ultimate reality, and maintaining harmony is the highest value. Consequently, the types of approaches that are most likely to be effective in Japan will take these realities into account, and present a witness that is a central part of authentic human relationships.

Much more so than temples, the church offers real possibilities for community and fellowship. I have personally found an approach that utilizes peer group witness in the context of small groups to be the most fruitful in my ministry. Japanese seem more likely to believe when they witness their own peers—significant others with whom they have a relationship—joined together in witness. This is in contrast to typical Western approaches to evangelism (even friendship evangelism) which are usually based on the individual evangelist preaching the gospel. As an alternative model, I propose group-based evangelism whereby teams of Japanese believers target people with similar interests and evangelize them after developing fairly intimate ingroup relationships. It is not easy for a Japanese individual to resist conforming to ingroup pressure, especially when the "pressure" is love! In such a context one seems much more likely to get a serious hearing of the message, not to mention encouragement in the decision-making process. I have found that this method has worked better than the above approach, though the relationships must be authentic and these take time and adequate opportunity to build. Obviously, the Japanese social nexus must also be considered and prayed over, so that Spirit-directed relationships are developed and a proper hearing of the gospel can take place.

Fear of Men Versus Fear of God

There have been numerous occasions, in my experience as an evangelist in Japan, when people rejected the appeal to trust in Christ expressly because they did not want to betray their core group affiliation. In some of these cases it seemed that they actually had come to believe orthodox doctrine, but in counting the social costs, could not bring themselves to make a clear decision to identify as a Christian. In most cases, this has been a reluctance to cause conflict in the family. (I also know several baptized believers who have avoided telling their family for the same reason.) Of course, counting the cost of following Jesus as Lord is an essential step in the conversion process. Jesus call to follow Him meant that He was sometimes asking individuals to forsake even family to gain a right relationship with God. Japanese seem particularly prone to fearing the negative evaluation of family and peers, and may feel driven to maintain harmony at all costs, even if it means rejecting Christ's offer of eternal life.

It needs to be stated that the public and private modes (*ura/ omote* and *tatemae/honne*) of behavior in Japan are merely social conventions. Most of the time, there is nothing wrong with going along with the group, fitting in, being reserved in sharing opinions, or generously giving up one's rights for the benefit of others. There is even a great deal of Christlike humility in this behavior. However, we must also recognize that there are times when these social conventions (*tatemae*) compel people to ignore their hearts and capitulate to what they perceive to be other's expectations. Suppressing one's Self so completely that it leads to a refusal stand up for the truth or inner convictions is a kind of dishonesty. Compromise with sins such as idolatry is a constant temptation in Japan.

At the very least, Christians are to speak honestly because of their new identity: "Do not lie to each other, since you have taken off your *old self* with its practices and have put on the *new self*, which is being renewed in knowledge in the image of its Creator" (Col. 3:9-10 NIV, emphasis mine).[10] Once a believer receives his new identity in Christ, the Lord demands that we speak the truth in love as He does, as well as casting aside every other kind of sin. In the final analysis, this aspect of Japanese culture may be inescapable, but if people transfer their ultimate allegiance to the Lordship of Christ and receive adequate support from the body of Christ, compromise with the world need not be inevitable.

Believers are free forever from condemnation from God (Rom. 8:1). Therefore, one might ask: Does it really matter if others in the world (who stand condemned) do not approve? If God is for us, who can be against us? This is the conclusion of a mature believer, secure in his salvation in Christ. But when Japanese seekers choose to turn away from following Christ due to their fear of harming relationships with their social group or family, in the final analysis they are fearing man, not God. Fear of social ostracism, persecution, and even death does not belong in the heart of the truly faithful, who know they have already died with Christ (Rom. 6:1-6). Moreover, when believers develop a healthy fear of God, they are motivated to persuade others to be believers as well (2 Cor. 5:11). It should be recognized that developing a healthy fear of God (over man) is an imperative for believers everywhere.

The Non-Self Versus the Need for Personal Responsibility and Individual Faith

Callaway writes, "Until a Buddhist is willing to grant the objective reality of individual personalities...he can never be led to believe he has disobeyed God....For a Buddhist to admit this, however, would be to give up belief in the validity of the doctrine of *muga*, and to give up the doctrine of *muga* would mean to cease being Buddhist" (1957, 253). However, I would argue that most Japanese are not really monistic idealists; they are merely culturally buddhistic, but have a restrained sense of self, and a sense of personal identity strongly influenced by others.

Yet in my experience, many Japanese have a very hard time admitting they are personally sinners. This is partly a misunderstanding of the word sin (*tsumi*), which connotes crimes or other evil acts that most people honestly deny committing. Moreover, Japanese usually hold to a strongly humanistic view of mankind (rooted in Neo-Confucianism), where most (Japanese) people are thought to be born sinless and good. If people do commit sin, it is a "mistake" due to lack of understanding (proper education).

There is a tendency to deny the reality of evil in the world. With Japan's low crime rate, many people pridefully feel Japan is almost free of *tsumi.* [11] Obviously, adequate attention should be given to sin, as a broken relationship with God, in our theology and certainly in our gospel presentation. Japanese need help understanding the holiness of God and mankind's responsibility for sinning against Him. Until they sense their own personal culpability, no individual will likely seek a Savior.

Individuals are important to God and God grants each person some uniqueness. Jesus taught that there is joy when *even one* sinner personally repents (Luke 15:10). Naturally, in our normal way of describing it, God judges people as individuals for their own *personal* sins and one can receive salvation only by making a *personal* decision to believe in Christ's unique claim: "Unless you believe that I AM you shall die in your sins" (John 8:24 *My paraphrase from the Greek*). Redemption ensures that each believer has a direct and personal relationship with God—a broken relationship restored to harmony and wholeness, but also one of dependency.

In a culture which favors group consensus in decision making, it is obviously better if seekers have Christians within their ingroup encouraging them to follow Christ. Nevertheless, a decision to trust in Christ for salvation must ultimately be made *personally*. However, this is not to say that people cannot come to Christ together in groups. Rather than seeing Japanese groupism or lack of individuality as a barrier to personal decisions for Christ, more effort should be made to reach whole groups of people, such as households or affiliation groups, together, whenever possible. Still, there are times when people seem to want to believe, but hold back because others in their family may not approve. At this point we cannot err in urging the individual to decide apart from the group. The Catholic novelist Endō Shūsaku is worth quoting at length here:

> When the history of Japanese Christianity as written by foreigners is studied, we find the claim that Christianity stressed the self-awakening of the individual, but I am not entirely in agreement with this opinion. What I mean by this is that the larger structure of Japan's agricultural villages was at work in the belief patterns of that time and that we can see the tendency of belief or familiarity being effected in terms of large and small

village groups.

> If the head or leader of a village believed in Christianity, the rest of the villagers would also believe, and if the village head drifted away from his belief, the rest of the village would also follow suit. Here also I feel we can see the strong relationship of the Japanese to their village group and to their religion (Endö 1985, 11-12).

But Endö further warns, "And while there were indeed some individuals who persevered in their individual belief in Christianity, for the most part, *there was a very strong tendency for people to give up their belief* if the head of the village made up his mind to abandon Christianity...[because] belief was promulgated *in village units rather than on the individual level*" (1985, 13, emphasis mine).

Indeed, not only did large numbers of Japanese Catholics recant during the official ban and persecution that began under Hideyoshi, [12] but whole churches in the Protestant camp—often following the example of their Japanese pastors—succumbed to idol worship during the war years under the pressures of state Shintö. These churches have been proven to be among the slowest growing. However, one sociologist notes rightly that "On the whole Japanese Christians tend to be individuals rather than whole families, and their children do not necessarily follow their example. It has become a 'personal religion', rather than an association of the continuing family...their families and communities are less able to understand such a seemingly selfish religion, and sometimes Christians are ostracised for their behaviour" (Hendry 1987, 114-115).

The Believer's Identity in Christ

There is strong pressure on all people to conform to the world's way of sin. Although this study has shown that the problem can be acute among the Japanese, who tend towards compromise even when it conflicts with internally held principles, strong-willed individualists are equally prone to sin and could benefit from more group-based accountability. All believers need a transformed mind and a new identity, under the power of the Holy Spirit. Romans 12:2 warns believers: "Do not *conform* any longer to the pattern of this world, but be *transformed* by the *renew-*

ing of your mind" (NIV, emphasis mine). Moreover, Christians have been bought with a price and now are no longer their own; they belong to God (1 Cor. 6:19-20). Since in Christ "all died," believers "should no longer live for themselves"—or any group— but for Christ (2 Cor. 5:14-15 NIV).

Although the Japanese normally find their identity through belongingness, rather than individual distinction, Japanese Christians need to discover their new identity in Christ. The doctrine of the identity of the believer in Christ is most marked in the writings of Paul, a man who also underwent a radical transformation in his identity, from an ultra-loyal member of a self-righteous national religion to a loyal servant of Christ. Paul testifies powerfully to his change of heart in Galatians 2:20 (NIV, vv. 19-20 in Gk.) where he declares, "*I have been crucified with Christ and I no longer live, but Christ lives in me. The life I live in the body, I live by faith in the Son of God, who loved me and gave Himself for me.*" This verse immediately stands out as unusual because the words "I" and "me" (all *watashi* in Japanese) appear six times in one sentence—extremely emphatic in Japanese in light of the tendency to omit the singular personal pronoun. I would like to suggest this verse as an identity statement *par excellence*: It is at once both Paul's "Declaration of Dependence" (*amae?*) on Christ and contains a concise summation of the gospel. It also affirms the crucial fact that *God loves the individual*, who is here seen as so significant that God is willing to die even *for the one* ("for me"). Yet Paul's old identity as Saul of Tarsus, sinful but self-righteous, has passed away ("I no longer live") and has been replaced entirely by that of Christ.

Perhaps to the surprise of Westerners, Paul expressly tells us that the believer is *not* to regard himself as an *independent* being. Believers are to see themselves as slaves of God (Rom. 6:22). Paul pointedly asks, "Do you not know that...you are not your own?" (1 Cor. 6:19 NIV). Salvation for any person, if anything, is to a more dependent life. What is key here is the object of our dependency. Jesus Christ is the Lord.

Identification with Christ is so complete that Paul declares believers have been crucified, died, been buried, raised, and made alive with Him (Rom. 6:1-6; Col. 2:12-13; Gal. 2:19-20), also linking this spiritual truth with the entry ritual of water baptism. Although Paul may not have known a people quite like the Japanese, he was inspired to write the Colossians to exhort them (and the whole church) to change their way of thinking and realize who they really had become. Having died with Christ, and having been raised with Him, believers are now to set their minds (*phronos*) "on things above, not on things that are on earth" (Col. 3:2 NASB), to derive their identity from Christ, not the world. He describes the transformation as an accomplished fact, which the believer must accept, explaining, "For you died and your life is now hidden with Christ in God" (3:3 NIV). In summary, being *firmly rooted* in Christ, believers are being built up in Him (Col. 2:7).

Every believer in Christ, regardless of background or nationality, must undergo this complete renewal in thinking that includes not only a change in worldview, but a radical new identity in Christ. Believers have been placed "in Christ" by God (1 Cor. 1:30), who thus established our identity in Him by sealing us with His Holy Spirit (2 Cor. 1:21-22; Eph. 1:13-14). In fact, not only are believers *in Christ*, but Christ is said to be *in the believer* (Col. 1:27; cf., Rom. 8:9-10; 1 Cor. 6:19), a "mystery" understood in light of the close association of God the Holy Spirit with Christ (e.g., Rom. 8:9; Acts 16:7; Phil. 1:19; 1 Pet. 1:11). We are given the very mind of Christ (1 Cor. 2:16; contra Jp. *busshin*, lit. "Buddha heart") and become partakers of the divine nature (2 Pet. 1:4).

In conclusion, Japanese Christians can be thankful for the national identity in which they were born as a result of God's sovereign will, recognizing that His revealed purpose has been that they should seek Him (Acts 17:27). Nevertheless, through redemption believers become citizens of heaven (Phil. 3:20) and are to begin thinking of themselves as seated there with Christ (Eph. 2:6).

Towards a Boom Strategy for a Church Planting Movement in Japan

Church planting movements are an act of God which a growing number of missiologists are discovering are more likely to occur when certain conditions and factors encourage them (Garrison 1999). Praying and planning toward that end is nothing other than good stewardship of the church's commission to make disciples among all nations. Group conversions, if genuine, are especially desirable.

One potentially helpful area that may have been neglected in missions studies on Japan is the nature of how certain items or ideas become popularized and gain a widespread public acceptance, sometimes overnight, in what is popularly called a "boom." Usually this term is applied to fashion items, such as clothing styles, music, or technology, but ideas can also become popular and quickly sweep the whole nation by storm. It is safe to say that although the rise and fall of popular fashion is a phenomenon common to the whole world, probably no developed country experiences the boom effect quite like Japan, where the popularity of an item can saturate the whole country in a heartbeat. A recent example would be in the rapid switchover to new generations of cell phone technology by most of the populace within just a few months.

The *Nihonjinron* genre of literature is one example of an "idea boom" that gained widespread acceptance and which has endured for over a decade. Religious researchers also recognized a boom in the popularity of new religions that became a phenomenon in the 1980's. During that time, choosing a sect was, for some, seen as a kind of fashion item. (This might have continued indefinitely if it were not for the Aum Supreme Truth cult's terrorist activities that swiftly changed public opinion from interest to suspicion and fear in 1995.) The evidence is compelling that even religions can become part of a boom.

What is important to understand here is the *power of the group-based culture* of Japan in generating mass movements. If a sufficiently large portion of certain segments of the population (for example, teenage girls) begins to adopt and promote an item, at some point a *critical mass* is achieved and *momentum* develops to produce a nationwide movement that cannot be contained. Marketing researchers understand this phenomenon well and use it to their benefit. In fact, there are companies in Japan whose sole job is to work to produce booms! Because of its social nature and strong tendency for uniformity, allowing mass acceptance of popular ideas as well as the power of the group in decision making, Japan could arguably hold unexpected potential for rapid and wide-spread conversions to Christianity—if God chooses to work through these social realities, increasing people's willingness to consider the gospel. Achieving a critical mass in witness would seem to be key. (What is certain is that God is not hindered by the barriers foreign missionaries may perceive.) At any rate, missiologists should investigate this social phenomenon further because the social realities of Japan, rather than being barriers to CPMs, could hold potential for a mass movement to Christ. A Christian boom would be a real boon!

For those of us hoping to see church planting movements arising and sweeping throughout the Buddhist world, Japan could arguably play a significant role. This vision of the future is admittedly about as far from the traditional image of Japan, as hopelessly closed and resistant, as one could get. But one merely needs to consider Japan's closest cultural neighbor—South Korea—to see that widespread acceptance of Christianity is not impossible, but already a reality in the region. When Japan's role throughout Asia, as one of influence in spreading popular culture, is also considered, the potential in thinking about booms missiologically becomes clearer, and demands further research. However, the key to the boom phenomenon in Japan likely lies first in understanding the nature of its group-based culture, including the attitudes of its individuals who favor consensus and find their identity within these peer groups.

Some practical recommendations for evangelizing the Japanese:

1) Don't underestimate the power Christian peer group pressure can have in Japan. Encourage Japanese believers to join together in their witness and mobilize them to attempt group-based evangelism together.

2) Work on earning the right to be heard—develop trust among non-Christians through building authentic relationships.

3) Whenever possible, integrate seekers into body life (cell group

or otherwise) *even before they believe.* Work hard to insure that they feel part of the group and can identify with it.

4) Help seekers to recognize their *personal* responsibility before God and their need to make a *personal* decision to believe. If necessary, build up the individual by communicating that you value their true feelings.

5) Teach people constantly about their identity in Christ as soon as they believe!

6) Plant churches with solid principles of reproduction built into their DNA. Pray earnestly for and believe that the day of momentum will come, for a CPM to be launched, and that the gospel of Christ will become a boom in Japan!

Notes

1 Doi, writing in a more suspect Nihonjinron vein and quoting from the Declaration of Independence, rejects the idea that all men are equal out of hand: "It is in fact highly doubtful that all men are created equal....Rather, it is fair to suggest that Americans promote equality precisely because of what is in fact an extremely naive belief in universal equality as self-evident truth" (1985, 51). For Doi, a Japanese, that men are not equal is obvious. He goes on to critique American-style independence, lamenting that in America, "No one else, not even parents, can be depended on." But Kōsaka maintains that "The virtue of non-self-assertiveness that was once respected is now either inappropriate or insufficient for modern society." He also notes that "democracy" was originally translated as heiminshugi ("equal-people-ism"), a term which did not resonate well in hierarchical Japan. This was later changed to its current form minshushugi ("people-rule-ism") (1967, 256).

2 I am not sure if this is emic or etic description, but as an insider, Nakane, seems to have unraveled something here. It is generally recognized that Western logical approaches and apologetics are not as fruitful in a Japanese context as emotional appeals, particularly when in the context of a senior (sempai) to junior (kōhai) relationship.

3 Sadly, some Japanese in Barnlund's study reported having almost no contact with either parent, and a number recalled never touching or being touched by their fathers. In no case did any American in his study approach that degree of physical isolation. This "distant father" syndrome is a widespread phenomenon in Japan, due in part to men working overly long hours and their reticence to communicate or show emotions. Exactly how this affects the identity and emotional development of children is not clear to me, but my personal experience in counseling Japanese suggests that it is a major issue in need of further study.

4 Tobin argues that the dual self-consciousness is developed even earlier and what is learned in Japanese preschool is actually when it is appropriate to shift. See this alternative theory in his "Japanese Preschools and the Pedagogy of Selfhood" (1992).

5 The Nichiren Shöshü sect is still quite formidable, mainly because of the emergence of an offshoot new religion called Söka Gakkai, which amassed millions of followers in the twentieth century. For an excellent Christian response to various schools of Japanese Buddhism, see Callaway (1957, 1976).

6 For a good discussion of the history of Buddhist thinking about human personality, see Kalupahanna 1992, 68-77.

7 For example, because worshipping an ancestor by name is an affirmation of the dead's continued existence, it is logically an implicit denial of reincarnation and having achieved a Buddhist "non-self" state of enlightenment.

8 At least two-thirds of the Japanese claim no religious affiliation or religious faith. Only thirty-one percent could say that the soul certainly exists after death. When asked what sect one belongs to, a Japanese might answer, "I don't know. No one in our household has died yet." One survey revealed that forty-three percent of people did not even know the name of the sect or temple to which they belonged (Reader 1993, 143).

9 Uchimura is well known even among non-Christian Japanese. Although he gained notoriety at his refusal to worship the Emperor, later he began the Mukyökai ("Non-Church") movement, which Japanese Evangelicals have rejected as unorthodox and radical. Mukyökai was a reaction to overly Western Christianity in the pre-war years, but rather than contextualizing in its mission and creating a growing indigenous church, it has unfortunately rejected practices such as baptism, the Lord's Supper, and evangelism. Still, one must consider Uchimura's refusal to be identified too closely with the Western church while at the same time finding a sense of affiliation with Japanese Buddhist leaders: "My friends are Hönen rather than Wesley, Shinran rather than Moody....The heart with which I turn to Jesus...is not the heart with which English and Americans believe in Christ" (see Lee 1999, 4).

10 The two most popular Japanese Bibles translate this as "old man" and "new man" respectively.

11 The crime rate is rising, but even the crime statistics need qualification, because Japanese laws are not necessarily God's laws. Murders are still rare, but the widespread acceptance of sins like adultery, abortion, and even child pornography indicate a culture given over to depravity and falling far short of even Buddhist standards of proper conduct.

12 Even among those who did not recant, but who went underground as *Kakure Kirishitan* ("Hidden Christians"), many—if not most—abandoned orthodox Catholicism for a syncretistic mixture of Catholicism, Buddhism, and Shintö.

Bibliography

Bachnik, Jane. 1992. *Kejime*: Defining a Shifting Self in Multiple Organizational Modes. *Japanese Sense of Self.* Edited by Nancy Rosenburger. Cambridge: Cambridge University Press.

Barnlund, Dean C. 1975. *Public and Private Self in Japan and the United States: Communicative Styles of Two Cultures.* San Francisco: Intercultural Press.

Befu Harumi. 1980. *The Group Model of Japanese Society and an Alternative.* Houston: Rice University Studies, No. 66.

———. 2001. *Hegemony of Homogeneity: An Anthropological Analysis of Nihonjinron.* Melbourne: Trans Pacific Press.

Ben-Dasan, Isaiah [Yamamoto Shichihei]. 1972. *The Japanese and the Jews.* Translated by Richard L. Gage. Tokyo: Weatherhill.

Benedict, Ruth. 1946. *The Chrysanthemum and the Sword: Patterns of Japanese Culture.* Boston: Houghton Mifflin.

Callaway, Tucker N. 1957. *Japanese Buddhism and Christianity.* Tokyo: Shinkyö Shuppansha.

———. 1976. Zen Way—Jesus Way. Tokyo: Tuttle.

Caudill, William and David W. Plath. 1986. Who Sleeps with Whom? Parent-Child Involvement in Urban Japanese Families. In *Japanese Culture and Behavior: Selected Readings.* Edited by Takie Sugiyama Lebra and William P. Lebra. Honolulu: University of Hawaii Press, 62-79.

——— and Helen Weinstein. Maternal Care and Infant Behavior in Japan and America. 1986. *Japanese Culture and Behavior: Selected Readings.* Edited by in Takie Sugiyama Lebra and William P. Lebra. Honolulu: University of Hawaii Press.

Clark, Paul P. 1985. Understanding the Resistance of Japan to Christianity: A Beginning Point for Developing Better Cross-cultural Communication and Evangelism Strategies. D. Miss. diss., Trinity Evangelical Divinity School.

Davis, Winston. 1992. *Japanese Religion and Society: Paradigms of Structure and Change.* Albany: State Univ. of New York Press.

De Barry, William Theodore, ed. 1958. *Sources of Japanese Tradition.* Vol. 1. New York: Columbia Univ. Press.

De Vos, George A. 1973a. Achievement Orientation, Social Self-Identity and Japanese Economic Growth. *Socialization for Achievement: Essays on the Cultural Psychology of the Japanese.* Berkeley: Univ. of California Press, 187-200.

_____. 1973b. *Socialization for Achievement: Essays on the Cultural Psychology of the Japanese.* Berkeley: Univ. of California Press.

Doi Takeo. 1971. *Amae no Közö [The Structure of Dependence].* Tökyö: Köbundö.

_____. 1973. *Omote and Ura:* Concepts Derived from the Japanese 2-Fold Structure of Consciousness. *Journal of Nervous and Mental Disease.* (157:258-261).

_____. 1985. *Omote to Ura [Front and Back].* Tökyö: Köbundö.

_____. 1986. *The Anatomy of Self: The Individual versus Society.* Translated by Mark A. Harbison. Tokyo: Kodansha.

Dyer, Stanley. 1982. Japan's Group Consciousness as It Relates to Evangelism. Unpublished D. Miss. diss., Trinity Evangelical Divinity School.

Endö Shüsaku. 1985. Nihonjin no Shükyö Ishiki [Religious Consciousness of the Japanese]. NHK Kokusaikyoku Bunka Purojekuto. *Nihon no Kokoro* [The Heart of Japan], bilingual edition. Translated by Don Kenny. Tokyo: Ködansha, 6-21.

Eyler, Marvin Lee. 1996. Japanese Social Formation and Religious Themes and the Development of a New Model Church in Japan. D.Miss. diss., Fuller Theological Seminary.

Furuya Yasuo, trans. and ed. 1997. *A History of Japanese Theology.* Grand Rapids: William B. Eerdmans.

Garrison, David. 1999. *Church Planting Movements.* Richmond: International Mission Board, Southern Baptist Convention.

Hendry, Joy. 1986. *Becoming Japanese: The World of the Pre-School Child.* Honolulu: Univ. of Hawaii Press.

_____. 1987. *Understanding Japanese Society.* London: Croom Helm.

Hori Ichirö. 1967. The Appearance of Individual Self-consciousness in Japanese Religion and Its Historical Transformations. *The Japanese Mind: Essentials of Japanese Philosophy and Culture.* Edited by Charles A. Moore. Honolulu: Univ. of Hawaii.

Kalupahanna, David J. 1992. *A History of Buddhist Philosophy: Continuities and Discontinuities.* Honolulu: Univ. of Hawaii Press.

Kawashima Takeyoshi. 1967. The Status of the Individual in the Notion of Law, Right, and Social Order in Japan. *The Japanese Mind: Essentials of Japanese Philosophy and Culture.* Edited by Charles A. Moore. Honolulu: Univ. of Hawaii.

Kitagawa, Joseph M. 1987. *On Understanding Japanese Religion.* Princeton: Princeton University Press.

Kösaka Masaaki. 1967. The Status and the Role of the Individual in Japanese Society. *The Japanese Mind: Essentials of Japanese Philosophy and Culture.* Edited by Charles A. Moore. Honolulu: Univ. of Hawaii, 245-261.

Kuwayama Takami. 1992. The Reference Other Orientation. *Japanese Sense of Self.*

Edited by Nancy Rosenburger. Cambridge: Cambridge University Press.

Lebra, Takie Sugiyama and William P. Lebra, eds. 1976. *Japanese Patterns of Behavior.* Honolulu: University of Hawaii Press.

_____. 1986a. *Japanese Culture and Behavior: Selected Readings.* Honolulu: University of Hawaii Press.

_____. 1986b. Self-Reconstruction in Japanese Religious Psychotherapy. *Japanese Culture and Behavior: Selected Readings.* Edited by Takie Sugiyama Lebra and William P. Lebra. Honolulu: University of Hawaii Press, 354-368.

_____. 1992. *Self in Japanese Culture. Japanese Sense of Self.* Edited by Nancy Rosenburger Cambridge: Cambridge University Press, 105-120.

Lee, Robert. 1999. *The Clash of Civilizations: An Intrusive Gospel in Japanese Civilization.* Christian Mission and Modern Culture Series. Harrisburg: Trinity Press International.

Lewis, Catherine C. 1995. *Educating Hearts and Minds: Reflections on Japanese Preschool and Elementary Education.* Cambridge: Cambridge University Press.

McVeigh, Brian. 2000. *Wearing Ideology: State, Schooling and Self-Presentation in Japan.* Oxford: Berg.

Miller, Alan S., and Kanazawa Satoshi. 2000. *Order by Accident: The Origins and Consequences of Conformity in Contemporary Japan.* Boulder: Westview Press.

Moore, Charles A., ed. 1967. *The Japanese Mind: Essentials of Japanese Philosophy and Culture.* Honolulu: Univ. of Hawaii.

Mullins, Mark R. 1993. *Religion & Society in Modern Japan: Selected Readings.* Edited by Shimazono Susumu, and Paul L. Swanson. Berkeley: Asian Humanities Press.

_____, 1998. *Christianity Made in Japan: A Study of Indigenous Movements.* Honolulu: Univ. of Hawaii Press.

Nakamura Hajime. 1964. *Ways of Thinking of Eastern Peoples.* Philip P. Wiener, ed. Honolulu: Univ. of Hawaii Press.

_____. 1967. Consciousness of the Individual and the Universal among Japanese. *The Japanese Mind: Essentials of Japanese Philosophy and Culture.* Edited by Charles A. Moore. Honolulu: Univ. of Hawaii, 179-200.

Nakane Chie. 1970. *Japanese Society.* Berkeley: University of California Press.

Odagaki Masaya. 1997. Theology after 1970. *A History of Japanese Theology.* Edited and translated by Furuya Yasuo. Grand Rapids: William B. Eerdmans.

Peak, Lois. 1991. *Learning to Go to School in Japan: The Transition from Home to Preschool Life.* Berkeley: University of California Press.

Picken, Stuart D. B. 1979. *Nihonjin no Jisatsu: Seiyö to no Hikaku.* Tokyo.

Reader, Ian. 1993. Buddhism as a Religion of the Family: Contemporary Images in

Sōtō Zen. *Religion & Society in Modern Japan: Selected Readings.* Edited by Mark R. Mullins, Shimazono Susumu, and Paul L. Swanson. Berkeley: Asian Humanities Press, 139-156.

Rohlen, Thomas P. 1983. *Japan's High Schools.* Berkeley: Univ. of California Press.

Rosenberger, Nancy, ed. 1992. *Japanese Sense of Self.* Cambridge: Cambridge University Press.

Smith, Robert J. 1974. *Ancestor Worship in Contemporary Japan.* Stanford, CA: Stanford University Press.

_____. 1983. *Japanese Society: Tradition, Self and the Social Order.* Cambridge: Cambridge University Press.

Tobin, Joseph. 1992. *Japanese Preschools and the Pedagogy of Selfhood.* Japanese Sense of Self. Edited by Nancy Rosenburger. Cambridge: Cambridge University Press, 21-39.

Ueda Yoshifumi. 1967. The Status of the Individual in Mahāyāna Buddhist Philosophy. *The Japanese Mind: Essentials of Japanese Philosophy and Culture.* Edited by Charles A. Moore. Honolulu: University of Hawaii, 164-178.

Watanabe Shoko. 1968. *Japanese Buddhism: A Critical Appraisal.* Tokyo: Kokusai Bunka Shinkokai.

Williams, Paul. 1989. *Mahāyāna Buddhism: The Doctrinal Foundations.* London: Routledge.

Yagi Seiichi. 1997. The Third Generation, 1945–1970. *A History of Japanese Theology.* Edited and translated by Furuya Yasuo. Grand Rapids: William B. Eerdmans.

Yamaguchi Katsumasa. 1997. "Jibun wo Ai Suru: Seisho-Shingakuteki, Rinshōteki Hihan" [Self-Love: A Biblical, Theological, and Clinical Critique]. Bummyakuka Kenkyūka [Research Association for Contextualization]: *R.A.C. Journal,* 3:17-25.

Yamazaki Masakazu. 1994. *Individualism and the Japanese: An Alternative Approach to Cultural Comparison.* Tokyo: Japan Echo Incorporated.